Teen
Dreams

Dedicated to the memory of

Selena Ulrich

(1976–2004)

Teen Dreams

Reading Teen Film from Heathers *to* Veronica Mars

Roz Kaveney

I.B. TAURIS

LONDON · NEW YORK

Published in 2006 by I.B. Tauris & Co Ltd
6 Salem Road, London W2 4BU
175 Fifth Avenue, New York NY 10010
www.ibtauris.com

In the United States of America and in Canada distributed by
Palgrave Macmillan, a division of St Martin's Press
175 Fifth Avenue, New York NY 10010

ISBN 10: 1 84511 184 2
ISBN 13: 978 1 84511 184 7

A full CIP record for this book is available from the British Library
A full CIP record for this book is available from the Library of Congress

Library of Congress catalog card: available

Typeset in Adobe Garamond by Steve Tribe, Andover
Printed and bound in Great Britain by TJ International Ltd, Padstow, Cornwall

Contents

Acknowledgements

*E*arly in this project, I asked the readers of my Live Journal to list their favourite teen films for me and had an extensive and helpful response. The resulting watching list included many films that I do not specifically mention in what follows: this should not be taken as meaning that I did not watch them with pleasure, or that they added nothing to my sense of the evolution of the modern teen genre.

My thanks are especially due to Jennifer Stoy, Veronica Schanoes and Sally Connolly, who acted as the first readers of these chapters, made many helpful comments and stopped me making a fool of myself in a variety of ways. Jennifer Stoy was particularly insistent on my watching *Veronica Mars* from an early stage – my thanks are due to her for this and also to Simon, Lesley and Marcus who facilitated my viewing of the actual episodes.

Thanks are also due to Leyte Jefferson, and her Live Journal correspondents, for listing films about ethnic minority teenagers for me (even if the result of their labours was to convince me that these were a separate subject that I should avoid in the present book).

Robert Hillenbrand clarified a quotation from the *Thousand Nights and One Night* for me.

As always, my thanks to Philippa Brewster, Susan Lawson and everyone else at I.B. Tauris, and to Steve Tribe, a copy editor with an almost preternatural gift for working out what I meant to say.

The months during which I have been working on this book have been especially trying and Paule has been an unfailing source of support.

Teen Dreams

The critic at the prom

*F*or large parts of the developed world, and much of the rest of it,
America provides, through the lens of Hollywood, significant parts of
the vocabulary of our dreams. This is one of the reasons why America is
so loved and so deeply hated – people who have never visited it, and who
do not speak its language, nonetheless walk its streets and ride its plains at
night. This applies even when we do not entirely understand the context of
what we are seeing on the screen, let alone the version of it that continues
to play inside our heads.

To give one example, one of my friends was entirely surprised when she
visited New York for the first time and saw steam rising up from vents in
the street in the early morning. She had seen it a thousand times in the
movies and had assumed it was a special effect, a piece of noir cinematic
cliché. It had never occurred to her that it was what actually happens on
cold days when the warm air of subways and other cut-and-cover tunnels
rises up through ventilation. It was something uncanny because familiar
but misunderstood.

Through films and television, and most especially through the teen genre
of the last two decades, many of us are acquainted with an adolescence

that has nothing in common with anything we actually experienced. The boys are all handsome, the girls are all beautiful, even the ones who wear glasses and talk of themselves as geeks and losers – many of them appear oddly physically mature for their years. They watch American football from bleachers, with illuminated scoreboards and scantily clad cheerleaders jumping up and down and chanting their hearts out. They go to homecoming, or their senior prom, looking oddly dignified in tuxedos and evening dress; they sign each others' yearbooks and endlessly vote for each other to be Student Body President, or Homecoming Queen, or Person Most Likely to Succeed. They inhabit an entire sequence of ritual years which has little or nothing to do with the lives of anyone outside the United States of America. Yet sometimes it seems as real to us as our own lives of GCSEs, UCAS forms and Sixth Form Common Rooms.

We find ourselves caught up in nostalgia for things that never happened to us. This is partly a matter of the potency of cheap music:

> I know that you're in love with him
> 'coz I saw you dancing in the gym.
> You both kicked off your shoes,
> Now I dig those rhythm and blues

or

> She'll have fun fun fun
> 'Til Daddy takes her T-bird away

Our imaginations have been colonized. Which is part of what cultural imperialism means, but also gives us an outsider's sense of how utterly weird and stylized much of this material actually is. We foreigners talk to our American friends and suddenly they will talk about what happened to them at homecoming or their prom, and we realize that they live in another country and they do things differently there, and yet we know what they are talking about because we heard the songs and saw the movies and the television shows.

My own interest in these films dates back to the 1980s, when release of the first of them coincided with the happenstance that I was undergoing a second adolescence in my mid-thirties (for reasons not relevant here). They became oddly parallel to my feelings and my clashes with other people. This book is, in some measure, a payment of a debt to work that helped me understand my life during a difficult transition.

The subject of this book is the movie and television genre that deals with the lives of American teenagers and most especially with their interactions in and around High School. Many of the best films in which teenagers appear are not part of this genre, which, I would argue, has, in the form in which it currently exists, a specific time and place and origin. It also has a specific racial mix, a specific set of class biases and a very interesting set of takes on gender and sexuality. It also has a set of tropes and genre rules which are subject to refinement and revisionism in that constant dialectical process of recall and echo which is the very nature of genre material. It is only when that dialectical process of metonymy kicks in that we can describe what we are considering as belonging to a genre. Similar material that lacks this process may be closely linked to the genre – its cousin, perhaps – but it does not belong to it. I am as keen in what follows to explain why some work is not part of the genre as why some clearly is.

What do I mean when I describe films and television as belonging to this quite specific teen genre? I am, as far as is possible, being far more precise than would be the case if I were talking merely about a marketing category or a broad subject matter. I am describing a body of work which is in large part a creative response to the 1980s John Hughes films and to a lesser extent other films that appeared at roughly the same time. (Amy Heckerling's *Fast Times at Ridgemont High* (1982) is influential in one particular area in that it took over from its source material, an article by the young Cameron Crowe, the habit of taxonomizing teen tribes and thus created what I have called elsewhere 'the anthropology shot'.)

The Hughes films – and it may simply have been a matter of there being six films by the same writer/director that appeared in cinemas over a three-year period – created or crystallized many stock expectations and character types that we find in the canonical work of the teen genre over the ensuing two decades. The Hughes films all take place in Illinois suburbs and thus suburbia became one of the standard expectations; they have a tendency to favour outsiders and underdogs, and so this became a standard expectation, even where it's one that is often subverted through revisionist approaches. Other films from within the same time frame – the early John Cusack vehicles for example – are not as important because they left less in the way of direct progeny. The Hughes films might not have been the best of their time, but they were the fittest, in a Darwinian sense, not least because they were the films which sparked response in the form of later, better films like *Heathers* (1989) when other films of the same period did not.

There are some very significant films from the 1950s and later which deal with the lives of teenagers and with which teenagers identified, and which to some extent still form a part of the folk memory of what it is to be a teenager both in the USA and outside it. Nicholas Ray's *Rebel Without a Cause* (1955) produced in James Dean an icon of doomed youth that will probably last as long as the movies do, and will always be echoed whenever pretty young people slick down their hair, wear a leather jacket and pout a bit. Bad boys from J.D. in *Heathers* to the vampires Spike and Angel in the television show *Buffy the Vampire Slayer* (1997–2003) are among Dean's posthumous progeny. The films in which he appeared – but most especially *Rebel...* which is the only one in which he played a teenager as such – are the prehistory from which the teen genre evolved. *Rebel...* is a classic example of a movie about teenagers which continues to have resonance within the teen movie genre as a part of vocabulary, while not in essence being part of a genre which did not exist for another thirty-plus years and might well not have come about without it.

One of the reasons for this is that *Rebel Without a Cause*, like many other serious films with teenagers in them, is a film that considers teenagers as a social problem to be understood and solved, rather than the teen years as a transitory phenomenon to be enjoyed and celebrated. Films about juvenile delinquents, or the problems of inner-city schooling, are about teenagers, quite centrally, and often described teen styles of their time in a way that meant teenagers keen to be cool flocked to them to check their personal styles against what Hollywood was offering. Ultimately, though, these films were all too serious-minded – they were directed at forming opinion in the way that many liberal films about the racial question were in the same period. They were not so much for teenagers, or African-Americans, as in favour of them.

This applies even when the purpose of making the films was not quite so high-minded as all that. Films that consider and discuss social problems generate, almost automatically, films which merely display them. Some films about teenagers were not so much Problem films as exploitation films which separated out the interest of teenagers in seeing themselves represented, but never went much further. The various 'Gidget' films (1959–1986) are entertaining, lightweight and not especially interesting.

Much of what might have become a teen movie genre in the 1950s and especially the 1960s was instead a sequence of vehicles for rock singers. These are no more teen movies than were the various musicals in which an increasingly implausibly adolescent group of stars like Judy Garland and Mickey Rooney agreed to do the show right here in the barn. Yet in their sense of the controlled anarchic, and their often sceptical attitude to authorities who prevent young people being dancing fools, they help prefigure the anti-authoritarian strain that has been present in the modern teen genre since John Hughes' *The Breakfast Club* (1985). The teen movie as created by Hughes proved at least as effective as the vehicles at shifting product.

Modern vehicle films, like *Crossroads* (2002) with Britney Spears, often have a relationship with teen-genre material, but that relationship is a loose one. *Crossroads* is a road movie and a showbiz movie long before it is a teen movie, even though it shares the genre's habit of polymorphous sexual subtext.

Such films are essentially a sub-division of the showbiz film or the back-stage musical, a worthwhile sub-genre in its own right. There are grey areas here and a case could be made that *Flashdance* (1983), say, has a stronger connection than I am prepared to acknowledge with the genre as defined by Hughes. At such times, I would argue, the deciding point about ancestry and inclusion has to be whether films form more than an incidental part of the standard vocabulary of the body of genre. The question becomes far more of an issue when we consider later films about wannabe dancers confronting serious difficulties such as *Save the Last Dance* (2001). Another closely linked genre which I have chosen to exclude is the age-swap fantasy – even though Coppola's *Peggy Sue Got Married* (1986) is an interesting precursor film in its own right, and the two versions of *Freaky Friday* (1976 and 2003) both have much of interest to say about mothers and daughters and how they perceive each other's lives.

I am far from sure, applying the same principle, that coming-out movies like *The Incredibly True Adventures of Two Girls in Love* (1995) or *But I'm a Cheerleader* (1999) belong in this study either. They have much in common with films that are clearly teen movies by my reckoning – the bitchy friends in the first have much in common with the standard clique of popular girls I discuss below in the chapter 'The Heirs of Heather', while the whole subject matter of the second (the shipping-off of queer youth to be re-educated in Christian camps) is central to *Saved!* (2004) which I discuss in that chapter. As I argue below, the teen movie proper has no axe to grind in its polymorphous portrayal of sexual chemistry. *But I'm a Cheerleader* is a witty polemic which never pretends to be anything else; *Saved!* is equally witty and scores as many polemical points, but it does so in a less direct way.

I would argue that contemporary films about teenagers which treat them as a problem to be solved are outside the genre, even if they are often closely linked to it imaginatively. Gus Van Sant's *Elephant* (2003) is a non-linear portrayal of a couple of disaffected youths who enter their high school and execute a number of their schoolfellows, in a more or less arbitrary way. Part of the trouble with it is that it is in a degree of bad faith in its simple attempts to pathologize the murderers – like Nazi guards in the Holocaust documentary that obsesses them, they play Beethoven before pulling out their rifles.

There are a couple of points where *Elephant* draws very heavily on the pieties of the genre teen movie. The boy the killers spare by persuading him not to enter the school they are about to make a free-fire zone is singled out by them precisely because he is the carer of an alcoholic father – just like Molly Ringwald in *Pretty in Pink* (1986), I found myself saying as I watched. Had Van Sant chosen to present this, and the selection of the beautiful and popular for death, as a consequence of watching teen movies, rather than bringing in Nazis, I might have been more impressed. The other thing that *Elephant* does well, in a way common in genre teen films, is its presentation of the internal geography of the school. When the killing starts, we know where we are.

Which, in a very different sense, is the reason why this book does not consider the extensive body of teen slasher movies. There has been a constant interplay between the genre teen movie and the teen slasher genre – they share many stock characters and many of the same cast members. As a general rule, though, there are crucial distinctions, among them being two rather different sets of moral rules. In a teen movie, virginity and its loss is a serious matter, but it is rarely a matter of life and death; in a teen slasher movie, to have sex is to move yourself up the list of likely victims. Obviously there are exceptions here – *Cherry Falls* (2000) has a slasher who specifically targets virgins, creating a rampage towards sexual intercourse among its characters. *The Faculty* (1998) makes a particularly close study of teen genre stock characters simply because, as a reworking of *Invasion of the Body Snatchers* (1956 and 1978), it needs to pay particular attention to individuality before it is destroyed.

Many of the films and TV shows I discuss below are comedies or at least have a light touch. I am reluctant however to make comedy a necessary part of my definition, because such key films as *The Breakfast Club* and *Cruel Intentions* (1999), and such important television as *Buffy the Vampire Slayer* and *Veronica Mars* (2004), would be excluded if I did. At the same time, all of them have that lightness of touch I think of as helping define the teen genre, whereas a truly great show about teenagers like *My So-Called Life* (1994–1995) has an earnestness which inclines me to exclude it. The same applies to less good shows like *Dawson's Creek* (1998–2004) and *The OC* (2003–). I am aware that I may be wrong here – and my sole excuse is that those of us interested in this topic are in the early stages of taxonomy, definition and the creation of a provisional canon.

My omission of what we may as well call the Daft Dude comedies – most especially the two 'Bill and Ted' movies (1989 and 1991) – is purely due to the constraints of space; I hope to write about them some other time.

I have also, and rather more reluctantly, left to one side the body of films that deal primarily with African-American teenagers and those of other ethnicities. Where these are not social problem dramas in which teenagers are discussed rather than celebrated, they generally belong to an entirely separate genre with its own set of expectations and rules. Where the teen genre is suburban or small-town, the genre of films that centres on teenage and post-teen African-Americans is urban. Where the standard economic assumption of the teen genre is that teenagers are given a small but real disposable income by their parents, and poorer teens who have to work for the money they spend are an exception, if a common one, the stock assumption of the African-American genre is that you work for your money, or otherwise hustle for it. Economic necessity is a plot point in the teen genre; it is essential background in the African-American one.

There are, regularly, non-white characters in teen genre movies and television, though almost never in central roles. Cher's best friend Dionne in *Clueless* (1995) is African-American and the cheerleader Whitney in *Bring It On* (2000) is East Asian – but in neither case is the film even marginally about them, nor does their ethnicity feature even in passing. That occasionally insightful comedy *Not Another Teen Movie* (2001) parodies this generally, and most particularly in its manifestation in the egregious Freddie Prinz vehicle *She's All That* (1999), with an African-American character whose duties consist of standing around listening to the other characters and saying 'Damn!' or 'This is whacked!' at appropriate intervals. At a party he evicts another black character – there cannot be two on-screen at the same time. This is fair comment and criticism of a genre whose record in this respect is far from impeccable, even when such films as *Cruel Intentions* and *Bring It On* manage to say worthwhile things about race and ethnicity in the modern USA.

One of the shared and defining aspects of genre teen films and television programmes is a free-floating atmosphere of sexual chemistry, much of it having to do with same-sex interactions that do not as a rule involve actual sexual activity, but clearly involve a level of romantic and sometimes erotic emotion that is not adequately described by terms like homosociality and bonding. Something of the sort is observable, as we shall see, even as early in this account as the films of John Hughes, where, given his essentially Midwestern, suburban and Catholic world-view, one would not entirely expect it. It has, as one would expect, a significant presence in the sophisticated and more than slightly camp *Heathers*, and in almost all of the films and shows that *Heathers* influenced. It continues to be significantly present in such more recent films as *Mean Girls* (2004) and the television show *Veronica Mars*. It is, almost without exception, absent from the African-American films.

One possibility which should not be dismissed out of hand is that I, and many other critics with a progressive social agenda and minority sexual tastes, am engaged in perverse imaginings about films that are entirely innocent in their representation of exclusively heterosexual teenagers. I freely admit to having been involved over the last few years in a fan-fiction sub-culture in which hints from shows are expanded into fan-generated erotic fiction – it seems to me impossible fully to understand much current popular culture without acquaintance with fan sub-cultures. I would argue, and have endeavoured to maintain this argument through close examination of texts that often only make entire sense if viewed in this way, that the evidence is in my favour. If it walks like a duck… Besides, I have the authority of Joss Whedon himself who stated, a propos of his television show *Buffy the Vampire Slayer*, that 'all the relationships on the show are sort of romantic. (Hence the BYO Subtext principle.)' If we accept that this is true about *Buffy*, it is reasonable to suppose it true of other texts consumed in the same marketplace by the same audience.

A paranoid view of this is possible and has been offered by the American Christian Right, when they can spare time from finding Satanic influence in the Harry Potter books. Subtext, and the development of a young audience that looks for subtext, is part of an attempt culturally to normalize bisexuality. One can think of reasons other than the maintenance of a strictly heterosexual standard for Donald Wildmon and his acolytes to wish to discourage the development of an audience in the habit of nuanced readings of text. And indeed, from a secularist liberal standpoint, if there were a conspiracy to preach gender equality and sexual tolerance through popular media, I for one would be entirely happy about it.

However, there are other, less romantic, pragmatic reasons for the presence of a bisexual subtext in teen movies. The marketing of films and television aimed at a teenage audience, especially in the USA, is predicated on their receiving a rating which means that their target audience can go and see them, or watch them without parental concern. The teen audience is as prone to expect sexiness in its media as it is in its music: as Joss Whedon's Xander usefully says, 'I'm a teenage boy – linoleum makes me think about sex.'

One of the ways of putting sexiness back into films from which actual sex has perforce to be largely extracted for the sake of ratings is to put it back in, in the form of non-overt interactions – straight and gay. Anyone who can actually remember being a teenager – which seemingly is not as common as it might be – will be aware of the sheer complexity of sexual identity in the middle teens, and of the strong element of voyeurism in much of intra-teen discussion of sexual variety. Knowing about sex is one of the ways in which teenagers are hip and cool among themselves. When, in *Cruel Intentions*, Kathryn corrupts Cecile with the idea that everyone else is having sex, that sexual activity is a secret club of cool other people doing it a lot, she is playing to a standard fantasy and anxiety.

One of the things that the teen genre accurately portrays is that same-sex romantic behaviour of a reasonably intense kind is not incompatible with a theoretical homophobia that may extend to actual violence. Homosexuality is what other people do and is about sexual organs; same-sex romance is pure. One of the attractive things about the teen genre as it has developed is that this sort of thing is mocked as hypocrisy – as in *Bring It On* and *Mean Girls* – if not actually punished, as in *Heathers*.

There is, of course, a certain feedback inherent in all of this. Whedon, commenting on the relationship between Faith and Buffy from Season Three of *Buffy* on, has said that it was when fan-fiction writers and fan commentators saw an element of sexual obsession in the younger Slayer's jealousy of the older one that he and the other writers looked again at what they had already written, and what Eliza Dushku and Sarah Michelle Gellar had acted on-screen, and realized that the fannish interpretation made sense. When Rob Thomas, creator and often writer of *Veronica Mars*, plays complex games in which the subtextual erotic behaviour of his characters is in part represented through quotation from earlier films and shows, we have reached a point in which subtext, so-called slashiness, has become a genre rule.

These games about sexuality are but one of the areas, albeit a particularly important one, in which the central films and television programmes of the teen genre are thick texts. In my introduction to *From Alien to The Matrix: Reading Science Fiction Film*, I suggested that thick texts are ones from which we learn to treat works of art as provisional, contingent and collective compromises, which we read as positioned within the context of a generic metatext. The films and shows I have selected for consideration in the chapters that follow are ones that seem to me useful to a sense of the teen genre as a metatextual endeavour.

They are also cute, sexy, funny and sharp, films that entertained me and that I wanted to write about. Criticism is an intellectual endeavour and a serious one – it should not, however, restrict itself to works and a critical manner that are ponderous and glum. It should hang with the popular kids and get to go to the prom.

John Hughes

and the creation of a genre

*A*ny discussion of the teen movie has to pay proper attention to the films of John Hughes and most especially to *The Breakfast Club*. A favourite film of most of those who experienced it as teenagers, *The Breakfast Club* is at least as influential as *Heathers* on every teen film that follows it, and is in many respects the film to which *Heathers* is a retort. Of Hughes' other films for this market, the wonderful and anarchic comedy *Ferris Bueller's Day Off* (1986) is one of the best films made for a US commercial market to deal with teen male friendship.

The teen romantic comedies *Pretty in Pink* and *Some Kind of Wonderful* (1987) are at least important enough to have created some much parodied and imitated clichés. *The Breakfast Club*, *Pretty in Pink* and the more problematic *Sixteen Candles* (1984) made Molly Ringwald an iconic enough representative of young love that her appearance as a grumpy thirty-something cynic in the deeply uneven *Not Another Teen Movie* is almost funny in itself and in the absence of actual funny lines.

All three films have an obsessive quality in their portrayal of Ringwald as an icon of innocence. This has worn badly, but it was sufficiently notable at the time that, a decade later, *Buffy the Vampire Slayer* can make a joke about watching 'part of the Ringwald oeuvre' without anyone's having any doubt about what is meant. Hughes has compared Ringwald to the leggy tomboyish redheads in Norman Rockwell's *Saturday Evening Post* paintings of the small-town American dream and this is clearly what she signifies for him.

It is easy to attack Hughes for his easy and over-schematic psychologizing, his lack of complication and subtext, and his deep sentimentality. Much of what followed him in the genre has been considerably more sophisticated but all of it built on his achievements, if only, as with *Heathers*, by radically dissenting from their style and morality. The mere fact that films consciously imitated him, or consciously subverted tropes that he established, is crucial to the existence of teen films as a genre rather than merely a marketing niche. After Hughes, teen movies would always be knowing, had lost that blandness of affect, and lack of recursiveness and reference, which is often termed innocence.

The crucial thing about *The Breakfast Club* is that the film that had such an influence on the genre was not, in a real sense, the film that Hughes originally made. The film he delivered to Universal Pictures was two and a half hours long and it was radically trimmed for release at 97 minutes; it is important to remember this at the various points at which the film's narrative seems incoherent and various characters' arcs under-developed. Since it was made at a point in time where DVDs and Directors' Cuts were not even being thought of, Universal are believed to have destroyed the negatives of the deleted scenes. Hughes is apparently in possession of a copy of his original cut. In the absence, for the moment, of publicly available further information on this bare set of facts, this chapter will proceed on the basis of the version of the film that we all saw and continue to see.

The set-up of *The Breakfast Club* is very stagy – it is significant that the script was rehearsed by the cast as if it were a play before shooting. It is largely set on a single set, a school library in which five representative samples of high school types are confined for the duration of a Saturday's detention. Normally these are people who would hardly interact at all – their interaction here is partly brought about by boredom, partly as a form of transgression. They have been forbidden by the school's principal to talk during the eight hours they are stuck together and the thrill of transgressing this rule is enough to trump the standard rules of high school life.

The kids in detention are a laboratory sample, subjected to testing and refining; this sort of set-up is often referred to in television as a 'bottle episode'. The film belongs in a category of closed-community dramas which explore the tensions of personal interactions and describe a specific sub-culture or place – though they are rather more important films, *Twelve Angry Men* (1957) and *Black Narcissus* (1947) are equally artificial, equally stagy.

We know the sort of film this is, almost from the beginning. It will be an ensemble piece, something like an opera, in which each character, pair of characters or group of characters will sooner or later express their inner feelings, show off their public selves or enter into clashes and reconciliations. It is almost inevitable, given that the film's exposition establishes the differences between the five principal young characters, that the film's resolution will reconcile them and that much of its action will be devoted to the dialectical personal clashes whereby this reconciliation will be achieved. Hughes' originality here is primarily that he took this sort of schematic structure and applied it to contemporary American teenagers and their problems; it is also impressive that he did this without using adaptation of some previous text as a fallback skeletal structure.

Each of the characters is at once an individual and a type and the reasons they are in detention are equally a combination of the quirky and the stereotypical. Claire (Hughes' favourite young actress, Molly Ringwald) is a 'princess' spoiled by her father with presents like the diamond earrings she is wearing – she has been given detention because she skipped out of class to go shopping. She is a virgin, a fact that she reveals at one of the film's many slightly synthetic climaxes; virginity is less a statement here about morality or personal integrity as it is about a failure yet to engage with life.

Claire is vapid not because of any particular failing on her part, but because her potential is as yet unexplored. She is someone whose life has been built around consumerism, both as the thing she does and the thing she is for. Bender suggests to her that the logical development of her life is that she will become overweight in adulthood: 'There's fat people that were once thin but became fat … so when you look at 'em you can sorta see that thin person inside. You see, you're gonna get married, you're gonna squeeze out a few puppies and then, uh…' Claire is, in a real sense, a figure of America, as are all of her companions with the possible exception of Allison – even Claire's name, with its connotation of light, is potentially a reference to Winthrop's famous 'city on a hill' sermon and its representation of Americans as a light to the world.

Bender (Judd Nelson) is the school's 'criminal' – he is an antisocial cut-up, who rebels against authority automatically and temperamentally rather than because of any ideological perspective. (The grumpy robot in Matt Groening's futuristic television cartoon *Futurama* was named after this character.) He set off a fire alarm and proceeds to accumulate further detentions by constantly answering back to the principal – the element of psychosis in both participants in these confrontations is one of the film's most disturbing aspects.

Both he and Principal Vernon are obsessed with not backing down – Vernon has the power to impose detentions every Saturday until Bender leaves the school and it is as important to him that he do so as it is to Bender not to care. We experience this as a failure on Vernon's part – he has no compassion and no interest in why Bender is as anti-social and alienated as he appears to be – but Hughes avoids sentimentality to the extent that Bender is genuinely irritating and at times menacing in his behaviour.

Bender is a rebel without a cause but, more importantly, without a clue; when Brando, in László Benedek's *The Wild One* (1953) is asked what he is rebelling against, he answers, 'What have you got?' For a good liberal like Hughes, this is not so much a boast of nihilism as a symptom of disadvantage and social exclusion. Bender is, as the joke in *West Side Story* would have it, 'depraved on account of he's deprived.' We spend much of the film waiting for the revelation of why he is as he is and in a sense, dramatic as his exposition of his personal problems is, it comes as no especial surprise.

He has sniped constantly at the happy family lives that he assumes the others have – it is mockery and mimicry of his perception of Brian's life that leads to his eventual breakdown and revelation that he is constantly criticized and beaten by his parents. His showing of a cigarette burn is genuinely shocking, because it demonstrates that this violence goes considerably farther even than he has thus far revealed. The fact that the abuse is merely physical, not sexual, reflects the different preoccupations of the 1980s.

Yet Bender's name implies, really simplistically, that he is capable of change because flexible; he is the reed, not the oak. He can joke about his home life – after teasing Claire over the expensive diamond earrings that she got for Christmas, he reveals that this last Christmas was unusually good for him, since his father gave him a carton of cigarettes as a present. Later still, he even acknowledges that the random brutality of his father and

Andrew's expectations of bullying have something in common – 'I think your old man and my old man should get together and go bowling.'

Another possible interpretation of his name comes from the phrase 'to go on a bender', to be involved in blind alcoholic excess. Since this does not seem to be a part of his behaviour patterns, and his delinquency seems to consist of calculated, if ill-considered, moves, I raise this possibility merely to dismiss it.

Andrew (Emilio Estevez) is a member of the school's wrestling team – he is doing detention for bullying a classmate. What is most disturbing about this is that he did it less because he felt any great desire to than because he felt it incumbent on him; bullying is part of his social role which he feels obliged to live up to. Specifically, it is behaviour he has learned from other jocks including his father.

The act he committed was not merely beating a weaker kid up – it was in taping the other boy's buttocks together – he, and indeed the film's authority figures, seem bizarrely unaware of the sexual implications of this act. Like the far more outrageous bullies of *Heathers*, he is free with accusations of homosexuality, calling Bender a 'faggot'; Bender ripostes in kind suggesting that this is uncalled for from someone whose principal skill is grappling with other boys on the floor and wearing a uniform that includes tights. Still, Andrew's name does link him fairly straightforwardly to masculinity and its discontents since the name Andrew does derive from the Greek for man.[1]

One of the areas in which the film's moral standpoint seems most questionable is the degree to which Andrew is allowed off the moral hook simply by discovering that other sorts of people have feelings and that he might like them outside the standard social roles of school. Any move from that to deciding that bullying is wrong because it hurts actual people's actual feelings is implicit rather than deeply felt. Inasmuch as Andrew is, like the others, a case study in an aspect of the American grain, this is worrying – this tendency to thuggery, as American as apple pie, is not simply a problem to be resolved, it is a sin to be repented. One of the weaknesses of Hughes' analysis is that he has a liberal's capacity for noting down problems, but not the capacity of the best liberals to be as stern in their moralism as anyone else.

Brian – whose name seems to have become the stock name for anxious nerds with a high grade-point average (Brian in the television show *My So-Called Life*, for example) and whose type pervades the genre – has become anxious about falling grades and contemplated suicide. He is in detention because the only firearm he could obtain was a flare gun, and it went off in his locker. Ironically, he has got himself in academic trouble by doing a non-academic subject for which he has no talent whatever – one of the film's intelligent comments on the problems of American education is that the cult of the grade-point average privileges consistent mediocrity over specialized talent:

> Brian Johnson: I'm a fucking idiot because I can't make a lamp?
>
> John Bender: No. You're a genius because you can't make a lamp.

Brian's name is either an ironic reference to the Irish heroes and kings of that name or, more probably, a reference to his intellect via the standard typo for it.

Brian is at once the least unlikeable and the most pathetic of the five. He wants to be liked by people he has no especial fellow-feeling for, and he tries to argue that the various academic activities clubs to which he belongs are as important to the school as the social and sports elites to which Claire and Andrew belong. Which, of course, in a sane world they would be, but these characters are not living in that world. It is a resolution for him that the others trust him enough to act as the spokesman for the entire group: where the other four pair off, he ends up alone, but his voice ends the film.

The other point that needs to be made here is that Anthony Michael Hall, who plays Brian, is almost as much an iconic figure in the films of John Hughes as Molly Ringwald, appearing in *Sixteen Candles* and *Weird Science* (1985) in roles similar in nature to Brian, though rather less sympathetic. Hughes always casts him as the pitiably unattractive youth who compounds a lack of physical presence by an obsessive quality both in his intellectual interests and his sexual ones. The decision to pose him as the moral centre here is, given Hughes' tendency to stereotype, an interesting one.

Allison (Ally Sheedy) is a proto-Goth with shapeless dark clothes, a hedge of hair to hide behind and masses of dark eye make-up. For much of the film she refuses to communicate with the others save by strange birdlike animal noises and grunts. Even when she does start talking, roughly a third of the way through the film, she is an unreliable narrator of her own life, claiming to a sexual promiscuity that is not in fact a part of her character: 'I never did it either. I'm not a nymphomaniac. I'm a compulsive liar.' We learn about her reason for being in detention last of all – and the answer to the problem posed is, simply, that she is not, and has come into school on a Saturday simply because she has nothing better to do.

All of the others have social roles that they hide behind as if they were masks. For Allison, the mask is her social role. Bender is defined, which is to say limited, by his delinquency; Allison is similarly defined and limited by her teen version of art-school bohemianism. This lack of sympathy for the bohemian is engrained in the more suburban type of American liberalism. (The cartoons of the popular Jules Feiffer include as one of the running characters a dancer who performs as 'Spring' or 'the decline of the West'. Feiffer's mockery is at once patronizing and philistine about an American avant-garde that had, in the dances of Martha Graham and Merce Cunningham achieved real distinction.)

We never find out what specifically is wrong with Allison's life – she talks about keeping her bag full because of the possibility that she may need to decide to run away. She also describes her home life as 'unsatisfactory'. Her quirkiness extends to her diet, she throws away the meat from her sandwich, replacing it with crushed crisps and sugar. In a more recent film, we would expect it to be explicit that she has an eating disorder, or that she has been sexually abused; two decades after it was made, we experience the more open and innocent *The Breakfast Club* as refreshingly reticent in its handling of these possibilities. Allison may be 'a basket case' but she is also something rather more, whose options are not closed.

The film has two other named characters. (There are also the largely silent parents who drop their children off at the beginning and who collect most of them at the end. These set up, in a couple of cases like Claire and Brian, a sense of the pressures they are under which means that we regard their accounts as truthful.) Vernon (Paul Gleason) is a classic example of the schoolteacher who has come to hate the children with whom he works – he is superficially handsome but his insecurities have made him an unpleasant bully without a sense of humour.

He postures in front of a mirror, priding himself on his physique, and yet is physically clumsy, accidentally pouring over his desk the coffee he has brought in from home. Generally, the film sets him up as an obnoxious figure of fun in a way that foreshadows what Hughes was to do with another officious bully in the far more overtly comic *Ferris Bueller's Day*

Off. Vernon's first name is Richard, which, of course, enables Bender to refer to him as Dick; he is almost automatically a figure of threatened adult masculinity. Mount Vernon was George Washington's home – it is a surname that lends authority.

In his interactions with Bender, Vernon comes close to being something rather worse than a bully – one of these days he is going to snap and use his full capacity for physical violence against one of the Benders of this world and then his life will be changed forever. He boasts to Bender that he will not use physical brutality against him because of its consequences:

> I make thirty-one thousand dollars a year and I have a home and
> I am not going to throw it away on some punk like you

before making the bizarre and improbable threat that one day, when Bender is no longer at school, Vernon will find him and brutalize him. How much more likely, we have to ask, is the converse of this?

Vernon offers Bender the chance to retaliate with physical violence and accuses him of being 'a gutless turd' when the smaller youth declines. What kind of man takes pleasure from this sort of petty triumph? There are times when Hughes, in setting up of the adult authority figure for our mockery and disdain, goes too far – or given actual authority figures in the real world, perhaps he doesn't.

Vernon consistently ends up allowing Bender to control the terms of their engagement – by reacting to Bender's insolence – the 'eat my shorts' later to be associated with Bart Simpson and the imputation that Vernon has copied his wardrobe from Barry Manilow – with threats and physical intimidation. He confirms not only Bender's own attitude to authority figures, but looks like a bully to the other adolescents. By constantly increasing the number of detentions Bender will be punished with – to a point where he loses count and has to have his figures corrected by a Brian still eager at this early stage to ingratiate himself with authority – he comes to look petty. This scene with his tiresomely macho 'don't mess with the bull, young man, you'll get the horns' is one of the moments from *The Breakfast Club* most parodied in *Not Another Teen Movie*, which brings back Paul Gleason almost two decades later for the purpose.

Similarly, when Bender closes and sabotages the door, Vernon's attempts to keep it open are almost as destructive as Bender's original act, spilling magazines from the rack he tries to use to jam it open. Bender suggests that he is blocking the exits and contravening the fire regulations ('unwise at this juncture in your career') and Vernon has to be reminded by Brian that there is in fact a fire door at the other end of the library of the school of which he is principal. Both in their confrontation in the gym, when Bender uses basketball control to evade him, and in Bender's escape from the closet in which Vernon illegally confines him, Bender creates a situation in which Vernon makes himself look silly. One of the film's strengths is the combination of neurosis and authority that Paul Gleason brings to the part – it asks the valid question of whether the delinquent is as dangerous as the authority who is trying to control him.

Vernon is contrasted with the happy-go-lucky figure of Carl the Janitor (John Kapelos) who drifts through life and in and out of the plot of the film without either passion or commitment. In an establishing shot, we learn from one of the photographs on the wall that he was, when younger, one of the school's sporting heroes. He is a reminder of what is at stake – people who make a mess of their lives at school may well end up becoming janitors – and that it does not necessarily matter all that much. As we see him, Carl is a far happier man than the over-achieving Vernon and is less likely to explode. He is also a realist about what can be expected from the younger generation:

> Richard Vernon: Now this is the thought that wakes me up in the middle of the night. That when I get older, these kids are going to take care of me.
>
> Carl: I wouldn't count on it.

Rather more telling is the other moment when Carl has Vernon at a disadvantage and exploits it. Vernon has gone into the basement and is going through confidential files, discovering, it seems, that Bender has been diagnosed with incipient mental illness, a fact he is clearly considering using in their next confrontation. Carl points out to him that the files are confidential and extorts fifty dollars for his silence.

The occasional interventions and interactions of Vernon and Carl are in the film primarily to break up what might otherwise seem like a very simplistic three-act structure. In this structure, the five adolescents are introduced, come to personal epiphanies through conflict and start trying to resolve their personal problems with the help of their co-detainees. These acts are also broken up by sequences like their attempt to get back to the library after a group departure without crossing the path of the prowling Vernon, their consumption of Bender's joint and their subsequent breakout into wild dancing, or in Andrew's case spectacular gymnastics. In its deeply structured layout, and its assumption that all problems can be cured by facing up to them, *The Breakfast Club* is a deeply Apollonian film, but it does have an occasional place for the Dionysiac.

A critical problem created by the knowledge that the film has been so ruthlessly trimmed is this – what can look like serious imbalances in its structure may simply be points at which scenes necessary to that structure were removed. In a film as stagy and artificial as *The Breakfast Club*, it is a serious weakness when situations once established have no pay-off. For example, except for his discovery of Brian's essay in the library in a single establishing shot that leads to Brian's concluding voiceover, Vernon disappears from the film for its last third.

Some of the workings through of the personal issues between the five may also be among what ended up on the cutting room floor. At first, for example, Andrew responds to Bender's verbal aggression with an altogether disproportionate amount of physical aggression ('If I lose my temper, you're totaled man!') and with insults based as much on their respective positions in the school's social hierarchy as anything else. He is genuinely outraged as well as nonplussed when Bender indicates that he finds such considerations laughable. Later on, they sit around together smoking dope with Brian and Claire as if this had never happened. Watched naively, it does not occur to us that this is a radical shift; considered, and in the context of the film's often laborious working through of its issues and relationships, the jump may have been a good decision by the studio about pacing.

Again, possibly as a result of cuts, there are what seem like inconsistencies in the film's resolution. At quite a late point in the film, Claire expresses serious doubts that any friendship they may have achieved is going to last past the day among the social peer pressures they encounter, that she and Andrew will continue to ignore the others in the halls. Further, she argues that it isn't just the case with the socially successful kids. She says to Bender, 'What would your friends say if we were walking down the hall together. They'd laugh their asses off and you'd probably tell them you were doing it with me so they'd forgive you for being seen with me.'

Brian is appalled at what she says but it is significant that, when he says he is not like her, his example of someone to whom he would be seen talking is Allison and not Bender. Bender gets very angry with Claire and his anger and her tears are the closest the film comes to foreshadowing their later pairing. In the event, the issue of peer-group pressure, which is the whole subject of *Heathers*, is dropped when the dialogue takes a sideways turn into Brian's trauma about grades and the reason why he is in detention. It is implicitly addressed by the shared dancing and by the election of Brian to speak for the whole group, but it remains an issue that the film as it stands fails to resolve at a level of force equivalent to that at which it raised it.

The eventual pairing-off of Claire and Bender and of Allison and Andrew looks, in the film as shown, quite arbitrary and almost an afterthought. These are the pairings you would not expect, but this breaking of the natural order of high school romance is not earned by preparation; the odd lingering glance cast by Allison in Andrew's direction hardly counts. Claire's interest in Bender is even more sudden; their earlier antagonism is, quite simply, not flirtatious banter but expressive, if genuine, considered dislike. The fact that their eventual pairing-off is preceded by Bender's sexual fondling of Claire when hiding under her desk is more indicative of Hughes' sometimes Neanderthal sexual politics than it is of a growing relationship between them.

Sometimes, of course, the growing bond between the five is represented purely in terms of the anarchic, and it is this sense of carnival that almost allows these pairings to become plausible. As the film wears on, the other young people become complicit in Bender's rebellions; they cover for his escape from the cupboard in which Vernon has locked him, even when he molests Claire. They join him in smoking his dope, even after he has hidden it from Vernon in Brian's underpants; they play loud music and they dance. Andrew does gymnastics and Allison gives out a high scream, which literally breaks down barriers in the shape of a glass door. If the five are here on a Saturday to learn discipline, then Vernon has clearly failed altogether.

At the beginning of the film, Vernon tells them to write an essay about why they are here. Their eventual refusal to do as he has ordered, and instead to delegate a joint statement to Brian is one of the most hopeful aspects of the film's portrayal of their growth and development. Sometimes deciding to disobey orders is the right thing to do.

The encounter between the five has enabled them to transcend the standard divisions of high school, even if a peer-mandated 'normality' of strict social division eventually reasserts itself beyond the confines of the plot. Hughes seriously considered that there could be later films which picked up these characters down the years and showed whether the interaction between them had lasting effects, which presumes that it did. None of these films, however, ever moved, as far as it is known, beyond the pipe-dream stage.

One of the film's weaknesses is its assumption that all of the problems of its five iconic teenagers have quick and simple fixes, that the sudden commitment involved in Claire's giving Bender one of her matched set of diamond earrings will reassure him to the point where he becomes a better and saner person, and is an act of self-sacrifice on her part which will simply transform her. The makeover that Claire performs on Allison is symbolic of this whole approach – it is at the same time entirely superficial and entirely reductive; she pushes Allison's hair back and secures it with a white band, and removes the heavy eye-liner replacing it with softly feathered eye-shadow. Suddenly, we are supposed to believe, boys see Allison in an entirely new light, and suddenly she has discovered the wonderful world of femininity and feminine solidarity:

Claire:	You know, you look a lot better without all that black shit under your eyes.
Allison Reynolds:	Hey, I like all that black shit… Why are you being so nice to me?
Claire:	Because you're letting me.

And, almost immediately, Allison and Andrew are a couple, simply because she changes her look. This is even more trite than the stock trope of the intellectual woman removing her glasses and suddenly becoming a ravishing beauty. The makeover scene has become another of the stock tropes of the teen genre in, for example, *Clueless* and *Jawbreaker* (1999), where it assumes more importance in the plot.

On the other hand, some of this obsession with the neat and the potentially meretriciously pat pays off. The pay-off to Vernon's demand that the five write him a thousand-word essay on who they are and why they are here is a good example of this; they delegate Brian to speak for them and he delivers the film's culminating message:

Dear Mr. Vernon: We accept the fact that we had to sacrifice a whole Saturday in detention for whatever it is we did wrong, but we think you're crazy for making us write an essay telling you

who we think we are. You see us as you want to see us: in the
simplest terms, in the most convenient definitions. But what we
found out is that each one of us is a brain, and an athlete, and
a basket case, a princess, and a criminal. Does that answer your
question? Sincerely yours, The Breakfast Club.

It is attractive that at the end of the film the five of them have transcended
the stereotypes into which school society and Vernon, as the principal who
determines the ethos of the school, place them. It is, however, somewhat
dishonest of a screenplay which has made a point of establishing them as
representatives of types to then tick off the adult world for doing so. One
of Hughes' besetting sins as writer and director is a desire to have his cake
and eat it.

This is very visibly the case in the three films he made which centre on
Molly Ringwald, and most egregiously so in the case of *Sixteen Candles*,
which combines a sentimentally comic foreplot with a darker subplot
of whose full implications Hughes seems unaware. Again, the notional
subject is the artificiality of the social divisions of American high schools
and in particular the arbitrary effect of an age standard which means that
girls always date boys their own age or older. *Sixteen Candles* was pitched
to Universal Studios at the same time as *The Breakfast Club* and, with its
large cast and many sets, was a far more expensive film.

The social comedy of the foregrounded plot is an effective given – in the
bustle of the preparations for her sister's wedding the following day, Sam's
parents have forgotten her birthday. Much of what follows is mean spirited
– there are jokes about the inability of the bride's family to cope with the
complex Slavic name of their future in-laws and jokes about the younger
brother's inability to cope with female physiology. However, the central
given is an effective reversal – Sam (Molly Ringwald) is an American
princess who for once is being denied something which she is entitled to
expect. Ringwald's performance in this role is effective but without much
nuance; she is considerably more interesting as Claire.

She is also in pursuit of something she is not necessarily entitled to
– Jake Ryan (Justin Henry), who is not only older but also taken. Even
she does not regard this as a serious goal – Jake is 'her ideal' rather than
someone she is actively pursuing. She writes down her interest and the
piece of paper falls into Jake's hands. To the surprise of the friend in
whom he confides, Jake indicates that he is actually more interested in

the comparatively asexual love on offer from Sam than he is in his existing girlfriend, the worldly and attractive Caroline.

What we turn out to have here is that old standard of European culture, the clash between sacred and profane love, the Madonna and the whore. It is significant that Jake gets to acknowledge his largely chaste devotion to Sam outside the church where her sister has just got married. The quiet meal to which he sweeps her away is a scene dominated by the sixteen candles that signify her missed birthday but also impart to their romance a quasi-sacramental character. The scene is shot through what appears literally to be a rose-tinted lens. And, of course, it is necessary to trash other more carnal devotions in the course of the film in order to make us swallow this sentimentalized romance.

Hughes sets up moments of silly farce in order to create moments of fake suspense – Jake is told by the Chinese house guest of Sam's family that she is at the church at a wedding. Long Duk Dong manages to be verbally and implausibly confused about precisely who is getting married and sends Jake into a panic at the possibility that he might lose Sam before declaring himself. Long is generally one of the film's embodiments of that spirit of comic anarchy which is elsewhere one of Hughes' strengths. The party scenes and the generalized wrecking of the house of Jake's parents have a certain vigour, though far less than the equivalent scenes in *Weird Science* or the far more interesting anarchy of *Ferris Bueller's Day Off*.

In a parallel plot, Sam is herself pursued by a younger boy, Ted (Anthony Michael Hall), referred to by himself for no obvious reason as Farmer Ted and by everyone else as 'the Geek'. The double standard is alive and well in this film – Sam's pursuit of Jake is seen as legitimate and the Geek's of her as seedy and obsessive, yet his desire to lose his virginity at almost any cost to himself and others is endorsed by the film. He boasts about his non-existent relationship with Sam to his even more pathetic friends, one of whom is played by John Cusack, who within a year or so was playing the romantic lead in this sort of film. Success with women is essential to homosocial bonding and validation even among social pariahs. (See also John Hughes' other film on this theme, *Weird Science*.)

There are touching moments here. At a school dance that evening Sam ends up crying on the Geek's shoulders about her parents forgetting her birthday and her feelings for the unattainable Jake and he does the right thing and tells her that Jake shares her feelings – which are almost immediately undercut by sour comedy. The Geek asks to borrow her underpants so that he can pretend to his friends that he has had intercourse with her and immediately betrays her trust by exhibiting the underwear for money to all the boys in his year.

Irritating as Hughes can be when his comedy is sentimental, he is even less attractive when the comedy is sour and sexual. The film approaches the entirely unacceptable in several comedic areas such as the handling of the Chinese house guest – we get the funny oriental name joke (Long Duk Dong) and the funny oriental pronunciation joke. He trails along to the dance with Sam and becomes sexually entangled with Marlene, a gawky yet voracious female athlete. It is viewed as intrinsically funny that these two should entwine and, whenever the comedy flags elsewhere, the camera wanders back to them. Long Duk Dong ends up humiliatingly dropped semi-conscious at the kerb outside Sam's house to face the enquiries of the older generation and does not get to go with them to the wedding – purely so that he is there as a plot function to confuse Jake.

Caroline has to be punished by Hughes for being bold and sexual and Sam's rival. She organizes a wild post-dance party at Jake's house and gets drunk. It is clear that he has a genuine grievance against her; her friends more or less wreck his parents' house, though it is Long Duk Dong and Marlene who do the most damage. The reasons why Jake rejects Caroline, though, are explicitly because their relationship is almost entirely sexual:

> She's beautiful and she's built and all that; I'm just not interested any more … She's totally insensitive … She doesn't know shit about love … I want a serious girlfriend. Someone I can love that's gonna love me back.

He abandons her in order to go and telephone Sam, whom he really, and chastely, loves, even though her grandparents view his attempts to contact her in the middle of the night in a somewhat darker light.

In the film's sourest note, he hands Caroline over to the Geek to take home in his parents' car, giving the young boy effective carte blanche to exploit her sexually along the way: 'She's so blitzed she won't know the difference' – a point he proves by simply reassuring her when she confusedly awakes that he is the Geek and the Geek is him. He makes the Geek promise actually to deliver her and not 'leave her in a parking lot somewhere'. There are limits even to the misogyny of this plot and it is a good thing that those limits are made explicit, though in the event the specifics of those limits are ironic. Let us be clear, however softened in the event, this is a film in which date rape is seen as a reasonable response to inappropriate female behaviour.

Nonetheless, the Geek insists on taking the paralytically drunk Caroline with him to the house of his friends, where he has them photograph him with her – sexuality is a shared homosocial act and has to be recorded in trophy pictures. Significantly they regard his acquisition of the Ryan family's Rolls-Royce as a triumph almost equivalent to his acquiring of the prom queen – trophies are branded commodities.

Hughes manages to soften this plot in an unlikely way – the Geek and Caroline wake up, in a parking lot across from a church and it is clear to both of them that they have had sex.

Geek:	Do you know if I enjoyed it? Am I nuts, of course I enjoyed it. I mean um, what I meant was, uh, did you?
Caroline:	You know, I have this weird feeling I did.

Haviland Morris manages to give Caroline a surprising amount of dignity at this moment as well as sexual purring. In a later scene, Caroline talks attractively about how the nicest thing of all was waking up in the Geek's arms; when Jake turns up, Haviland Morris plays the scene as if she is letting him down gently as much as him telling her that he is leaving her. Her performance earlier in the film is standard comic drunken airhead; she manages to redeem this potentially highly offensive subplot by incredibly sensitive playing.

Anthony Michael Hall as the Geek manages to be quite singularly unlikeable, as are his cohorts with their crude nerdish humour:

Geek:	Just get it [a camera] and come out front.
Bruce:	UFO?
Geek:	It's better.
Bryce:	Extraterrestrial?
Geek:	It's better.
Bryce:	Female Extraterrestrial?
Geek:	It's better. Now sssh.
Bryce:	How do you tell it's a female extraterrestrial?
Cliff:	'Cause it's got tits.

They are gauche and cowardly and weirdly venal, all three of them. The Geek exploits the moment of empathy between him and Sam to humiliate her and make money. He would rather boast about a non-existent sexual bond between them than enjoy genuine intimacy. The only exception to this is his behaviour in his occasional moments of sensitivity. If we are to take it that having sex with Caroline has changed him for the better, then that is not entirely satisfactory, since what has happened is still sex with a women out of her head on drink.

The similar character that Anthony Michael Hall plays in Hughes' other teen film of 1985, *Weird Science*, is redeemed by a more complex mechanism, though one which is only marginally less distasteful. Gary (Hall) and his friend Wyatt (Ilan Mitchell-Smith) are gauche twerps oppressed by the bullies Ian and Max at school, and by Wyatt's brutish brother Chet at home. The only reason that their parents are not high on their list of adversaries is that their emotionally abusive fathers do not regularly brutalize them. They have a vivid fantasy life about the future they may one day attain, a future where they have parties that people come to, where they date girls, and where they explore city night life with panache.

In spite of its title, and the use of computer hacking as a plot mechanism, *Weird Science* is a fantasy about two youths who manage to summon a genie and get all of their wishes to scarily come true. 'Lisa' (Kelly LeBrock) is clearly more a magical being than an android of any kind – she is Mary Poppins as a centrefold model. She fulfils their wishes, but for the most part in ways that they have not expected or asked for and she is a figure of wild anarchic magic that scares as much as it delights them.

When, for example, she feels they need it, she summons a group of Mad Max style mutant bikers and puts Gary and Wyatt in a situation where they have to discover a certain inner courage, after some gross displays of cowardice. Inevitably, because this is a very American film, the mutants' mockery is not what inspires them; it is their molestation of Deb and Hilly, the two girls of their own age whom Gary and Wyatt have been enabled by Lisa to start noticing. And, equally predictably, their answer to the biker mutants is to point very large guns at their hideous faces. Gary, indeed, points the very large gun that earlier on Lisa has pointed at his father when rebuking his parents for never praising him.

Some of the comedy is interesting and well-observed; when Lisa takes Gary and Wyatt into a blues club in the city, its elderly hip denizens pick up the youths' basic likeableness and are more amused than otherwise by their drunken attempts to pick up the blues fans' idiolect. Some of what makes them unacceptable is that they think of themselves as victims – the moment they start to realize that they have done something extraordinary, they begin to stop feeling sorry for themselves. Lisa is not a mere deus ex machina, in other words; she is a metaphor for Gary and Wyatt's growing sense of themselves.

There are some things she does for Gary and Wyatt that they are incapable of doing for themselves. When Chet returns to find the detritus of a party and Gary and Wyatt in bed with their respective girlfriends, he turns exceptionally nasty and starts belting the youths with the barrels of his loaded shotgun. It is not realistic for Gary and Wyatt to stand up to him – he is a figure of real malevolence. Lisa, on the other hand, can simply turn him into a giant turd with a wave of her hand and extort promises of better behaviour, just as she can place Wyatt's grandparents into frozen stasis when they turn up and make a scene in the middle of the party.

One does not think of John Hughes as any sort of Freudian, but it does have to be mentioned that much of this lends itself to a very crude Freudian reading. It is a coming-of-age movie, after all, in which two youths are uncertain of their sexuality and are constantly humiliated in specifically sexual ways by Max and Ian, and by Chet. Chet regularly refers to them as girls and Max and Ian pull down their gym shorts exposing them to the gym full of older girls that Gary and Wyatt were fantasizing about. And in this context, the various large guns are clearly relevant.

When Gary and Wyatt offer to make superwomen for Max and Ian, the process that created Lisa goes wrong and they end up with a phallic Pershing missile thrusting through the floor. And then there are all those guns, and Chet's transformation. If there were any doubt that the sexually aggressive English-accented Lisa were in some sense a phallic fantasy woman, it should probably disappear in the film's last moments when she turns up as the new gym instructor at the school, and demands press-ups from a male gym class.

One of the things that stops this film being more than marginally offensive – and I now find it somewhat less so than I remembered it – is the sheer gusto that Kelly LeBrock brings to her portrayal of Lisa. She may affect submission to Gary and Wyatt's desires, but it is always on her own terms and with a distinct edge of genial contempt for their more idiotic fantasies. She always has an edge of mild menace in her dealings, even with them, though more especially with their various enemies. Hughes is never one to avoid the obvious, but the deliberate references to various films from the Frankenstein mythos – cries of 'It's alive' coming from the television – never seem cheap or gratuitous. When they try to repeat her creation, they are acting as Sorcerer's Apprentices, making magic that they do not understand or control. The fact that they produce a nuclear missile is again hardly subtle, but is a reasonable if not reasoned statement about the urge to control and create irresponsibly and where it leaves us.

Lisa showers with them and they realize that they are simply not up to coping with the fulfilment of that particular fantasy; she drives them around in fast cars and throws the sort of party of which they'd always dreamed, and they do not entirely cope with the fantasy. And yet her mere presence on their arms is enough to impress the likes of Max and Ian. Above all, it is the fact that she clearly genuinely likes her creators/summoners, that makes us notice that their very rough edges are being wiped away as we watch. This is a film about the importance of status in high school society – Hughes placed class firmly if crudely on the agenda in all of these films – and it takes magic here to break down rigid rules.

This is a film in which two very unappealing young men mutate into something approaching good looks, partly by hairdressing and better clothes, but also by the way they hold themselves and react to other people. In *Sixteen Candles*, Anthony Michael Hall never gets to sustain the moments of sensitivity Hughes gives him; here he gives a more nuanced portrayal of someone learning better. He is also genuinely funny in large parts of the film – his drunken attempts to fit in at the blues' club are a delight.

One of the major lessons that Lisa teaches them is that they realize they cannot keep her, that they have to tell her that they have moved on to actual relationships with actual girls. It is not that Lisa is in any sense a toy, a childish thing that they need to put away, it is that Gary and Wyatt's relationship with her is such a toy. Lisa will continue to be in their lives, we learn, but very much on her own terms.

She undoes all the physical chaos her creation and her party have produced. The fact that the last bits of order to be restored – furniture scurrying to its original place – happens as Wyatt's parents enter the house is a nice piece of comic timing. Hughes was to do something similar and subtler in the last moments of *Ferris Bueller's Day Off*. Lisa is a productive figure of misrule and one of the most attractive creations of Hughes' teen films.

There followed, in 1986, the first of two films which Hughes wrote and Howard Deutch, a jobbing director previously known for music videos and trailers, directed, for Paramount rather than for Universal. *Pretty in Pink* forms a diptych with *Some Kind of Wonderful* in other respects as well. Both deal with the theme of class and popularity which *The Breakfast Club* and the other Hughes films of 1985 had raised, and both of them deal with the question of generosity and of loving someone who does not love you back.

Pretty in Pink starts with a sequence that fetishizes Molly Ringwald to an uncomfortable degree, as Andie, a high school senior from the wrong side of the tracks, dresses for a day at school in one of the idiosyncratic outfits she runs up for herself. The camera runs itself lovingly up her long legs as she puts white stockings on them and lingers on the texture of her brocade waistcoat. She is a self-consciously wacky teen who compensates with personal style for lack of money and a father, Jack Walsh (Harry Dean Stanton), who has drifted into indolence and implied alcoholism as a result of the departure of his wife. Much is made, not very subtly, of the extent to which Andie has had to become her father's parent – one of the weaknesses of the film is this tendency to make Andie perfect and victimized in every possible way.

Andie is sneered at for her poverty and clothes by the rich kids at the school she attends. She protests at one point when sent to the principal that the school does nothing to prevent the constant niggling persecution she and others undergo, and that they are punished when all they do is fight back. He acknowledges that she is right, by letting her off detention, and extending this to the friend she was defending, but has no obvious answer to the problem. The film is clear that the social pressures of class weigh on staff as much as pupils and that the rich kids whose families own the nice houses past which Andie sometimes drives her car have a measure of impunity.

One of these rich kids, the appalling and loudmouthed Steff (James Spader), propositions Andie and she rejects him as much for the way he pro-positions her as for who he is – he leans on her car door preventing her from getting into it. Andie has her pride, even though she wants desperately to have a boyfriend who will take her to the prom. She knows how things work well enough to know that Steff just wants her as a disposable object of sexual exploitation, because that is what girls from her side of the tracks mean to boys from the rich suburbs. When she starts dating Steff's nicer friend Blane, there is a real question about what he expects from her and what she is prepared to give him, that only has its teeth drawn by his vague effeteness.

One of the major threats to Andie is her own sense of social shame – it matters to her that people whose clothes sense and taste in music she rightly despises consider her and her friends to be freaks. (The clothes of the preppy boys in this film are one of its aspects that have not worn well, whereas her admirer Duckie and her employer and friend Iona still look eccentrically stylish and Andie's outfits have a period charm.) She and Blane have their first real row not over his dragging her to a party where she is ostracized and insulted, nor her taking him to a club where something similar happens to him, but over his seemingly harmless request that he take her home. She is ashamed of the poor housing in which she and her father live, even though she knows that Blane is entirely aware in the abstract of where she lives. Similarly, her original instinct is to look at prom dresses she cannot afford, and only later does she have the strength to make a dress for herself from the fabric of one dress her father bought for her and one Iona gave her.

The young Spader, looking something like Christopher Walken, is convincingly slimy at this point and rather better than Craig Sheffer in the equivalent role of Hardy in *Some Kind of Wonderful*. There are some deeply sentimental aspects to the way in which John Hughes writes his upper-middle-class characters. It is a given that they are essentially weak bullies who will always crumble if properly challenged, because their parents do not give them the attentive devotion that even a flawed parent like Jack Walsh can deliver. Hughes' capacity for Christmas-cracker-slogan moralizing and psychologizing is a factor in his enduring popularity with young audiences, and is one of the reasons why people often grow out of his films.

Andie is loved, hopelessly, by her best friend Duckie (Jon Cryer), an equally poor boy with a similarly bizarre taste in clothes. He is an aspiring hipster with a pork-pie hat, a DA hairstyle and dark glasses, who rides around on a small bike because he is too poor to run a car. He is also physically frail – shorter even than Andie – which makes the scene late in the movie where he physically attacks Steff for disrespecting her all the more impressive. Because Duckie is a boy, the film does not play with the implications of possibly queer sexuality and androgyny that apply to the similar figure of Watts in *Some Kind of Wonderful* – he is very carefully coded as heterosexual. (His name, which might imply otherwise to a UK audience, is of course a reference to his hairstyle rather than any implied campness.)

Andie has a substitute mother and best girlfriend in the shape of Iona (Annie Potts), the woman in her thirties who runs the record store where Andie works in her spare time and whose equally bizarre fashion sense makes her Andie's mentor in eccentricity and fearlessness. Iona is keen that Andie attend the prom, talking of a friend, who does not seem to be herself, who did not go, and spent her life feeling that she missed something. When she gives Andie her old prom dress to cut up and restyle, it is a deliberate handing on of a torch.

Iona is also, like Andie's father, an awful warning of what happens when relationships go wrong. Jack's wife left him and Andie because, as Andie says, she just did not love them enough to stay. Iona has a history of violent boyfriends and is touchingly happy when she finds herself dating a pleasant vet yuppy who likes her in spite of her beehive hairdos and cheongsam dresses. She is a role model in sticking to your guns and pursuing your sense of your own identity.

In what might seem a piece of radicalism, the character whose identity is most threatened in *Pretty in Pink* is none of these, but rather Blane (Andrew McCarthy), Andie's object of desire and Steff's best friend. Blane is genuinely attracted to Andie and has genuine feelings for her, but he has not the strength of character to persist in the relationship when he is threatened with social death by Steff and their clique, and finds himself made unwelcome by Andie's friends Iona and Duckie, and uncomfortable in the club where they hang out.

Steff's motiveless malignity is coded as effetely heterosexual – he puts on a display of studliness with his girlfriend as a way of making Blane and Andie more uncomfortable at his party – but his need is to own his friends, and in particular to own Blane. Blane's eventual decision to apologize to Andie at the prom they were supposed to attend together is a rejection of Steff at something like the last point at which Blane could possibly retain any self-respect. As in *Some Kind of Wonderful*, personal autonomy is threatened by the pursuit of status and approval. At one point, Blane responds to Steff's arguments by saying, 'What are you, my mother?' It is clear beyond the joke that he is aware that Steff is saying what his parents would say.

Blane's cowardice and his callous betrayal of Andie when he withdraws his invitation to the prom are hard to forgive, which makes the ending of this film rather more problematic than that of *Some Kind of Wonderful*. His virtue is almost passive – he attends the prom alone as does Andie, but she does not realize this, until Duckie, who has also attended alone in order to give Andie at least the appearance of a date, generously points this out to her.

I do find myself wondering whether anyone really likes this ending as much as that of *Some Kind of Wonderful*, where the generosity of Amanda and Watts is equivalent and they compete as to which of them will give up Keith to the other. It never seems to occur to Blane that he might do something equivalent – in the end, his class privilege extends to expecting to be forgiven and getting what he expects. The film ends where it has to with Blane and Andie kissing in the car park to which they have taken refuge from the prom – I find their future together unimaginable because implausible. It is necessary for Andie to get her man because anything else means that the Steffs of this world win, but Blane is a hollow enough figure to make this victory also hollow – Andrew McCarthy does not give him much in the way of charisma save slightly weaselly good looks.

Where *Pretty in Pink* is at its best is in the liveliness of the scenes with Iona and Duckie – who are, it hardly needs saying, classic examples of Hughes' identification of moral uprightness with the anarchic and eccentric – and the sheer loving loathsomeness of the portrayal of the preppy world of Steff and Blane. This is a deeply Manichean film in which the total hipness of the heroine's friends is constantly stressed: the only one of the evil preppies to have even a hint of the same level of stylishness is one played by the young Gina Gershon, who can never be uncool.

From its first moments, *Some Kind of Wonderful* announces itself as being, in a variety of ways, more interesting than most of the other John Hughes teen movies, perhaps even than its immediate predecessor and thematic stablemate. *Pretty in Pink* was, after all, Deutch's first film, and he had learnt from the experience. The Paramount fanfare fades into a crashing drum solo and the screen flashes between Watts (Mary Stuart Masterson) playing her drums, Keith (Eric Stolz) walking moodily along the freight tracks that dominate much of the film and Amanda Jones (Lea Thompson) kissing Hardy (Craig Sheffer) with an unfeigned passion whose complexities we only learn about later.

Clearly we are being told that these young people are on each other's minds and one of the interesting things about the film is that the story it tells about them comes across as only one of the possibilities. Much of what is strongest about the film comes from this sense of human potentialities which may or may not be explored. Of all the John Hughes films, it is the one which has most potential for a polymorphously sexual reading – the sexuality of the central characters is never in serious doubt at a surface level, and yet the issue is raised at the same time verbally, in the usual sexual insults, and in lingering glances and irrational rivalries that can be taken as implying complex subtext.

Also, of course, it takes some aspects of the relationships in *Pretty in Pink* and reverses the genders. Steff's role is split between Shane and Hardy, for example, and Watts is to some extent an equivalent of Duckie. On the other hand, Amanda is radically different from Blane, and Keith a more dour and brooding person than Andie. Yet ultimately both films are about class, autonomy and generosity, themes that Hughes felt able to go back to, and preach sermons on, without repeating himself.

To summarize briefly: Keith is a talented youth who wants to go to art school and whose blue-collar father wants him to be the first of the family not to have to wash his hands when he comes in from work. He is the best friend and beloved of the orphaned Watts, a short-haired woman drummer assumed by most people at their school to be a lesbian. He nurses a crush on Amanda, who like him and Watts comes from a poor background, but has bought her way into the popular rich crowd at their school with her looks, charms and sexual favours. At one point in this, he gets detention to be near her, only to find that she has weaselled out of it; this brings him into contact with Duncan and the school's hoodlum element.

When Amanda breaks with her obnoxious lover Hardy, Keith asks her out and she agrees, originally to make a point to Hardy and secondly because she cannot bring herself to hurt Keith's feelings, even when she is dropped by her friends for not doing so. Hardy asks them to his party, planning to humiliate and beat Keith: Keith gets wind of this plan and assumes Amanda to be complicit in it; he nonetheless goes through with an elaborate date plan, spending his college fund on diamond earrings for her and getting Watts to chauffeur them. In the course of the evening, he and Amanda confront each other with the way they have used each other and he realizes she has no part in Hardy's plan. He nonetheless stands up to Hardy knowing he will be beaten and Amanda offers herself for humiliation in an attempt to save him. They are rescued by Duncan and his gang who turn the tables on Hardy. Amanda renounces Keith and tells him to give the earrings to Watts.

Written and produced by John Hughes, Howard Deutch's direction and the central performances give the film a little more subtlety than, say,

Sixteen Candles. One of its other strengths is the fact that, far more even than *The Breakfast Club* and like *Pretty in Pink*, it is a film about class. All three of the central characters are kids from, quite literally, the wrong side of the tracks, tracks which are shown literally for a moment in *Pretty in Pink* but in prolonged sequences here. The difference is that Amanda Jones has managed to buy into the style and popularity of her friend Shane and her boyfriend Hardy, whereas Keith's talent for art and Watts' mild androgyny make them mutually dependent pariahs at school. This is a film about deciding what you really want, and it is as much about Amanda as it is about Keith and Watts.

Even more than *Pretty in Pink*, *Some Kind of Wonderful* is a film about autonomy. Amanda has sold hers out for what she comes to see as far too little – as she learns when Shane drops her for not breaking her date with Keith. One of the crucial points in her personal character arc is the moment when she resents being referred to as Hardy's property in front of other people. Early in the film she talks of preferring to be with someone for the wrong reasons than alone for the right ones; at the film's end she reverses this choice. Her decision to be alone and unpopular is one rarely made in teen films and comes to seem not only an admirable choice but a plausible one. Her name means 'she who must be loved', and she moves past the lack of choice compelled by that name into a genuine regard for her self and her own choices.

Lea Thompson is fetishized in the film in the way Molly Ringwald was in the earlier one – her character takes her very name from a Rolling Stones track, 'Miss Amanda Jones'. Unlike almost any other princess figure in a high school movie – even Veronica in Waters and Lehman's *Heathers* – Amanda is a self-made figure from the same background as the social pariahs. Thompson and Deutch were to work together on later films and eventually married.

Earlier in the film, Amanda senses the inherent wrongness of the path she has chosen and has no very obvious way of escaping from it. She is a status symbol for Hardy, and her lower-class status makes her one with fewer ways of negotiating with him when he mauls her, or when he gets her into trouble by persuading her to leave school property, or when he humiliates Keith for looking at her. She knows that to cease to be Hardy's girlfriend is to forfeit the social status she has acquired.

When Hardy pushes her too far, she revolts and walks away from him. She takes Keith's offer of a date without thinking about its implications.

Pressured by Shane and the other 'popular' girls to cancel the date, she resists less out of a desire to protect her autonomy from them than out of an awareness of how much it would crush him. Soon, she finds herself dropped by Shane in a scene which elegantly and succinctly portrays the school-yard malice which other films – *Heathers* for example – spend their entire length dissecting. Quite literally, in the value system to which she sold herself for status, if she is dating Keith, she no longer exists.

And if she no longer exists, she is open to real sexual jeopardy. This is in the end a 1980s film in which nothing too bad can happen or even be seriously threatened. However, when she offers to give herself back to Hardy in order to protect Keith from a beating, it is clear that she knows that the consequences for her may be more than humiliating. Her generosity to Keith, who had earlier tried to humiliate her by giving her the ultimate date and by putting his entire future into a gift of jewellery, is remarkable given that he has put himself into jeopardy purely to make a point. Deutch gives this scene momentarily a real sense of menace and jeopardy of which Hughes by himself would not have been capable.

Watts has autonomy, and values it, but pushes her own pride far too hard in the name of proving the fact. She is an outsider, who wears boys underwear out of poverty and sharing with a brood of brothers, and is proud enough to allow the girls with whom she shares a locker room to assume that she is making a statement about her sexuality. She will let Duncan accuse her of being a lesbian, but threatens him when he calls Keith a faggot; she is tiny and yet formidable – her threats to Duncan are somehow not entirely ludicrous. Much of the time she wears her androgyny as a successful claiming of power – 'It's the eighties – I can be whatever I want' – and is socially at ease; dressed in her chauffeur's uniform, she fleeces restaurant waiters in a game of dice.

She does not value herself enough, even so – this is a film from the era of self-esteem – and more especially she discounts her own right to pursue Keith whom she loves because she is not the conventionally attractive womanly girl that Amanda is. Her instrument is the drum set – the raw power of her drumming indicates the level of passion that lies under her cool exterior and of course her name also reflects the extent to which she is about power, her own power that she does not value enough. (Also, of course, one of the standard descriptions of eccentricity and autonomy is that people are seen to be 'marching to their own drum'.) And because of that low self-esteem, she underestimates Amanda – this is in part a film about two young women who behave with real generosity to each other in the end and have to learn to accept that the other has done so.

It is, nonetheless, a film of its period and the means by which they express that generosity has to be which of them walks away with Keith. This is probably the closest that John Hughes ever came to making a feminist film, but that is not very close – it is in the end all about the boy.

Keith's autonomy is primarily threatened by his father's attempts to insist that he go to business school rather than art college. He is obsessed with his autonomy in other respects though, resenting interference in his emotional life from both his sister and from Watts. He comes for a while almost to hate Amanda under the mistaken impression that she has betrayed him, not so much because of the betrayal but because he resents loving someone who does not love him back.

There is also the morally ambiguous aspect of the situation. Keith is attracted to Amanda partly because she is a valuable possession who automatically confers status on him, and partly because she is a glamorous aesthetic object of whom he does a painting that is one of his best pieces of work. In a very real sense, he wants to own her, rather than love her. This is an intelligent film about sexual objectification precisely because its hero is as guilty of it as its villain.

She also represents a means of revolt against his father. His father is obsessed with status and fears Keith's artistic talent as something that might stop him making money. Keith's objectified version of the real Amanda is a possession so valuable that he can focus his revolt on her, spending his accumulated college funds on an evening with her and on the earrings which set his brand on her. Again, this is entirely understandable and entirely wrong – he is trying to get autonomy for himself but is attacking someone else's autonomy in order to get it.

He is also behaving in a fundamentally abusive way to his best friend, using the advice she gives him out of selfless love to pursue the object of his desire. One of the ways in which Eric Stolz makes this potentially dislikeable trait tolerable is by showing the extent to which Keith is leading a life of quiet desperation – early in the film he walks the train tracks and only steps off them when a slow-moving freight train is within inches of crushing him. It is never stated specifically that he is struggling with a death wish, but this and his preparedness to give himself up for a serious beating at the hands of Hardy and his minions make it clear that he is. The power to allow himself to be seriously injured is a sort of power and he is prepared to go for that option if there is no other option available to him.

His near-abusive mistreatment of the older of his two sisters for her obsessive testing of his boundary issues by coming into his room and trespassing in his emotional life is similarly a pursuit of the wrong kind of autonomy. It is the latter, her trading on his relationship with Amanda and intention of attending Hardy's party to give herself status with her own younger crowd, that leads to her discovery of Hardy's true intentions and ability to warn him. Significantly, she has to come into his room to do so – and for once he accepts her right to do so – and she gets wrong the important detail of Amanda's complicity. (This last is a necessary plot point from which it is impossible to extract any psychological significance. She needs to get it wrong so that he demonstrate his lack of trust for the woman he thinks of himself as loving, but there is no especial reason for her to do so save that she assumes Hardy is telling the truth to his friends when she eavesdrops.)

Hardy, on the other hand, has considerable autonomy and abuses it, both by lying to his girlfriend and by refusing to take responsibility for even his own acts of violence. He wants his minions to beat up Keith on the pathetically weak excuse that he is the party's host and cannot take the time. Autonomy then is only in this film valuable if it is threatened and not taken for granted; it has an intimate connection with class privilege and the lack of it.

At the same time, Hardy, like the other kids from the right side of the tracks, is obsessed with maintaining the social order of high school hierarchy. He has to humiliate Keith at every turn because Keith is a figure whose talent and whose refusal to be cowed threaten order. And Hardy is punished for this by an irruption of anarchy into his home. When Duncan promises Keith that he will not harm Hardy, just scare him and perhaps hurt him 'this much' showing a thin gap between thumb and finger, it is because Duncan does not need to do more than he has done to break Hardy's power forever.

Some Kind of Wonderful, a title which spells out the mood of quiet joy that pervades its ending, is also a film about generosity and gratitude. Watts sacrifices her own feelings for Keith, who has no apparent consciousness of them. Amanda is similarly gracious at the film's end; she gives Keith up to Watts even though there is enough feeling between them that she could have hung on to him, and even though at this point in the film she has nothing else. She has sacrificed her friendships with rich girls like Shane to her complex feelings for Keith, but she knows that he doesn't love her.

All of which would be lachrymose to an almost unbearable extent were the film's portrayal of emotion not happily undercut by minor characters who go about their business less affected by these concerns than the more sensitive central characters. Duncan is the film's embodiment of the sort of anarchy Hughes always likes – he is set up as an illusory threat in the opening sequences but rapidly becomes Keith's friend, after his own fashion. (Weevil in the 2004 television show *Veronica Mars* is fairly clearly drawn from the Duncan mould and very productively so.)

When Amanda ends up with detention for leaving school with Hardy, Keith, who has been spying on them, sets out to get detention himself in order to be near her. In the event, because this is stalker behaviour for which he should not profit, she talks her way out of detention by flirting with the relevant male teacher and Keith finds himself confined in a room with Duncan, and the other school stoners and hoodlums. The visual reference here is to middle-class offenders finding themselves in a cell with violent gangbangers. And since such scenes regularly culminate in attempted or actual male rape, we are entitled to see a sexual threat in Duncan's broad leer at the younger man he has called a faggot a few scenes earlier.

Later, in a crucial scene, he congratulates Keith on successfully persuading Amanda to go out with him. Earlier, he had accused Keith of homosexuality merely for being an artist and now he shows him his own macabre cartoon drawing, a tattoo design of a skeleton girl with a mullet and a rose in her teeth – 'That's a picture of my girlfriend,' he says with a leer and we realize at a stroke that Duncan is a more complex figure than he appears. He is a skinhead, but not in a sectarian way – his posse includes blacks and stoners; he is a trickster figure rather than any actual teen delinquent that ever existed.

For Keith to date Amanda, Duncan says, is a piece of successful class warfare, to take back someone who has crossed the tracks into acceptance and non-pariahdom. He and his friends help facilitate Keith's ultimate date fantasy – they arrange for him and Amanda to be served hamburgers in the swanky restaurant they go to and they set up a brightly lit open-air concert arena for them to talk in. Above all, Duncan has persuaded his janitor father to hang Keith's portrait of her in pride of place and give Keith and Amanda access to the gallery at night; he has made a free gift of his territory to his friend.

His eventual arrival, with his gang, just in time to humiliate Hardy and rescue Keith, is something he does because he can, and because he wants to, not because anyone has asked him to. It is a piece of generosity, in other words, though also a way to pursue class warfare in a tricksterish way. It is one of several especially satisfying moments in this exceptionally likeable film. It needs also to be noted that both this film and *Pretty in Pink* have, perhaps because of Howard Deutch's earlier involvement in the music industry, two of the most attractive and undated rock music scores of the Hughes canon, indeed of the entire teen genre, using non-mainstream bands like the Jesus and Mary Chain and the Psychedelic Furs. For once, hip teens are shown as listening to the edgy music that hip teens of their period might actually regard as worthwhile, something that was not to happen again in the genre until the early years of *Buffy the Vampire Slayer* on TV.

Hughes' other film of 1986, *Ferris Bueller's Day Off* for Universal, is paradoxically the most accomplished of his teen movies and the least influential; it goes farther than any of the other five in exploring the farcical elements which were increasingly to dominate his work as writer and director. At the same time, it continues the exploration of the anarchic which is always present in his teen films and here dominates even more entirely than it did in *Weird Science*. It also, alas, contains material that foreshadows the sad decline of Hughes' work over the last two decades.

In brief, Ferris Bueller (Matthew Broderick) is a talented manipulator and trickster who decides to take a day off school and to persuade his girlfriend, Sloane (Mia Sara), and his best friend to go with him to Chicago for adventures. Attempts to expose his various deceits by his sister and by the school principal result in the comic humiliation of the latter. Ferris escapes various unforeseen consequences of his own actions through a mixture of talent, luck, the eventual assistance of his sister and the self-sacrifice of his best friend.

The predicament of his friend Cameron Frye (Alan Buck) is not radically different from those of the troubled teens of *The Breakfast Club* – his oppression by an uncaring father is as soulfully described – and there are moments of serious emotion amid the comedy that link the film momentarily to the more romantic *Pretty in Pink* and *Some Kind of Wonderful*. In one of the film's few moments of stillness and sadness, Ferris expresses his concern that, at college, Cameron will wreck his life by marrying the wrong girl, because of his lack of self-esteem. Cameron's eventual decision to take responsibility for the destruction of his father's car, is not so much a matter of Ferris getting away with things one more time, because he tries to insist on taking the blame, as of Cameron making a decision to confront his father once and for all with no conceivable chance of backing down.

Part of the point of this day is Ferris exploiting Cameron, and part of it is his determination to show his friend a good time. Not all of the good time is boisterous; in a scene of touching innocence, the trio of Ferris, Sloane and Cameron join a crocodile of small children touring the art museum. The film lingers over Cameron's sense of wonder at the technique of Seurat's *La Grande Jatte* as much as over Sloane and Ferris necking in front of a Chagall. This ought to seem like a moment of ghastly good taste, but actually it reminds us that Cameron has an inner life of which his friend is largely unaware.

A reading of the film in which a part of Cameron's problem is that he is in love with his oblivious friend is not entirely far-fetched. When Cameron discovers how many miles have been put on the Ferrari he screams and lapses into catatonia, and eventually topples, still apparently catatonic, into a deep swimming pool. When Ferris saves him from drowning, Cameron says 'My hero', gazing at him sappily until Ferris turns the whole moment into horseplay, into which he drags Sloane. Hughes' intrinsic conservative blinkeredness sometimes frees the material to follow its own direction. As with the relationships in *Pretty in Pink* and *Some Kind of Wonderful*, there is subtext here.

The misfortunes of the Dean of Students, Ed Rooney (Jeffrey Jones) are more comprehensively humiliating than those of Dick Vernon in *The Breakfast Club*, and closer to those of the unfortunate burglars in the *Home Alone* series that Hughes was to script. He remains, especially in Jones' capable hands, a convincing portrait of a man determined to win small victories over the petty rebellions of teenagers. Rooney, far more even than Vernon, believes himself capable of wrecking a rebellious student's life and actively wants to do so; he sees himself as a Clint Eastwood figure and is prepared to do anything to trap Ferris, including illegal entry into the Bueller home. Everything that happens to him is entirely deserved.

Ferris himself is the sort of young man who is popular less for anything specific he does, than for what he is, which is cool. Indeed, in its cartoony way, *Ferris Bueller's Day Off* comes closer than most teen films to defining what cool is. It is not just that Ferris gets away with things and lives a life almost as unscathed as that of Bugs Bunny; it is that he does so with style, taking risks for their own sake as well as for the opportunities they bring him. 'You can never go too far,' he says to Cameron and Sloane, and his entire existence is bound up with that motto. It is typical of the clash in Hughes' work between conservatism and anarchy that Ferris's recklessness is admirable and successful, whereas the reckless disregard for limits of Dean Rooney has consequences.

It is clear from the school scenes that Ferris's popularity is based partly on his outrageous lies about himself and partly on the way he is prepared to teach others his techniques – one boy says excitedly, 'He's getting me out of summer school.' He is, both at school and in the course of his trip to Chicago, a Lord of Misrule, and an even more effective trickster figure than Lisa in *Weird Science*. Both his sister Jeanie (Jennifer Grey) and Dean Rooney hate him for this – Jeanie because Ferris gets away with things she would never dare do, Rooney because of his not entirely wrong assumption that 'he gives the good kids bad ideas. The last thing I need at this point in my career is fifteen hundred Ferris Bueller disciples running around these halls.'

Ferris's capacity to impose his will on the world exists in small things like his persuading Cameron to impersonate Sloane's father on the phone and bigger things like persuading Cameron to steal his father's lovingly restored Ferrari for their day trip to Chicago. In Chicago, he is working on a broader canvas than he is used to, and takes over a German-American parade, first miming to Danke Schön and then to a version of 'Twist and Shout' that literally sets all of Chicago, white and black, dancing – including his own father, in his office high above the street. This scene is simply gorgeous in its management of large crowds and its sense that what we are being shown is an apotheosis; Ferris is normally merely a trickster, but here he becomes Dionysus for a few minutes. It is the most perfectly achieved moment Hughes has ever managed, before or since, and part of its pleasure is thinking back to the mildly embarrassing dancing of *The Breakfast Club* and the clumsily shot wild parties of *Weird Science* and *Sixteen Candles* and seeing him finally get something entirely right.

In the real world, Ferris would never get away with as much as he does, but this is the world of farce, where much of the time luck as well as ingenuity is on his side. One of the strengths of the film is that Ferris is shown to be less in control than he would like to believe – coincidence is only ever ultimately his friend. Parking attendants take the Ferrari for a thousand-mile drive; his father uses the same Chicago restaurant; Rooney's obsessive pursuit of Ferris persists past the point at which a sane man would have been fooled by Ferris's ploys.

Sometimes Ferris is saved by coincidences as unlikely as those which might trap him – he and Cameron are visible on screen when a hot-dog vendor watches the match they are attending on television at the same time as Rooney is using his napkins to wipe his face clean. Rooney is too preoccupied to notice, because he has just mistaken a slightly butch girl for Ferris and had milkshake blown into his face with her straw. (And if we choose to see this as a specifically sexual humiliation, the more Freudian bits of *Weird Science* entitle us to this view.)

More often, Ferris is saved by people not because of his plots and schemes, but because they genuinely like him. His sister Jeanie has spent most of the film trying to find a chance to inform against him – she gets a speeding ticket trying to get herself and their mother home ahead of Ferris – and yet saves him when he is finally trapped by the by now demented Rooney. This is partly because of the lecture she has got from a drug-addled youth she made out with in the police station – the youth is played by Charlie Sheen, which explains her good mood – and partly because she realises that Rooney was the intruder she kicked in the face. In the end, she finds it easy to decide which side she is on.

Both she and Rooney are sent into a constant slow burn by the cult of Ferris. One of the film's rare subtleties is the way his claims to be ill snowball out of control so that, for example, his father fails to see a story about it in the newspaper he is reading and Jeanie, waiting for the police after Rooney's home invasion, is pestered by a stripogram sent for Ferris. Much of this material is outrageous and some of it is almost subliminal.

It is a tribute to the charm of Matthew Broderick as an actor that the film gets away with material that breaks the Fourth Wall and which might have made Ferris seem unbearably smug. He constantly addresses the camera and the audience, explaining many of his scams – how he gives himself the clammy hands that convince his parents that he is genuinely ill – and expressing his somewhat patronizing if clearly accurate views about Cameron's self-hatred. Comparison with purported earlier versions of the script available online would seem to indicate that some of this material was cut – a scene where Ferris loots the sofa and his siblings' rooms and his father's coats for funds, for example – and one cannot wish it otherwise. (One would have to do an exhaustive study of films that break through the Fourth Wall, but it is quite probable that the now common trope of the post-credits zinger, now common in adventure films like *Pirates of the Carribbean*, was brought back into currency by Ferris's post-credits appearance telling the audience to stop watching him and go home.)

The finished film is far from perfect. The handling of a snooty maître d' in the Chicago restaurant skirts homophobia and the parking attendants are ethnic lowlife clichés, however joyful their speeding of the Ferrari on the Chicago freeway to the tune of John Williams' *Star Wars* theme. Sloane is under-characterized – the truly romantic relationship in the film is the friendship between Ferris and Cameron – even though Mia Sara does what she can with some moments of bonding with Cameron and Sloane's final ecstatic 'He's going to marry me' as Ferris disappears into the distance.

The humiliations heaped on Rooney are too numerous and a point of diminishing returns is reached at some points. It is funny when he abuses, on the phone, Sloane's supposed father, whom he assumes to be Ferris, only to realize Ferris is ringing him on another line and start grovelling – to, as we then realize, Cameron. It is funny when he is kicked in the face by Jeanie as the intruder he in fact is. On the other hand, many of the slapstick gags involving the Bueller family dog and the compost heap and the water barrel are redundant, however funny Jeffery Jones' slow burn is. The dog in particular foreshadows how much of Hughes' time was to be wasted on the entirely worthless *Beethoven* films.

What is quite wonderful, though, is the over-the-credits sequence of Rooney getting a lift on the school bus when his car has been towed away, and having to sit at the back with unpopular kids who offer him Gummi Bears. It goes without saying that at least one of these young unpopular children has 'Save Ferris' scrawled on his schoolbooks. Rooney is returned by implication to his own schooldays when, we intuit, he was never popular or cool. (This is a trope which crops up in the television series *Buffy*, where the equally unpleasant Principal Snyder (Armin Shimerman) is mocked as someone who never got a date, and regresses under magical influence into an irritating nerd who wants desperately to hang with the cool kids.)

What *Ferris Bueller* brings to the teen genre, ultimately, is a sense of how it is possible to be cool and popular without being rich or a sports hero. Unlike the heroes of *Weird Science*, Ferris is computer savvy without being a nerd or a geek – it is a skill he has taken the trouble to learn. (Willow in *Buffy* starts off as shy and unpopular, but does not discard her fascination with skill when she gains confidence, and Veronica Mars, in the show of the same name, has much of Ferris's ability to use computers as a part of her elaborate plots.) Some of the finest moments in later teen film draw on Ferris's blithe Dionysian fervour – the elaborate courtship by song in *10 Things I Hate About You* (1999) draws usefully on the 'Twist and Shout' sequence in *Ferris Bueller's Day Off.*

What then were John Hughes' crucial contributions to the teen film and why can he be seen as crystallizing it as a genre?

The Hughes films are effective at shifting product, let us be clear, but by accumulating soundtracks from a number of sources rather than by featuring music centrally. The soundtrack albums from *Pretty in Pink* and *Some Kind of Wonderful* are still useful starting points for an understanding of late 1980s American independent rock music. As suggested above, this probably has as much to do with Howard Deutch as it does with John Hughes himself, the soundtracks of whose other four films are less interesting.

Several of Hughes' six films bring a greater awareness of class to the teen movie – it is significant in *The Breakfast Club* and a prime motivator in *Pretty in Pink* and *Some Kind of Wonderful*. If it is a version of class awareness that owes more to Frank Capra than to Karl Marx, that is what one would expect.

His films are good on dysfunctional families and the way that parental expectations cripple adolescents – again, this is not so much an original perception as one he brought comprehensively into the material that future genre teen films would consider. Hughes' values are sexually conservative to the point of being vanilla, and yet the sexual unease of the mid 1980s nonetheless imports a free-floating eroticism to these films which sometimes manifests itself as implied gay subtext. Again, this is often a feature of later teen films, though rarely any more explicitly than in Hughes.

He brings together motifs – the Child who is Parent, the Lord of Misrule, the Humiliation of the Obsessive Authority Figure and that Authority Figure's Persecution of the Weak, the Rich Kid who Meddles, the Hierarchy of High School – in forms that crystallize them for later use. The anthropology shot is not a Hughes invention, though he uses it, more or less, in *Pretty in Pink*, but his awareness of its potential is signalled by the selection of types in *The Breakfast Club* and the School Secretary's slightly bizarre reeling off of the tribes in *Ferris Bueller's Day Off.* 'Sportos, motorheads, geeks, sluts, pinheads, dweebies, wonkers, richies.'

Above all, though often ponderously, Hughes took teenagers seriously and this seriousness manifests in the way that their problems and traumas are often complex back stories rather than mere givens. We simply know much more about the six members of *The Breakfast Club* than about the characters of earlier teen films and presumably would have known even more if we had seen the longer version. Hughes' characters have, much of the time, sociological context and depth in time and historicized trauma and this is why his films retain our interest and have been the teen films that other teen films, from *Heathers* onwards, pick fights with. He took a nascent genre, and in at least four of his films demonstrated, however half-heartedly and sometimes clumsily, that it was one capable of generating thick texts.

Other teen films of the same period are remembered with equal affection, yet were less influential. Take for example, *Adventures in Babysitting* (1987), a film directed by Chris Columbus, who was to collaborate with Hughes on *Home Alone* (1990), and which is also set in Chicago, and also has a memorable soundtrack.

To summarize, Chris (Elisabeth Shue), stood up by her boyfriend, agrees to babysit young Sara; Sara's brother is infatuated with the older Chris. When her runaway friend Brenda asks to be rescued from Chicago bus station, Chris heads into the city with Sara, Brad and Brad's friend Doug. They get caught up in urban violence and crime and accidentally steal a copy of *Playboy* with gangland secrets inside and are pursued by gang boss Bleak and his more sympathetic minion Joe. They flee via a blues club – where both teenagers and gangsters are made to sing – and the subway where Brad is stabbed in the foot by a street-gang member – the subway gang is probably a reference to Walter Roy Hill's *The Warriors* (1979) and provokes Chris's most memorable line: 'Nobody fucks with the babysitter.'

They get off the train and take Brad to a hospital where his wound is stitched – a momentary misunderstanding means that Doug and Chris think he is dead and are thoroughly delighted when he proves not to be – Chris faints at his apparent resurrection. They crash a frat house party where Chris meets a nice student who helps them with their damaged car. The repairman points out that they are five dollars short and refuses to hand over the car until Sara, mistaking him for the comic book god Thor, pleads with him. Driving to the bus station, they spot the car of Chris's boyfriend; she confronts him and the girl he has taken out to dinner in her place. Sara is put in jeopardy by the gangsters and Joe changes sides, helping them get home ahead of Sara and Brad's parents.

Compared with Hughes, it possesses a degree of bad faith in that it plays with the anarchic, but its anarchic tendencies are controlled and that in the end an offensive normality is restored – where in Hughes the anarchic always effects permanent changes. Issues around race and age difference are raised only to be dropped in favour of a marginally improved status quo – the hellish inner city is where the suburban high school girl Chris goes on a night journey to acquire wisdom, but it is to the suburbs that she returns.

This use of the myth of journey outwards and return is part of a general adoption of mythic structures that reinforce white-bread values without significant irony, as does the film's play with the superhero motif via the child Sara's faith in the Marvel comics god Thor. In the course of the film we find not only the night journey, but other sorts of ordeal – the song contest, the voyage to the underworld, the raising from the dead. Anyone who doubts the conscious presence of mythic patterns in this film is advised to consider the presence of so many mythic tropes, embodied in seemingly mundane contexts, in so short a space. These make it a comprehensive set of allusions to Joseph Campbell's *The Hero with a Thousand Faces*, perhaps the most popular and accessible of 'keys to all mythologies'. All of these motifs are used to explore the anarchic and then move past it; there is also a burlesque element present in their application to a suburban teen situation, an element signalled in the film's poster, which parodies action adventure films.

What makes this an attractive enough film in its way is in part the score (which relies heavily on Chicago rhythm and blues and on such bands as Southside Johnny, who appears in person in the blues club); in part the comic pacing, which is exemplary; and in part the sheer charm and beauty of the young Elisabeth Shue, who has found in later life that this role defines her career as much as more highly praised adult performances in films like *Leaving Las Vegas*.

It is fashionable, and not without reason, to dismiss Columbus as a crowd-pleasing producer of pot boilers such as the *Home Alone* films and the first two films in the Harry Potter franchise, but *Adventures in Babysitting* plays to his strengths, such as they are. The farcical stuff – teenagers and gangsters alike crash the cocktail party Sara's parents are at – is handled competently, but without the brio of *Ferris Bueller's Day Off*. He has the knack of getting good, or at least acceptable, ensemble performances from groups of young actors – and is accomplished at providing just the right level of jeopardy to thrill young audiences without upsetting very young ones. Rationally, we know that Sara is in serious danger as she crawls around the sloping glass of a high building, but Columbus manages to make this less humanly upsetting than it ought to be. This is a useful symbol of the way the film plays with risk and then avoids its implications – Chris ends up with a vacuous older boy rather than with the black criminal Joe or Brad, who is admirable, classy and too young for her.

In the end, though, what the script lacks is any sense that these characters have a context or personal depth. Affection for the film attaches either to Shue, or to the simple fact that it deals with the universal fact of babysitting, or to its games with myth – a viable strategy for teen comedy, let us be clear, but one, outside of the Bill and Ted comedies, not otherwise taken. Entirely likeable as it is, *Adventures in Babysitting* remains a one-off, where the Hughes films have continued to resonate in other films and television shows for twenty years.

Note

1.   Whether or not an author's perhaps thoughtless choice of characters' names can be taken as necessarily implying the etymological and culturally associative subtext it is possible to draw from them is a question on which it is possible to waste much ink and time. When, as here, a film contains a cluster of names with such subtext, it seems to me to be a reasonable supposition that conscious or unconscious choices of a systematic nature are being made.

The Friends Who Are Bad for You

Heathers

Heathers is a long way from being the first – or even the first good – teen movie, though it was and remains one of the genre's highpoints and the genre's best example of a thick text. It is complex and intelligent both in its own right and as a response to earlier films both inside the teen genre and outside it; it was also a highly fertile influence.

It set much of the agenda for the teen, and most especially of the high school, films of the next decade and a half, both through its exuberant virtuoso display of linguistic invention and through its creation of what became stock tropes. It is also, most crucially, a demonstration of how rich a text a teen movie could present and still inhabit the genre.

A brief summary: a clique consisting of Heather Chandler (Kim Walker), Heather McNamara (Lisanne Falk), Heather Duke (Shannen Doherty) and Veronica Sawyer (Winona Ryder) dominate school life through beauty, bitchery and sexual favours. Veronica is quietly hostile to her friends, a hostility exploited by her new boyfriend, the nihilistic J.D. (Christian Slater), who enlists her originally unwitting support in a campaign of murders disguised as suicides that is intended to culminate in the blowing up of the school. She has come to see him as mad and bad, and shoots him; dying, he blows himself up.

It is worth remarking on the extent to which *Heathers* was a radical movie for its time and place. Though he claims now to have retreated from his earlier dislike for the John Hughes films, Daniel Waters very much saw *Heathers* when he wrote it as a deconstruction of the cosy pieties of *Sixteen Candles* and the rest, as 'the high school film to end high school films' that has in it all the things that a high school movie has. Both endings – the scripted one and the final one – refuse theodicy, the restoration of an assumed state of ordained normality, whereas most earlier teen movies that flirt with the anarchic (*Adventures in Babysitting*, for example) put everything back at the end more or less where they found it. *Heathers* starts and ends with scenes that are uncomfortable and uncanny. *Heathers* takes the stereotypes with which *The Breakfast Club* plays – the jock, the cheerleader – and shows them as opportunities for malicious behaviour rather than mere social roles; at various points, its villain/antihero J.D. indulges parodically in the sort of self-analysis which is the entire point of *The Breakfast Club*.

Winona Ryder testifies that her agent begged her not to appear in a movie that was thought of as a potential career killer and that she was dropped from other films by directors who disapproved of it. According to the DVD commentary by Daniel Waters and director Michael Lehman, various young actresses who were considered for the central roles were unable to appear because their parents refused to give them permission. The first love scene between J.D. and Veronica takes place in what was supposed to be a 7-11 store, but had to be built as a set because the supermarket chain got nervous about being associated with the project.

It is, in a sense, sublimely irrelevant to critical consideration how much *Heathers'* richness was a matter of conscious thought and how much a matter of good instinct. It is probable that Daniel Waters and Michael Lehman never sat down and thought through the extent to which *Heathers* uses fantastic tropes like the tempter and the Faustian pact, the extent to which it plays with the concept of liminality, the complexity of its sexual and social subtext or its demonstration in a few scenes that the social dynamics of its teen characters pervade adult discourse. This richness may in part derive from the fact that Waters originally wrote a far longer, more ambitious script (200 pages) and the film is a boiling down and simplification of that. And *Heathers* is all the more impressive a film for having so much to unpack.

Take the opening sequence, over the credits, with the anodyne 1950s

Doris Day song of adolescence growing into adulthood 'Que Sera, Sera' playing as Heather Chandler puts her hair through the red rosette scrunchee that is her signature, and comes later in the film to serve as the emblem of her power, a power which gets transferred with it. We rapidly realize that this film is going to be a long way away from the simple asexual pieties of a Doris Day movie. The three Heathers sip tea, and then walk over to the croquet green trampling someone else's roses as they go – in its first seconds, the film announces itself as dealing with cruelty and the transgression of boundaries.

In the DVD commentary, Waters and Lehman mention that this sequence was shot some weeks after the rest of the film – Lisanne Falk, who plays Heather McNamara, had cut her hair and has to wear an unbecoming wig – which implies it was an afterthought. If so, it was a happy one that crystallizes much of the film's material – the games of dominance, the cruelty, Veronica's not wholly appropriate sense of herself as Heather Chandler or J.D.'s victim rather than their accomplice.

The opening version of 'Que Sera, Sera' was in fact a follow-on from Waters and Lehman's desire to use the rough cast Sly Stone R&B version at the end, but that inspiration became a framing device and they wanted a different, more innocent version at the beginning. They wanted to use the Doris Day recording of 'Que Sera, Sera' for the irony implicit both in the song's words and its association with Day. In the event, Day's management were unprepared to give them the rights because of the film's bad language – producer Denise Di Novi's father had worked with Day, and she knew that Day always had a swear box for her session musicians. The version actually used at the beginning is by Syd Straw.

At this point, we do not know why the film has the title it does, and we find out as the three Heathers defer to each other over croquet shots that prove to be aimed at the head of Veronica who is buried up to her neck in the green. Before aiming her ball – the red one – Heather Chandler puts it to her mouth as if biting an apple, or more precisely the fruit of the Tree of Knowledge, the knowledge of 'real life' that she teaches. (Even at this point Heather Duke is distracted by the book she is reading. *Moby-Dick* was not the first choice for the book she obsessively reads – it was supposed to be J.D. Salinger's *The Catcher in the Rye*, but they were unable to get permission to use it.)

The image of Veronica as the target of the Heathers' croquet balls becomes especially poignant when we realize that the constant croquet games are one of the things that she brought to the group dynamic. It is on her lawn, and with her set, that they play, and the game is something that used to feature in her former friendship with Betty. When she plays croquet with a new friend, it is a significant act of infidelity to her relationship with the Heathers.

The three Heathers are an alliance of the power-hungry – by giving them the same name, Waters makes explicit that they are generic, that there are Heathers in every school, in every social setting. This is a point usefully made by the decision of the film's designer Rudy Dillonto to dress the three Heathers and Veronica in a teen version of 1980s padded shoulder power-dressing – when Veronica and two Heathers stalk down the cafeteria, they are genuinely formidable. There is a potential streak of misogyny in the script which never becomes dominant partly because of Denise Di Novi's good influence as producer and partly because of Winona Ryder's performance.

As the scene changes from this dream image to a shot of high school students with Veronica foregrounded, she utters her first lines:

> Dear Diary: Heather told me she teaches people life. She said
> 'Real life sucks losers dry. If you want to fuck with the eagles, you
> have to learn to fly.' I said, 'So you teach people how to spread
> their wings and fly?' She said, 'Yes.' I said, 'You're beautiful!'

From the start, her relationship with Heather Chandler, and to a lesser extent with the other two Heathers, is shown as a seduction and a temptation and a threat. Veronica is enchanted into giving her will over to another – and she makes the same mistake with J.D.

At the start of the film, Veronica has already sold her soul once – to become an associate of the three Heathers, she has ditched unfashionable friends like Betty Finn and is prepared to go on dates with the likes of Kurt and Ram. More crucially, though she protests for a moment at using her skills as a forger to humiliate the obese Martha Dunstock with a fake mash note from Kurt, she does it anyway. Waters remarks that this is something his sister used to do with her friends – given that their brother directed one of the other best films about teen girl malice, *Mean Girls*, the young Ms. Waters has a lot to answer for.

Veronica's relationship with Heather Chandler is precarious simply because she is Heather Chandler's ideal audience – Heather Duke and

Heather McNamara are perfect serfs, but lack the intelligence of Veronica and Heather Chandler. Heather Chandler needs Veronica and at the same time resents her, and needs to keep her under control. Just to demonstrate her power, Heather Chandler makes Heather Duke bend over as a writing table for Veronica – abasement becomes literally objectification. Heather Chandler is all about control, often sexual control – she even argues that the cruel prank will give Martha 'shower nozzle masturbation fantasies for a month', as if the prank were a favour instead of a public humiliation.

The forging of the note is the first of several forgeries important to *Heathers*' convoluted plot – the suicide notes, produced by Veronica, with which J.D. covers up his murders and the 'petitions' which are supposed to be a suicide note signed by the entire school. A forgery is by definition a theft of name and handwriting and therefore of identity. Forgeries thus relate thematically to the film's central theme of insincerity – J.D. and under his influence Veronica giggle at the phoney piety with which adults and schoolkids alike react to the 'suicides' and yet their own default response is to create something equally inauthentic. When Heather Chandler picks out Martha Dunstock as her victim, she deliberately distorts her name into Dumptruck – again, a theft of identity. The forgeries Veronica used to do for Heather Chandler are replaced by the forgeries she does for J.D., and they are equally malicious and are part of murder plots rather than mere social humiliation. Veronica eventually creates a sort of ultimate forgery – by faking her own death; if faking other people's writing is a sort of theft of their identity, that goes along with the stealing of their lives, then a fake suicide is a partial amends.

Veronica wants to be part of Heather Chandler's world, yet experiences their relationship as one of constant pain and humiliation. The world of the Heathers is one of constant minor cruelties and refusal of normal pieties in the name of brutal honesty – their use of deceptions reveals this honesty as hypocritical. This applies both at the personal level – Heather Duke is almost certainly right when she points out later in the film that the discarded Betty Finn would be just as prepared to sell people out if she got the chance – and at the level of the world outside. When the socially concerned pupils are calling out for spare lunch money to feed the Third World, Heather McNamara and Veronica joke about it:

Heather McNamara:　Do they even have Thanksgiving in Africa?

Veronica :	Oh sure, pilgrims, Indians, tater-tots – it's a real party continent.

Live Aid had been a mere four years earlier; this is a film whose cruel wit takes no prisoners.

At the moment when she participates in the act of malice towards Martha, she catches sight of J.D., and he stares knowingly back at her. He is, at one level, merely a disturbed charismatic teenager, but he is also Veronica's personal tempter. His name, Jason Dean, is cognate enough with James Dean to signal him as a teen rebel; his initials J.D., by which he is usually referred to, also stand, in common parlance, for juvenile delinquent. Waters confirms on the DVD commentary that these thoughts were in his mind: 'To be the world's coolest teenager you have to be a psychopath.'

They are also the initials of J.D. Salinger, the writer whose novel *The Catcher in the Rye* gave a voice to an entire generation of adolescent detectors of bad faith among both their peers and adults. *The Catcher in the Rye* has not, as far as I am aware, ever been especially associated with the sort of high school massacre that J.D. ends up planning. It was, though, the favourite book of Mark Chapman, who assassinated John Lennon, and of John Hinckley, who attempted the assassination of Ronald Reagan, both a few years before the production of *Heathers*, and thus has an association with random violence in the name of existential honesty.

As Veronica walks towards J.D., the soundtrack comes to include the harmonica chords that in American film so often stand for the open road and freedom, and establish what he means for her. The first words he utters are 'Greetings and salutations', an affectation which echoes Victorian translations of a stock Arabic greeting. Without stressing this point too far, it signals him as an exotic dragged out of any context normal to him and dumped in an Ohio high school – and his next words to Veronica ('Are you a Heather?') are a question that she spends the rest of the film answering.

This is as good a place as any to point out the extent to which J.D. is positioned throughout the film as a liminal being, as well as a very disturbed, if attractive, young man. His father has become rich through blowing things up and knocking things down – Mr Dean is a destroyer without any vestige of being a creator as well and J.D.'s name signals him as the rightful son of such a malign deity, in other words, the Antichrist. D is after all the letter that comes after C; it also stands for Damien. J.D. witnessed the death of his mother, who was apparently either murdered by his father or chose to commit suicide by wandering into a demolition site – this loss of a parent gives him a special relationship with the borderland of life and death.

(If this seems fanciful, it is worth remembering that St Veronica is the woman who wiped the face of Christ as he carried the cross, the towel retaining a perfect image. In *Heathers*, Veronica becomes the instrument through which J.D. tries to imprint his self-destructive image on the school. This may be relevant, or may not – Waters is religious enough that he turned up on the first day of shooting with the ashes from the Ash Wednesday service on his forehead – this is as likely to indicate very high Episcopalianism as specifically Roman Catholicism.)

Slater's performance is avowedly modelled on those given by Jack Nicholson in liminal roles such as a madman (in *One Flew Over the Cuckoo's Nest* (1975) or *The Shining* (1980)) and as a tempting devil (in *The Witches of Eastwick* (1987)). Nicholson has made something of a speciality of liminal beings – the Joker in Tim Burton's *Batman* (1989) is another example. As such, he was precisely the right influence for Slater here, though perhaps not again until he appeared in a stage version of *One Flew Over the Cuckoo's Nest* in London in 2005, which is why his career has been disappointing. As a liminal being, caught between states, J.D. is uncanny, and possessed of that particular wisdom which belongs to the uncanny; Slater captures perfectly that element in the script.

It is not surprising therefore that the very next thing J.D. says, in answer to her identification of herself as Veronica and invitation to take part in Heather Chandler's poll, is 'There are no stupid questions.' He has questioned her identity and she has reaffirmed it, but the question remains. When she asks him the poll question, however, he tells her, 'That's the stupidest question I ever heard.' The point is that the polls are one of the ways in which Heather Chandler manipulates her schoolmates, and asked by Veronica, it is a piece of folly in which she is subordinating her own identity to Heather Chandler's purposes.

He does answer her though, after a fashion. The question is 'You inherit five million dollars the same day aliens land on the earth and say they're gonna blow it up in two days. What do you do?' His answer – 'Probably row out to the middle of a lake somewhere, bring along a bottle of Tequila, my sax and… some bac' – significantly fails to address either the question of the money or the question of the aliens. It is an affirmation of solipsistic teen rebel status rather than an answer. What he and Heather

Chandler have in common is this obsession with last things as well as with manipulation and deceit. In this respect, as in much else, they are shadow doubles of each other, alike in their appeal to Veronica, their use of forgery and their destructiveness.

The poll – and the sequence in which we see a number of students answer it – provides the equivalent in *Heathers* of a stock shot of the teen film. (Standard early examples are present in both *Grease* (1978) and *Fast Times at Ridgemont High*, and a good later example is present in *10 Things I Hate About You*. Such shots establish a number of social groups among high school students and pan between them to demonstrate social divisions. This kind of shot can usefully be referred to as the anthropology shot and will be referred to as that hereafter.) We are not going to get to know more than a few key characters in a film, and yet we need to have a sense of the community that Heather Chandler seeks to dominate and J.D. seeks to destroy, both of them seeking Veronica's help to do so. Heather Chandler asks these seemingly meaningless questions as a way of finding out who people are – and they are economically in the script as a way of helping us do the same thing.

Waters, in interviews and commentary, refers to the fact that the screenplay for *Heathers* was originally far larger in scope – he jokes (?) that he intended it as a project for Stanley Kubrick and claims that this scene in particular was originally far longer. It was intended as a homage to the wedding scene in Coppola's *The Godfather* (1972) and the early barracks scenes in *Full Metal Jacket* (1987). Certainly Lehman learns from both those examples to keep his movement through a complex collection of major and minor characters snappy and fluid, through pans and cuts and the use of foreground and background. This is a very rich sequence.

Two more significant things happen in the first minutes of the film – we see the way in which the Heathers and Veronica use each other as instruments. Heather McNamara is bulimic and Veronica helps her vomit with a dextrous finger, remarking, 'True friend's work is never done.' (A cut to food being discarded from plates to waste bins in the cafeteria makes this far more graphic by implication.) And Kurt and Ram make the mistake of trying to bully J.D., accusing him of homosexuality as they do everyone they bully, and he pulls out a gun and shoots them, this time with blanks. It is a truly shocking moment because the looming chaos of stock bully behaviour is greeted with first equal, and when that does not work, greater, aggression.

Kurt and Ram are established instantly as unpleasant thugs and as playing entirely outside their league, both in their attempt to bully J.D. and in their sexual fantasies about the Heathers and Veronica:

Kurt:	I'm telling you man, it would be so righteous to be in a Veronica Sawyer/ Heather Chandler sandwich.
Ram:	Oh, hell yes. I wanna get a Heather, and put her on my johnson, and just start spinnin' her around like a goddamn pinwheel... Punch it in!

Sex is about control and aggression, and about fantasy; aggression has a weird component of the sexual.

This is one of the first times that a teen movie had specifically alluded to bullies' habit of imputing homosexuality to anyone they dislike, and makes far more significant use of it than *Some Kind of Wonderful*. *Heathers* is a film that takes bullying for granted rather than dealing with it as a central issue, but its perception of how bullying works is especially precise. Social policing in general and the enforcement of heterosexual norms in particular are shown as directly linked to homosociality; the ambiguities of intense same-sex friendships are mediated through an aggressive refusal and rejection of explicit homosexuality, or, more often, a model of 'the homosexual' which has everything to do with lack of status and power and little to do with sex. Given what happens to Kurt and Ram later, some real satirical scores are being set up for settlement here.

Many teen films overtly or covertly portray homosociality as having an erotic component, or at least a component of serious possessiveness. Among groups of girls in film, the standard form is wanting to approve new male partners on a basis of good looks and economic status; among boys, the desire is either actually to share girls or to share an often exaggerated account of sexual encounters. To quote *Grease*, in which the Pink Ladies can be seen as a marginally less unwholesome version of the Heathers, 'Tell me more, tell me more, did you get very far?/Tell me more, tell me more, but does he have a car?' The whole 'Summer Nights' number can be seen as an acting out of a heterosexual relationship in order to gain power through gaining the attention of an eroticized same-sex group.

The croquet matches in *Heathers* are one way in which female homosociality is acted out – it is after all a game which lends itself to sexual metaphor, with its hoops, greens, balls and cheating shots. There is also an eroticism attached to temptation – Heather Chandler and J.D. both seduce Veronica into being their tools. Even if Veronica's relationship with Heather Chandler is not explicitly positioned as sexual, it is significant that it exists as one in Kurt's sexual fantasies.

However, this erotic element is often seen as a chaotic or uncontrolled or dangerous thing – central characters who are coded as closeted and gay often end up dead or excluded because the standard comedic resolution of teen movies is almost always heteronormative. Heather Chandler ends up dead, as do the two jocks; Regina in *Mean Girls* ends up separated from her former friends and power base as a born-again jock in a world where the women who pile on top of her to celebrate victory may love her, but do not fear her. Those, like Veronica, who fall briefly under the spell of the powerful and sexually ambiguous end their stories freed from what is seen as bondage. Those few films in which homosexuality is seen as a happy ending use other strategies to get there.

The games with time – these various moments from a few minutes of time are presented out of order – continue the surreal aspects of the film's opening shots and make it less about linear reality than mental events. The film is not stuck in Veronica's consciousness – events are included that she hears about, but does not witness – but, even without any voiceover, its omniscient viewpoint can be taken as hers in retrospect. This is a film about how Veronica got to the end of its plot, and its shifts in time, and in and out of dream and daydream, remind us that it is a subjective and in some ways unreliable narrative.

Interestingly, Waters and Lehman attribute much of the film's success to the way Winona Ryder added sympathetic qualities to a character they had originally seen in far darker tones. She loved the script and loved Veronica and manages to make everything that Veronica says and does more human than it was originally written. Waters saw Veronica as less of a monster than J.D., but still morally culpable – Waters' Catholicism is relevant here – whereas Winona Ryder makes her far more a sleepwalker, far more unconscious of what she is getting herself into. Given this, it is appropriate that the monocle Waters had Veronica affect when writing her journal – a symbol of seeing clearly – was something that Ryder found it uncomfortable to wear, and which was accordingly dropped.

The two major features of the film's idiolect are established early – J.D. and Heather Chandler share habits of speech that Veronica largely imitates and those habits are a taste for scabrous paradox and a taste for speech broken down into effective minimalistic particles of sentences. Heather Chandler establishes her combination of aggression and wit with remarks like 'Fuck me gently with a chainsaw. Do I look like Mother Theresa?' and J.D.'s double entendre riposte to accusations of faggotry – 'They ... seem to have an open-door policy for assholes' – has something of the same dexterity. Exchanges like Veronica and J.D.'s 'Later ... Definitely' indicate that they are capable of using language for communicative effect not phatic stroking – the brutal brevity of the exchange is far sexier than any more prolonged discussion would be. Yet language is not everything; the look of jealous contempt that Heather Chandler shoots at J.D. as he and Veronica flirt conveys that these two are destined mortal enemies.

The other characters are far less verbally adroit – Kurt and Ram are positively brutish in their means of expression and the other characters, even when revealing themselves through inventive answers to the poll, have very little interesting or amusing to say. We do see why Veronica has attached herself to Heather Chandler and attaches herself to J.D. – it is because they are her equals in a way that Betty Finch never was. She has a moment of gentle nostalgia when Betty accosts her in the cafeteria, but is dragged away by Heather Chandler, dropping at Betty's feet the photographs of happier more innocent times that Betty has been showing her.

Later in the film, J.D. blackmails Heather Duke into being his cat's-paw by threatening to release photographs of her canoeing with Martha. *Heathers* is a film in which innocence was a time in which people failed to make the sort of social distinctions on which both Heather Chandler and J.D. pride themselves – social acceptability on the one hand and cool on the other – and therefore made friendships which are embarrassing in later life. Betrayed loyalty is one of the currencies in which high school life trades, and this is as much the case when Veronica sells out the Heathers to J.D. as it was when she sold out Betty to them.

This whole theme of the friends of one's younger schooldays that one leaves behind is one that plays out in various other films and, most especially, in television shows like *My So-Called Life* and *Freaks and Geeks* (1999–2000). In this, as in so much else, *Heathers* helped to set an agenda. Waters points out that Betty is signalled as Veronica's true friend of the heart both by her first name – Betty and Veronica are best friends in the

Archie comics – and by her surname – Tom Sawyer and Huck Finn in the novels of Mark Twain. If some of the non-canonical references I tease out in what follows seem implausible, it is worth bearing in mind that Waters consciously works at this level at least some of the time.

The next scene – another croquet game – establishes Heather Chandler's deep antipathy towards J.D. and Veronica's fascination with his anarchic behaviour. It also, via the gag of Heather Duke's outplaying Heather Chandler's tactical viciousness via a freak fluke shot, establishes that Heather Chandler is not nearly as in control as she would wish to be. The exchange about the college party she and Veronica are attending together re-establishes her as desiring control and getting it – she regards Veronica's attendance as an audition Veronica has to pass: 'I'm giving Veronica her shot, her first Remington party. You blow it tonight girl, and it's "keggers with kids" all next year.'

There follows, very briefly, the first of the scenes with her parents that help give Veronica some of the hinterland which explains why she is not as shallow as she aspires to be. The parents are shot, as are other adults at various points, with a wide-angle lens that makes them faintly grotesque, but they treat Veronica as an equal while trying to nurture her by feeding her pâté. They ask her about possible dates for the prom – one of the signs of the quality of this relationship is that she does not regard the question as intrusive – and she responds that there is a dark horse contender. J.D. is a dark horse in the sense of being a new possibility, but also, of course, in terms of being more sinister than she realizes. She abandons her parents for Heather Chandler as she has abandoned earlier good friends – 'Great pâté, but I gotta motor.'

The encounter between J.D. and Veronica at the convenience store – she is getting snacks for herself and Heather Chandler and J.D. just happens to be there at the same time – establishes a relationship between sexuality and consumption that crops up several times in the film. He talks of convenience food as something that he can reaffirm his solitary identity with in every new town; she is buying food to be eaten as a group, as a part of her relationship with Heather Chandler. More significantly, she flirtatiously suggests that he buy her a slushie – when he asks her coke or cherry, she responds cherry, indicating that she is still a virgin to the man with whom she already at some level intends to sleep. According to Waters and Lehman, the joke here was unintended – they did not know it was a laugh line until the film screened.

Their conversation also includes one of the film's defining exchanges as Veronica starts her journey away from Heather Chandler's orbit and into J.D.'s:

Veronica:	My life's not perfect. I don't really like my friends.
J.D.:	I… I don't really like your friends either.
Veronica:	Well, it's just like they're people I work with, and our job is being popular and shit.
J.D.:	Maybe it's time to take a vacation.

The perception that, in a high school context, being popular is a social role that transcends any personal relationships, that it is a way of being a celebrity whom everyone wants 'as a fuck or a friend' as Heather Chandler puts it, is one of the film's major contributions to the genre. It is echoed in *Cruel Intentions* and *Mean Girls*; it gives the show *Popular* (1999–2001) its title and its major subject, and is a key issue in *Buffy the Vampire Slayer*, both in its film and TV show incarnations. There is a direct choice Buffy has to make between being the stereotypically popular girl that her looks and personality suggest and the role of weird pariah with odd friends that her responsibilities in the parallel world of vampires and demons mandate from her.

Time goes screwy again, as the film shifts backwards and forwards between Veronica writing murderous fantasies in her diary and Veronica experiencing public humiliation at the Remington party. It is hard to say what offends Heather Chandler most – Veronica getting sick and vomiting, or Veronica refusing to have sex with Brad, the man Heather has selected for her. She tells Veronica that Brad has said she is acting like 'a cooze' (a cunt) – the script pinpoints the paradox that Veronica is accused of being a sexual receptacle for, precisely, refusing to be one.

This is one of the two or three occasions at which *Heathers* sets off against straightforward, if potentially abusive, heterosexual behaviour that odd form of homosociality in which the Heathers, or Kurt and Ram, quasi-erotically control or share heterosexual behaviour. Heather expects Veronica to have performed fellatio on one of the frat boys, as she has herself, and is disappointed and jealous that she has not, and that for Veronica it is a big deal, not something to be done and then washed out of her mouth with beer. Veronica's vomiting is clearly positioned alongside her refusal of casual oral sex and both are set against her hurting herself by burning her hand with a match. In an effective piece of multi-tasking screen-writing on the part of Waters, the match, thrown away, lights a wastebin whose flames supply a suitably hellish backdrop for Heather Chandler's threats of social death.

Back home, Veronica's murderous dreams of life without Heather are set beside her self-contempt for her betrayal of Betty: 'I sold her out for a bunch of Swatch-dogs and Diet Coke-heads.' She contemplates killing Heather Chandler: 'Killing Heather would be like offing the Wicked Witch of the West.' In another flashback, Heather Chandler threatens her with social disgrace after the weekend – 'Monday morning, you're history.' And it is at precisely this moment that, back in her bedroom again, J.D. sticks his head through the open window like a jack-in-the-box, just after she has announced her dream of a world without Heather Chandler, 'a world where I am free'. What he appears to offer is that world of freedom; what he is actually offering is something rather different.

In the immediate moment, what he offers is a game of croquet – which becomes, behind a fade, a game of strip croquet that culminates in sex. Croquet was an appropriate game for her and the Heathers to play, simply because it is a game that combines social pretension and social aggression – the fact that her sexual relationship with J.D. starts with more of the same is not the least disturbing aspect of the situation.[1] In a longer version of the scene, he points to the condoms they have used and says that they have killed their babies – love and death are fruitfully connected in this scene.

He suggests murder as a solution to her problem with Heather Chandler and she specifically and repeatedly rejects his idea, both in the abstract and when he suggests the drainpipe clearer. What she fails to understand is that her preferred plan – to make Heather violently sick, to make her 'puke her guts out' is verbally ambiguous enough that he can exploit it. Because she uses loose language, so can he – this obsession with the precise terms of engagement is a standard feature of the literature about Faustian pacts from Goethe onwards. The choice of a cleansing product to kill the evil Heather Chandler is profoundly resonant.

He prepares the poison cup, she the merely emetic one. He kisses her and she picks up the wrong cup while being kissed. Once she has left the room, he looks down and sees that she has left the harmless cup; he pauses for a moment, and then offers to be the one who takes the cup in. The DVD commentary states that he considers for a moment and then 'goes with the flow'; by implication, her making of the mistake has an element of unconscious murderousness about it, given how much she has talked about killing Heather Chandler before this point.

By the time they enter Heather Chandler's room, it is J.D. who is carrying the cup, with its lid behind his back; at the point when he offers it to Heather, he has taken the lid off. Veronica should know what is going on, but she has excuses for not realizing that she has made a fatal mistake. It is a matter of conjecture how clearly Waters and Lehman worked out the respective moral responsibilities of J.D. and Veronica, and how efficiently they blocked the scene; whether by design, or happy accident, they end up with something profoundly and effectively ambiguous.

This switching of cups is a staple of comedy – see Danny Kaye's *The Court Jester* (1956), for example – but is played darkly here; it also has its place at the heart of western high art in the shape of the substitution of love potion for poison in the first act of Wagner's *Tristan und Isolde*. The playing out of rivalry between J.D. and Heather Chandler for the possession of Veronica takes a traditional quasi-erotic form. She tries to recruit him as her ally momentarily by calling him Jesse James and by telling him about Heather's vomiting the night before.

J.D. persuades Heather to drink by appealing to her amour propre:

J.D.:	Umm… Veronica knew you'd have a hangover, so I whipped this up for you. It's a family recipe.
HC:	What did you do, put a phlegm globber in it or something? I'm not gonna drink that piss.
J.D.:	I knew this stuff'd be too intense for her.
HC:	Intense. Grow up! You think I'll drink it just because you call me chicken? [J.D. smiles wryly and nods] Just give me the cup, jerk. [HC drinks the contents, chokes] Corn nuts! [and falls head first through her glass table]

Significantly, though unremarkably, Heather Chandler is wearing her trademark scrunchee when continuing her threats to Veronica, but takes it off as she rises from the bed to take the fatal cup from J.D. She has put aside the object in which power resides, and has become vulnerable and mortal.

The ensuing exchange can be seen as using a stock paradox of love poetry:

Veronica:	I just killed my best friend.
J.D.:	And your worst enemy.
Veronica:	Same difference.

It is in an erotic context that friends and enemies are often the same person. And there is a similar ambiguity present when Veronica forges Heather Chandler's suicide note – Veronica and J.D. try to say what Heather would have said and so their new relationship becomes, in a real sense about her. They argue for example about whether she would have used the word 'myriad' which she had failed to get right in a test – both have insight on this. J.D. persuades Veronica that Heather would have wanted to use a word she failed on before to give her suicide note some weight – she asks him if he has done this before, and he doesn't answer.

One of the things that the film is about is mass consciousness and what follows Heather Chandler's death is an orgy of sentiment true and false among the school's faculty and pupils. One of the few genuinely touching things here is Heather McNamara's attempt to give one of Heather Chandler's Swatches to Veronica simply because it combines mourning with aggression: 'She'd want you to have it, Veronica. She always said you couldn't accessorise for shit.' Heather Duke is upset enough to forget to be bulimic. Their mourning, brief-lived as it is, is genuine because in character. And the Swatches for which Veronica metaphorically sold out Betty Finn become actual.

Not entirely plausibly, but very funnily, Heather Duke says, 'Oh, the humanity.' This is a quotation from the commentator who reported live on the explosion of the passenger airship Hindenburg with the loss of most on board. Waters refers to this in his commentary, while also pointing out that it has become a piece of shtick adopted by some stand-ups. It serves as a very effective contrast to the simplicity of Veronica's reaction – she walks into the shower room and gets into a shower fully clothed.

At one level, this is a reference to one of the stock tropes of the high school film – the voyeuristic scene in which girls shower and boys spy on them. The original idea, according to Waters, was to have a number of girls decide that what Veronica was doing, showering fully-clothed, was cool, and imitate her, to the consternation of a group of boys spying on them. In the event, the scene is very simple – just a stage direction in the script and the line 'Veronica… Veronica, what are you doing?' from Heather McNamara. What Veronica is doing, of course, is attempting to wash herself free of guilt, but whether it is guilt for helping kill Heather Chandler, or for letting herself be influenced by her in the first place, remains profoundly ambiguous. (Again, if there is a link between her name and a saint associated with the Passion of Christ, imagery around cleaning is appropriate. In the shower, she momentarily stretches out her arms as if crucified herself.)

Other students decide that Heather Chandler was a different and better person simply because her apparent suicide indicates to them that she was, like them, in pain. 'Sorry to hear about your friend. Thought she was your usual airhead bitch. Guess I was wrong. We all were,' says Tracey, whose smoked granny glasses indicate her desire to have an artistic temperament, before indulging in morbid speculation about the details of Heather Chandler's death: 'I heard it was really gnarly. She sucked down a bowl of multi-purpose deodorizing disinfectant, and then smash!'

An ex-boyfriend finds a way of making Heather Chandler's death an affirmation of his own worth – 'Heather and I used to go out, and she said I was boring, but now I realise I really wasn't boring, it's just that she was dissatisfied with her life' – and is praised for this by his teacher. Veronica, in her role of the authorial viewpoint truth-teller, stifles a laugh at the absurdity of this. One way in which Winona Ryder manages to make the role more telling is how she makes Veronica at this moment at once mocking and embarrassed by her capacity to mock. The laugh is sincere, and she turns it into a sob, the approved response. The insincerity of the entire proceeding is underlined by the question from one of the students: 'Are we going to be tested on this?'

The teachers are hardly better or more sincere – J.D. is not wrong about phoniness. One of them comments, as he predicted, that at least Heather Chandler had learned to use myriad correctly; the principal is mostly concerned that her death be recognized by a correct amount of time off for the students – as a non-cheerleader, she does not rate a half-day. Pauline Fleming, the teacher who claims to care, is equally the target of satire in her rebukes to the others:

> I find it profoundly disturbing that we're told of the tragic
> destruction of youth, and all we can think to talk about is

adequate mourning times and misused vocabulary words… We must revel in this revealing moment. Look, I suggest that we get everybody together, both students and teachers, in the cafeteria, and just… talk, and… feel, together.

Like the best satirists, Waters takes no particular side save that of language – Fleming talks a language of sensitivity that is actually all about showing off and ego.

The self-serving claptrap continues in the television interviews that many of the class give about Heather Chandler's death, watched and commentated on by Veronica and J.D. at his house. Whatever guilt Veronica was feeling earlier has disappeared, as she heckles the other Heathers and a variety of others for insincerity or effusiveness. She has caught from J.D. the attitude that insincerity is the worst possible sin, worse, in fact, than the murder they have committed.

At this point, she gets to meet J.D.'s father who acknowledges her in passing as he talks to his son about the inconveniences posed to his demolition business by conservationists of all kinds. As he talks, he exercises on a walking machine – in the book of Job, Satan walks about the earth, and this lower-rent demon uses a walking machine in his front room. They offer Veronica a meal, but she prefers to eat with her parents, spaghetti with lots of oregano – this is, I think, intended as a reminder that Veronica still has something clean and wholesome about herself.

J.D. responds by saying, 'Last time I saw my Mom, she was waving from a library window in Texas. Right Dad?' Later on we learn that his mother was specifically blown up by his father; here the implication is differently sinister, linking her death to that iconic moment, the assassination of John Fitzgerald Kennedy from a window in the Dallas book depository. One of the film's earliest showings took place in Dallas, where this joke fell as flat as one might expect – Waters is capable of stunningly deliberate moments of aggressively bad taste.

The ensuing scene with Veronica and her parents shows her again as grounded with people who mock each other's bad habits – her father's smoking – in a way that entirely lacks aggression and who take an interest in this boyfriend they have not met that she does not reject as intrusive. Again, she breaks off the meal for other commitments – last time it was to go out with Heather Chandler and now it is for the dead girl's funeral – and the line is the same: 'Great pâté, but I gotta motor.'

The funeral continues the film's implied rebuke to insincere pieties – in the commentary, Waters and Lehman and Di Novi talk about the extent to which the film was always less about teen suicide than about reactions to it, a reaction that often at the time approached sanctification. They mention being afraid of being accused of responsibility if there had been an epidemic of teen suicide after the film came out – this is one of the reasons for the change to the ending. The decision to dress the female members of the cast in a series of appalling hats is one of several points at which the scene starts the film's deliberate move further and more obviously into the surreal and grotesque. Heather Duke's big hat is particularly awful, though Winona Ryder's pill-box is subtly unpleasant.

At the heart of the insincerity and unwholesomeness is Glenn Shadix as Father Ripper. Shadix had played a different kind of vague campery as the interior decorator in *Beetlejuice* (1988), and his round features respond particularly cruelly to the wide-angle lens technique that *Heathers* mostly uses for its adult characters. His sermon here is a classic of misplaced ecclesiastical trendiness, and worth quoting in full:

> I blame not Heather, but rather a society that tells its youth that
> the answers can be found in the MTV video games. We must
> pray that the other teenagers of Sherwood, Ohio know the name
> of that righteous dude who can solve their problems. It's Jesus
> Christ, and he's in the book.

One of the reasons why Waters' religious life is relevant to his work on this script is that only a believer could be quite this uncomplicatedly acid. Here, as often elsewhere, J.D. is the truth-telling moral centre of the film as much as its villain – Christian Slater reacts to the sermon with a delicate raising of an eyebrow that says everything necessary.

This institutional insincerity is followed by the prayers of Heather Chandler's friends at her coffin. Interestingly, Heather McNamara is genuinely upset and speaks with a simplicity that is surprisingly touching for all its inarticulate crassness:

> Oh God, this is a tragic thing, and sometimes I have a hard time
> dealing with it and stuff. Please send Heather to Heaven and all
> that.

Heather Duke, by contrast, reveals that she hated Heather Chandler passionately and now feels no guilt about it at all:

> I prayed for the death of Heather Chandler many times, and I felt bad every time I did it, but I kept doing it anyway. Now I know you understood everything. Praise Jesus, Hallelujah.

Ram rebukes God – 'Why didja kill such hot snatch?' – in terms that indicate that he saw Heather Chandler purely as a means to a sexual end. And Veronica is vaguely guilty, vaguely glad she is gone – she has attained a level of honesty where she can at least admit to mixed feelings.

Once the funeral is over, Heather McNamara demonstrates that, whatever her feelings, it is now time for business as usual. She primps her curly hair in the water from a holy water stoup as if it were a convenient restroom sink and asks Veronica to come with her on a double date with Kurt and Ram. She refers to J.D. as 'Billy the Kid', at once demeaning him as immature and half recognizing his deadly outlaw status. When Veronica demurs, Heather McNamara says 'After all, I am your best friend,' indicating her intention of picking up where Heather Chandler left off.

In case we were in any doubt about Kurt and Ram being changed by Heather Chandler's death, they go after a younger boy who accidentally jostles them coming out of the church and force him to say that he loves to suck big dicks. They force him to claim homosexual identity in order to justify their brutalizing of him retrospectively. Bizarrely, some, notably the makers of *The Celluloid Closet* (1995), have seen this scene as an example of homophobia rather than as a fairly telling representation of it, and of how it contaminates all male interactions rather than just straight/gay ones. J.D. sees this going on and drives on past on his motorbike; his version of cool is one which involves sticking his neck out for nobody – he does not intervene protectively to help someone who cannot fight back as effectively as he did.

Ironically, given what we have just seen, the cut back to Heather McNamara and Veronica includes Heather claiming that Ram has 'been so sweet lately, consoling me and stuff. It'll be really very. Promise.' The promise is as worthless as that which presumably follows Veronica's expressed fear that 'It's not one of those nights when they get shit-faced and take us to a pasture to tip cows.' And of course it is.

Daniel Waters assures us, on the commentary, that bored teenagers, among them his friends, in rural communities do indeed engage in cow-tipping. The Kinsey Report (1948) indicated, probably equally reliably, that bored rural male teenagers do entirely other things to cows, which could not possibly have been included in a film. However, it is possible that the one antisocial activity stands in here for bestiality; certainly either is a bizarre thing to do on a double date with two girls.

Both girls sprayed with a nameless dark fluid, literally mud, as a cow falls – there is something deliberately pornographic about this. And instantly Ram jumps onto Heather McNamara getting her muddier; Kurt is so drunk that Veronica fends him off without having even to try. And suddenly, at the top of a rise, J.D. appears to pull her up and out of this mess, looming into the centre of the picture as if he were larger than life. And he takes what is going on entirely for granted – he has seen it all before in 'seven schools in seven states' and the only thing different is the combination of his locker. Like his satanic father, he has been going up and down the earth; Veronica asked him, after the death of Heather Chandler, 'Have you done this before?' and he significantly failed to answer.

The brief scene that follows between Veronica and the yearbook staff is a useful mechanism for planting information; it is the first we hear of the group Big Fun and their pop anthem 'Teen Suicide – Don't Do It' which is going to be crucial to the plot. Otherwise the scene is a fairly obvious discussion of the Heather Chandler suicide montage which is going to take pride of place in the yearbook – 'A two-page layout, with her suicide note right up here in the corner. It's more tasteful than it sounds.' The satirical point is being laboured here, however wittily and momentarily so.

Instantly, though, because this is a fast-moving script, we move on to the consequences of the previous night's date – Veronica escaped the consequences of offending Heather Chandler on a date, only to undergo even worse ones from the date with Heather McNamara. What is bizarre about the rumour is the extent to which the double standard operates – the 'swordfight in the mouth' scenario is seen as demonstrating that Veronica is a slut rather than implying anything about the two boys whose penises are supposed to have come into such very close contact.

She and J.D. concoct a revenge – she claims on the phone to Ram that the lies he and Kurt have been telling force her to confront her unconscious desire to have sex with them both. This is particularly ironic, since the plot she and J.D. have put together is actually a lethal trap for the two jocks, though one which Veronica allows herself to believe non-fatal. J.D. tells her that they are going to shoot Kurt and Ram with anaesthetic bullets. After ascertaining that Veronica studied French rather than German, he tells them that the bullets are called *Echt Luge* bullets, which is to say that he tells her, though she cannot understand, that he is lying. (Some transcripts render this as *Ich Luge*, 'I lie', rather than the DVD's subtitled *Echt Luge*, 'genuine lies'.)

Gay teenagers are statistically unusually prone to suicide during the high school years because of the homophobia of the school environment – there is a poetic justice, of a sort, to the two worst homophobes of all having their deaths set up as a fake lover's pact. The evidence of the pact J.D. provides is a coarse joke, but an effective one – porn, chocolates, a photo of Joan Crawford, mascara, another forged note, and a bottle of mineral water. Veronica rewards him for his intelligence with another kiss, at the very least.

This killing goes off as planned – Kurt almost gets away and Veronica has time to realize Ram is dead before shooting him. J.D. regards this as a useful wake-up call about what is actually going on – 'Look. You believed it, because you wanted to believe it. Your true feelings were to gross and icky for you to face' – whereas she demonstrates her real feelings by burning herself with a cigarette lighter. J.D., as prepared as Heather Chandler was to use people about whom he is supposed to care as objects of convenience, uses the hot point on her burned hand to light his cigarette.

At the same time, where in the aftermath of Heather Chandler's death, of which she was mostly innocent, she worried about consequences ('I'm gonna have to send my SAT scores to San Quentin instead of Stanford'), here she has the presence of mind to snog with J.D. when a passing police car pays them momentary attention before jumping to the conclusion J.D. has set up for them. Later, while J.D. is trying to justify the killing – 'Football season is over. Kurt and Ram had nothing to offer this school but date rapes and AIDS jokes' – she asks him to get her ice; her desire to feel pain is transitory.

'What a waste!' one of the cops says, and it is unclear whether he is talking about the standard heteronormative regret about gay men, or the loss of two football players. 'Oh, the humanity,' the other says, echoing, like Heather Duke, the Hindenburg explosion radio commentator. Like Heather Chandler's death before, the deaths of the two footballers – buried of course in their uniforms – become the occasion for a festival of phoney sentiment – 'I love my dead gay son' says Kurt's father, fiddling with the dead boy's football, and J.D. mocks him, accurately pointing out that he would not have welcomed so openly 'a son that had a limp wrist with a pulse'. Veronica nearly laughs at this – then sees Kurt's very young sister exhibiting genuine grief and is abashed. Here as at so many other points, Winona Ryder's performance softens the script.

One of the things which keeps Veronica from following J.D. all the way into madness is simply this habit of a conscience and the intelligence that lets her observe herself in a critical way. 'My teen angst bullshit has a body count,' she writes in her diary, before musing on the way that in death and public opinion, the supposedly suicidal Heather Chandler, Kurt and Ram have acquired the heart, the brain and the soul that they lacked in fact and in life.' Is this a reference to *The Wizard of Oz* (1939), in which Dorothy's three companions lack these? Almost certainly. She asks herself where her relationship with J.D. is going ('to prom or to hell?') and in the original draft of the script this proved a particularly salient question.

The suicide of the footballers has put Miss Fleming in her element – she is able to claim that the other teachers, by refusing to take her seriously, are in part responsible. Again, the film shows pious sentiment and counter-culture values as just another way in which people can impose their will on those around them. She demands that she gets to impose a mass counselling session on the student body – 'an unadulterated emotional outpour' – and this time the school principal decides to go along with her. The outbreak of suicides has left him at a loss, where 'sexually perverse photography exhibits involving tennis rackets' did not.

Miss Fleming takes over the cafeteria during lunch break with a television film crew in order to turn the school into 'one mighty circuit' in which everyone will clap hands and express their emotions, and talk about them on camera. Heather Duke briefly joins Veronica in cynical comment before joining in the moment she realizes that she can get her face on television. The ambitious Peter asks if he can have a video to send in with his Princeton application – no occasion is too sacred for someone not to try and made an opportunity out of it. Veronica uses it to make a fashion statement, arriving in black, with dark glasses that she removes once their statement has been made. 'Is this as good for you as it is for me?' J.D. asks her, implying that for him, mischief is the same thing as sex.

Meanwhile Martha hides under one of the tables rather than try to squeeze around it to join the group hug – she is shown as marginalized here as always – and suddenly J.D. is at her table, approaching her with his trademark 'Greetings and salutations' and setting in motion another piece of the plot. 'Don't let suicide get you down,' says Miss Fleming on the soundtrack, in a wonderful piece of crassness that foreshadows what happens to Martha.

The scene that follows is one in which J.D. pushes Veronica too far by glorying in the chaos he has created. 'Chaos is what killed the dinosaurs,' he says and, when she demurs, he points out that she is his accomplice in everything he has done – 'Tell it to the judge. Tell it to Kurt.' Then his father returns – 'The Beaver's home,' Veronica says in a sarcastic reference to the idealized father of a classic TV sitcom – full of the same glee we have just seen in his son, and boasting of his technique both in the courtroom and in demolishing a building. There is blatant misogyny in the way he talks of the conservationists he has defeated – 'We beat the bitches … The judge told them to slurp shit and die' – and a sexual glint in his eyes when he talks about the explosion while showing a video of it: 'I put a Norwegian in the boiler room. Masterful! And then, when that blew … it set off a pack of thermals I stuck upstairs. Some days it's great to be alive.' It is almost as if he just obliged his son and Veronica to watch him have sex.

There follows a moment of calm before a return to the storm that terminates the relationship. 'Do you like your father?' Veronica asks J.D. 'I've never given the matter much thought,' J.D. replies, before telling her how his mother, whom he did love, deliberately walked into a building just before his father detonated it. Waters specifically associates this exchange, with its revelation of a particularly vicious sort of primal scene – Freud linked mental disturbance to witnessing children having sex and it is clear from what preceded it that J.D.'s mother's death was sexually gratifying to J.D.'s father – to the stock pieties of John Hughes films about the relationship between single parents and their children. And then on the radio, a DJ plays Big Fun's 'Teenage Suicide – Don't Do It' threatening to kill himself if people keep requesting it, and J.D. pulls out his revolver and shoots the radio.

'That's it. We're breaking up,' says Veronica and J.D. grapples with her, effectively trying to rape her into submission in a scene that is menacing and disturbing. 'You can't bring them back,' he says, and she replies, 'I'm not trying to bring anyone back, except maybe myself.' She has realized that involvement with J.D. will ultimately involve her in an annihilation similar to that suffered by his mother. She mocks him, implying that destruction is sex for him as well as for his father – 'Stay home and … blow up a couple of toasters or something.' Is this a reference to the closing sequence of Antonioni's *Zabriskie Point* (1970)? In a way it doesn't matter, because the masturbation reference is telling enough without High Cinema complications.

Briefly, J.D. is at a disadvantage, but almost instantly he is back in control, in his role as tempter. He shows Heather Duke photographs of her and a thinner, younger Martha in the days when they used to go canoeing together. 'Is this blackmail?' she asks, and he does not dignify her question with an answer. His price – 'I'll ask you to do me a favour, it'll be one you'll enjoy' – is a reference to Brando as Don Corleone in *The Godfather* ('Someday, and that day may never come, I will ask you to do me a favour'). What he is offering her is the chance to replace Heather Chandler as the dominant female of the school. By giving her Heather Chandler's red scrunchee, and mocking her death in terms of Heather Duke's obsessive reading matter ('Moby-Dick drank some bad plankton'), he effectively makes her his accomplice as he earlier did Veronica. After all – and this point is not laboured in the film – how does she think he has the scrunchee?

In one of the moments of stillness Winona Ryder does so well, Veronica breaks into Heather Chandler's locker and looks at the detritus of a life. A sticker that says 'I shop therefore I am', a vanity plate that says 'Heather', a badge that says 'I want it all', some old school books – who would have expected Heather Chandler to keep a pre-Algebra textbook for years? – some slot machine photos of her and Veronica, and a keyring with a red slipper – a reference to the Hans Anderson story of the girl who danced herself to death? There is genuine pathos here interrupted by Heather Duke coming up behind her and putting her hands over her eyes. 'Guess who?' she asks and Veronica says, 'Heather.'

The look of desolate disappointment on her face when she turns round makes clear that for a moment of hope she thought it was not Heather Duke; she fingers the red scrunchee with a look of disapproval on her face. She knows that Heather Duke has made a deal with J.D. and stalks away; Heather Duke starts rummaging among Heather Chandler's possessions, taking a red bangle. Red is the colour of dominance in this film, and Heather Duke is seizing the perquisites that go with the leadership that J.D. has promised her.

Veronica tries to go back, to recapture the innocence of her friendship with Betty Finn, by playing croquet with her. Significantly, she tries to play it not to win by vicious manoeuvres, as she would with the Heathers or with J.D., but simply, for all her 'prepare to die' noises, to have fun. She and Betty chat; Betty is self-deprecating about not being as interesting as Veronica's new friends and Veronica chides her: 'Your daydreams are much better than my reality.' Betty though is merely being realistic – 'Nice guys finish last' – and shames Veronica out of patronizing her and into the ruthless winning shot which is her natural game. And, as Veronica does so, Heather Duke and Heather McNamara arrive, and shoo Betty away. 'I'm red,' Heather Duke announces; she has chosen to become the new alpha female.

In a very poignant little scene, Martha Dunstock sits alone in the gym drinking coke and wearing a Big Fun T-shirt, which on her becomes a sad little expression of aspiration. She tips the cup up for the last dregs and spills it over herself in what is clearly something like the last straw for her. We get to see Martha's desolate inner life for a moment here, and it is a telling rebuke to the pseudo-desperation around her; one of the things that *Heathers* is too rarely praised for is its occasional moments of understatement and subtlety.

The scene which follows is one of the weakest in the script simply because it makes its points entirely without nuance. Veronica's parents are watching a television news interview with Miss Fleming over film of the mass therapy session and Veronica gets progressively angry and upset, first heckling the screen – 'Cleansing synchronicity?' – and then turning it off. She complains that adults do not treat teenagers like human beings and that suicide is being made to sound cool, and her mother points out that the human condition is hard, before offering her some pâté. In the middle of the scene, we cut away to Martha, walking suicidally into traffic with the forged note supposedly from the dead Kurt pinned to her stained T-shirt – she is a rebuke to Veronica's posturing, another addition to the body count of her teen angst.

And almost at once we learn that Martha is a failure, even at suicides. Heather Duke walks in, mocks her – 'Just another example of a geek trying to imitate the popular people at school, failing miserably' – and tries to score some pâté. She is genuinely surprised when Veronica hits her. Shannen Doherty is impressive as Heather Duke, still probably the best thing she has ever done, simply because for the first part of the film she has to be a loyal serf to Heather Chandler and then step up as a serious contender to her vacated throne. Like Winona Ryder, Shannen Doherty was more or less the same age as the character she was playing and she turned in an exemplary performance.

She is also capable of a measure of real pain, even if it is only that Veronica has slapped her when she is supposed to be a loyal subordinate. Heather Duke has learned wit from Heather Chandler; Veronica may well snap, 'You're not funny' when Heather Duke says, 'Martha Dumptruck? Get crucial. She has dialled the suicide hotline since she was in diapers,' but in a cruel way she is.

Heather Duke has also learned ruthlessness – when Heather McNamara turns up on the radio phone-in, *Hot Probs*, at first not even bothering to disguise her name, and talking about Kurt's suicide and cheerleading and her divorced parents, Heather Duke says with glee, 'We'll crucify her,' taking Veronica's participation for granted. Lisanne Falk is touching in Heather McNamara's meltdown scenes, with the gently ridiculous pathos of her taking the name Tweety from a caged bird. The cartoon canary always escapes the cat, but not this one.

Heather Duke makes sure everyone knows about her former friend's breakdown. The washed out Heather McNamara sits listlessly in a classroom on whose chalkboard 'Poor little Heather' has been chalked, while Heather Duke is the centre of attention with her mockery of her broken friend, and Veronica sits on the sidelines, commenting in her diary:

> I cut off Heather Chandler's head, and Heather Duke's head has sprung right back in its place, like some mythological thing my eighth grade boyfriend would have known about.

Suddenly Heather McNamara runs from the room and we see her in the restroom struggling frantically with the childproof cap on a bottle of pills. Veronica, taking some sort of responsibility for the first time, dashes in, assumes she has already taken them, and grabs her by the throat in an attempt to save her life – it is somehow appropriate that when she does the right thing she gets it slightly wrong. And of course this takes place in a room full of sinks and towel machines – the cleaning motif is not overplayed in this film, but it does recur.

Nonetheless, Veronica successfully talks her friend out of suicide, partly by appealing to her individuality – 'If everyone jumped off a bridge, would you?' – partly by just being there for her as her friend. If friendship is expressed by going shopping together, that is not seen here as a bad thing;

Waters may occasionally feint at disapproving of the consumerism of the Heathers – 'I shop therefore I am' – but regards it as venial besides the power hunger that has come over Heather Duke. Denise Di Novi mentions on the DVD commentary her happiness at getting to show this one moment of female solidarity.

The ensuing scene between Heather Duke and J.D. is pitched very much in shadow as befits a scene of temptation. He has returned the compromising photos of her and Martha and she is burning them in the flame of a Bunsen burner; the past is something that can be erased. He suggests that she needs a shtick of her own to replace Heather Chandler's constant polling – and hands her a petition to get Big Fun to play at the school prom. Heather Duke makes him a present of the copy of *Moby-Dick* that when we first saw her was the only distinguishing feature about her – she does not need that touch of individuality any more. On the DVD commentary, Waters bemoans again at this point the fact that the litigiousness of its author prevented their getting to use *The Catcher in the Rye* as Heather Duke's book.

There follows a short montage of Heather Duke getting people to sign the petition and luxuriating in the attention and popularity it brings her. This alternates with a beautifully posed shot of her simply sitting on a window seat with her legs up, looking out of the window and basking in the sunlight. What is impressive about this is the way Shannen Doherty brings us for a moment into Heather Duke's interior life – becoming fully committed to what we recognize as evil has made her as happy as a cat.

Veronica confronts Heather Duke, who asks her to sign; Veronica refuses and there follows a battle of wills in which it is clear that friendship is in the balance. For Heather Duke now, as with Heather Chandler earlier, friendship consists in large part of complying with her wishes: it is not about mutual regard, it is about the power of one person over another. She has started copying Heather Chandler's trademark foulmouthedness and her astuteness about people – her suggestion that Betty Finn would sell out for popularity. Asked by Veronica why she is being such a megabitch, she answers, as Heather Chandler would have done, 'Because I can.' Where Heather Chandler's pithy obscenities involved boasting of an impregnable femininity – 'Fuck me with a chainsaw' – Heather Duke's power comes from a Faustian transaction with J.D. and has a gender-swapped quality – 'Why are you pulling my dick?' she asks Veronica.

She leaves and J.D. arrives still trying to get Veronica back. She mocks him and he fails to understand that her suggestion that they fake Heather Duke's suicide is sarcasm – he reveals that he has started marking up the copy of *Moby-Dick* with this in mind. Heather Duke has given up her individuality to him, and he instantly turns it into a potential weapon. He is not as smart as he thinks, though – this is a film whose perception of evil is always orthodox, and never Manichaean – and finds himself kneed in the crotch when he molests Veronica. He overreaches with her, and she humiliates him. Their estrangement is total, which puts her in jeopardy.

The film becomes progressively darker from this point on – Veronica's next scene with her parents lacks the carefree quality of their earlier interactions and what had earlier seemed a charming egalitarianism now seems vaguely feckless. J.D. has suggested to them that Veronica might commit suicide and their response is to catalogue all of the things against which he warned them. Their expressions are of bafflement and hurt as much as concern – and yet, there is a certain justice to this. Veronica's mood has become darker and darker as they have watched. They hand her a note – J.D. has learned to copy her handwriting as accurately as she copies everyone else's; this is a film in which power and identity are intimately linked.

Rather than try and talk to them, she rushes silently from the room, only to discover a Barbie, wearing a Big Fun T-shirt and nothing else, hanging from a noose in her room. She has made herself a perfect consumer and entirely inauthentic by becoming part of the Heathers clique and here he is using a plastic sexualized commodity to represent her in an act of sympathetic magic. Waters points to this as an Agatha Christie reference – in the often-filmed novel most often now referred to as *And Then There Were None*, the killer, who has faked his own death earlier, influences the last survivor into killing himself and this is clearly what J.D. has in mind.

She lies down and sleeps, in the time-honoured fashion of depressives. What follows is identified on the DVD commentary as real by Denise Di Novi, as perhaps fantasy by Waters – clearly it is fantasy since it involves J.D. coming to Veronica's room, something he does all over again a few minutes later after events have become surprisingly surreal. However, Di Novi can be forgiven the confusion a decade later – the dream is deliberately positioned as starting almost real and gradually becoming even more extreme. To labour the obvious, Heather Duke is alive at the end of the film, so a sequence in which she dies, and has a funeral, attended by ghosts, is clearly Veronica's dream. (It is implied in the version of the film's originally scripted ending present on the DVD that Heather Duke did actually die in that earlier version, as did the obnoxiously ambitious Peter – this may also help explain the confusion.) The exterior shot of J.D. lighting a cigarette in the street outside is one of the more obvious signals of the non-realism of what follows – it deliberately uses a palate far more garish than the other night shots earlier in the movie, with the flame of his lighter casting a reddish pink light on his face.

Veronica appears to awake from her torpor as J.D. reads to her from Heather Duke's copy of *Moby-Dick*; again, on the commentary, Waters and the others bemoan that they were unable to use *The Catcher in the Rye* at this point. First he reads a piece of Melville at his most anachronistic, then the single word 'Eskimo' – the book is full of Romantic agonizing that fits society's beliefs about teen angst. 'You're not a rebel,' she screams at him, 'you're fucking psychotic.' 'You say Tomato, I say Tomahto,' he replies with a shrug – Christian Slater is wonderful throughout this film but this is one of his best moments. He genuinely does not care whether or not he is mad, or whether she thinks he is. The studio wanted him more demonic at this point and Lehman and the others resisted them; the whole point of the performance is to keep J.D. almost likeable, almost a genuine temptation.

In one of the cuts that signals that what is happening is not real, he is suddenly pulling Veronica through a doorway into the kitchen of Heather Duke's house. Again, if there were any doubt this is not real, her bedroom appears to be attached to the kitchen with only a step up. The kitchen is the same set as the one used for Heather Chandler's house, but lit differently in an eerie steel blue – this was doubtless an economic decision, but it also makes a wonderful point about the interchangeability of these lives. Veronica says that if he kills Heather Duke, someone will take her place tomorrow and, in a still voice of resignation, 'that person could be me.'

He seizes a large kitchen knife and Veronica watches her own reflected features transfixed as she points out to him that the knife is dirty and Heather Duke would only kill herself with a clean one – cleanliness is again associated with Veronica. She refuses to forge a note and he seizes her hand and forces her to scrawl on a card; in fact, when you are faking a teen suicide, verisimilitude is not expected of you. The satiric point that the film started from is made very precisely here – teen suicide is a social expectation.

He rushes into a room where Heather Duke lies sleeping and Veronica finds herself unable to open the door to follow him in – again, this is a classic dream image of frustration and paralysis. The dream cuts instantly to a surreal version of the earlier funerals – Father Ripper and the corpse of Heather Duke are dressed in identical Paisley frocks and the mourners are all in white, wearing the cardboard glasses with which people view 3D movies. The only person dressed normally is Veronica; she is also the only person who seems to notice how far Ripper's sermon has tipped into the parodic with its patronizing piety. 'As she writes so eloquently in her suicide note, the way that life can suck!' he says, quoting J.D.'s perfunctory forgery. 'We'll all miss Sherwood's little Eskimo. Let's just hope she's rubbing noses with Jesus!'

Veronica, with a surreal red light behind her, finds herself talking to Heather Chandler, who is dressed in an exaggeratedly haute couture Wicked Queen outfit, and who mocks the dead Heather Duke for not getting as good a turnout for her funeral as she got. Her afterlife is boring, she remarks: 'If I have to sing Kumbaya one more time…' Even dead, Heather Chandler has no softness to her, no preparedness to play along with conventional pieties. She turns menacing, like a demon in a horror film; she has made Veronica's favourite, she says, taking the lid off the holy water stoup and revealing it to be full of boiling spaghetti. 'Dinner,' she says in a voice not her own, and plunges Veronica's face into it – and Veronica wakes up.

Having fooled us with a dream sequence that started so low key that even the film's producer and screenwriter got confused about whether it was real or not, they continue with a sequence that stretches the film's technique as a way of indicating that we are about to be tricked by a *coup de théâtre*. As Veronica writes what is to be her last diary entry, the camera looks down on her from ceiling height, whereas earlier entries have shown her more or less at eye level. J.D. dismounts his motorbike outside, shot in light almost as garish as that during his arrival in the dream and sticks a gun in his belt before climbing a ladder into Veronica's room. Previously his capacity to arrive in her room through the window was left uncanny and unexplained. He finds her hanging from a rafter. 'Let's see,' she wrote in her diary, 'how this son of a bitch reacts to a suicide he didn't perform himself.'

With his usual efficiency, Waters combines J.D.'s reaction to Veronica's apparent suicide with a piece of exposition. J.D. is annoyed and upset that Veronica is dead because he had planned to kill her himself, unless she took him back; he wants her because she is the perfect audience to his master stroke. He tears away the top layer of the petition – which was not even the final top layer, since Heather Duke persuaded people to sign the request for Big Fun to play at the prom with a variety of claims that they were, for example, signing for a hot tub in the cafeteria – and reveals a mass suicide note. Everyone in the school is going to die, and J.D. is making it look like the ultimate act of teen angst.

Once he is gone, and her mother has come into the room to call her down, one last time, for dinner, Veronica climbs down from her faked hanging, mocking her mother for being tense, and by implication mocking us for being fooled. There is a sense, of course, in which she has killed herself, just not literally; faking suicide is a way of trying it on for size, and then taking it back. Because we are not in on the trick, we experience this scene as a revival and a resurrection, even though we know that it is nothing of the kind at a literal level. Resurrection is, of course, one of the things that happens to the Hero with a Thousand Faces – we start to believe in Veronica's capacity to confront J.D. and win.

It was hardly necessary by this point to make any more satirical jibes at the sentimentalizing of teen suicide, but sometimes it is necessary to shoot fish in barrels and kick people when they are down. Miss Fleming expresses surprise when Veronica turns up at the school next day, because J.D. has told her Veronica killed herself. 'Whether to kill himself or not is the most important decision a teenager can make,' the teacher says earnestly as if the act of teen suicide were ever an appropriate existential option. 'Get a job,' Veronica says curtly, because Fleming has taken up emotional self-indulgence as a hobby and career, when she ought to be doing something better. Like the best satirists, Waters can be very judgemental and moralistic in his comments on the world of the touchy feely – in the original version of the script, this scene went on far longer and the point was far more intensely laboured.

The long sequence that follows, the next day, both pays respects to and subverts the action movie, though without any specific reference that would weaken its effect by making it merely parodic. The school is having another pep rally, so that we see all the surviving minor characters. Veronica spies on J.D. and guesses that he has followed his father's precepts, planting small bombs throughout the building, and a larger one in the basement boiler room, where she confronts him, carrying an unfeasibly large gun. It is J.D.'s gun, which he left behind distracted by her apparent suicide. Because he laid it aside, we never feel that she has borrowed his power, merely that she has legitimately acquired it.

None of what follows goes remotely as either of them expects. He is hardly cowed at all by her gun, and knocks her down, leaving her stunned – this is a film that precedes most action heroines and so the idea that a villain would simply use his strength to overpower a small girl was rare outside horror films. By the same token, he is not expecting her to get up again and hit him with a fire extinguisher – neither of them know the rules, which is why their grappling turns momentarily into his attempting to take her by force. J.D. still believes he can seduce her, despite all the evidence to the contrary.

Both of them fumble because this is a film in which the standard expectations of the action movie do not apply. His reaction on seeing her alive is a spoonerism ('I knew that loose was too noose') and she finds herself baffled when he tells her that she can stop the bomb by pressing the red button – when she looks at it, it has three buttons, all of them red. He gives her the finger, and she shoots it off – right up to this moment, it has never occurred to him that she might be serious in her preparedness to maim and kill him to stop him blowing up the school. And there is still a perverse sexiness to their interactions – he is not going to seduce her, ever again, because her sense of self is more important.

Like every movie psycho facing defeat, he has his little moment of self-justification, this one making reference to the way that the original script ended: 'The only place where different social types genuinely can get along with each other is in heaven.' He tells her how to turn off the bomb, if that's what she really wants. It is never all that clever implicitly to ask an armed woman in a movie Freud's famous question, because Veronica tells him what she wants, by shooting him several times: 'Cool guys like you out of my life.'

Somewhat mussed, she wanders through the continuing pep rally and out into the schoolyard, where she is joined by a mortally wounded J.D. Like all the best movie villains, he comes back, not yet quite dead and still dangerous. He recognizes that Veronica has power, power that he has not given her, and he challenges her before blowing himself up: 'Pretend I did blow up the school. All the schools. Now that you're dead, what are you gonna do with your life?' As he said earlier, there are no stupid questions, and the question he asks her is a saner version of the one Heather Chandler posed to everyone in her poll at the film's opening. For the moment, Veronica stands there, calmly waiting for him to die, with a cigarette in her mouth that his death will light – Waters points out that this is an intentional reference to the scene earlier when she deliberately burned her hand and he lit his cigarette off her pain. In the very last shot we see of J.D. before the explosion that kills him, he stretches out his arms as if he were being crucified.

The pep rally stops at the noise and Veronica, covered in grime wanders through the crowd until she comes up to Heather Duke. 'You look like hell,' Heather says. 'Yeah,' Veronica replies, 'I just got back,' underlining that she has been resurrected and has made the night journey all heroes and all liminal beings make sooner or later. She takes Heather Chandler's red scrunchee from Heather Duke's hair and puts it in her own. She kisses her former friend, smearing the pretender's immaculate cheek with her own grime. As mentioned previously, Waters attended the first day of shooting wearing the ashes of the Ash Wednesday service as a memento mori and this is clearly a recalling of that ritual, as well as a neat reversal of the film's regular mention of washing and cleaning.

As the film ends, Veronica walks away, not with Betty Finn, the friend she betrayed and neglected, but with the fat pariah Martha, whose suicide attempt has left her with a neck brace and a motorized wheelchair. If Veronica is 'the new sheriff', she is a leader of outsiders and the marginal. Like Veronica, the failed suicide Martha is now a liminal being, because they have both survived their own deaths. Martha has become the 'dark horse' with whom Veronica will spend the night of the prom, watching films and eating popcorn – not, you will note, playing croquet.

This ending was not the only one envisaged. In one version of the script, Martha shoots Veronica down, calling her Heather as she does so, and Veronica expires denying that identity with her last gasp. In another, the original one, J.D. does not come back after Veronica shoots him and it is Veronica who blows herself up, after contemplating first the cliques and bullying of her schoolfellows as they leave the rally and the natural world in the shape of a single beetle. The question 'What are you going to do with your life?' was in this version asked by her in a note she left in an open locker and which was found and read by Heather McNamara and Betty Finn, suddenly united in mourning.

There followed a grand finale – a school prom, with the slogan 'What a Waste. Oh the humanity', in which all the cliques blurred, and odd couples danced with each other, including the presidents of the USA and the USSR as well as Kurt and the cow he tipped. Martha sang elegiacally from the balcony and from higher up Veronica looked down at everyone, the living and the dead, glad to have redeemed them. Or something.

One always wants it to be the case that studio bosses gave orders which compromised the pure vision of the original creators, but in this case the studio bosses were probably right. Their concern that the film would be a disaster if the sympathetic central character killed herself and if there was just one associated imitator in the real world led to some serious second thoughts that made many of the same points more succinctly. The studio was also doubtless concerned about the extremely elaborate nature of this final surreal sequence, which demands a lot of space to labour satiric points, even though some of its jokes – Kurt and the cow – are moderately funny.

As the creators agree on the commentary, it was better for the film to be made than not, and New Line were not in a mood to negotiate. The ending as it stands is delicious and has a nice mythic ring to it – and it also enabled them to end with 'Que Sera, Sera' and thus to begin with it. Sometimes afterthoughts are the best ones.

One of the problems with *Heathers* is that, for several of its creators and stars, it serves as something of a finest hour. Denise Di Novi went on to produce several of Tim Burton's best films and Christian Slater has been reasonably successful in spite of trouble in his personal life. Winona Ryder's subsequent work has been chequered – she got an Academy Award Nomination in 1993 for Martin Scorsese's *The Age of Innocence* and was excellent in 1990 in Burton's *Edward Scissorhands*, but has not otherwise had that impressive a career. Shannen Doherty is best known for television work, most notably in *Charmed*, and for a much-publicised habit of being difficult to work with.

Waters and Lehman suffered the consequences of success – they were allowed on the strength of *Heathers* to make *Hudson Hawk* (1991), a detective romp starring Bruce Willis, which is nowhere near as bad as its reputation but, in fairness, it is hard to see how anything could be. What it does demonstrate is that without a studio leaning on them hard, both Waters and Lehman lack the capacity to see which ideas don't work and which only work if they go on too long. Secret agents named after candy bars is a joke of limited worth, and it was never a good idea to cast Sandra Bernhard and Richard E. Grant, perhaps the two most self-indulgent performers working regularly in film, as incestuous twin master criminals. Waters' most notable work since was on *Batman Returns* (1992), produced by Di Novi, and the underrated *Demolition Man* (1993). The virtues of *Heathers* include endless comic invention, startling language, excellent casting – they also include a capacity to cut all of these things down to a grinning death's head.

Note

1.   This does not do justice to the glamorous arcane evil that is croquet, but I would not presume to venture an opinion on the precisely nuanced semiotics of the game as played in Ohio.

The Heirs
of Heather

Cordelia, Nicole and
other mean girls

The mark that *Heathers* left most firmly established as a trope of the teen genre in movies and television was the theme of the snobbish social elite that the heroine wishes to be part of and then grows out of. Often this elite is identified with cheerleading, in a culture that values beauty and athleticism over brains – and with intrigues to become homecoming or prom queen. Part of the originality of *Bring It On*, which I will primarily deal with below, is that it sees a school's cheerleaders in a largely positive light as a group of people motivated by the desire to be good at what they do rather than by a desire to rule the roost. Significantly, only Heather McNamara was a cheerleader in *Heathers*; the film neither fully inhabits the cliché, nor refuses it altogether.

The absence of the cheerleading phenomenon from British schools is one of the reasons for the comparative absence of the trope of the popular clique from British teen film and television. There is a clique in the Sky fantasy show *Hex* (2004) which owes a clear debt to its American high school equivalents, but in the absence of any particular goal all they can do is sit around being sexually competitive and bitchy.

The television show *Popular* shown on WB features a group along the lines of the Heathers, the cheerleading squad called the Glamazons.

Significantly, the person who grows away from the group is its theoretical leader, Brooke, who becomes sickened by the treachery and double-dealing that go on among her henchpersons, though it is clear that for a long time she has allowed herself to turn a blind eye to Nicole's intrigues when they have served her own interests. It is explicit, in the episode 'Baby Don't Do It', when she briefly takes on apprentices from Junior High, that Nicole has read, and uses, Machiavelli, she refers to him as 'Nicole – I mean, Nicolo – Machiavelli'.

By the end of *Popular*'s second season, both Nicole and her rich but incompetent rival Mary Cherry have over-reached themselves into disgrace. It is not clear where the show would have gone in a third season had it not been cancelled, with Brooke suffering the physical consequences of a murderous assault on her by Nicole, and Nicole the legal ones.

Part of *Popular*'s originality is that it postulates a rival clique who suffer from the delusion that they are an outsider group – but are contrasted with genuine outsiders like the Tuna sisters and the geekish Emory. This rival group is quite as inward-turning and cliquish. When Carmen makes it onto the Glamazons on the strength of her dancing talent, and in spite of not sharing the clinical anorexia and bulimia of Brooke and Nicole, her friends support her, but are glad when she changes her mind. Similarly, Carmen and Lily, the school's vegetarian and animal rights activist, are concerned when Sam, the school's newspaper editor, becomes, in the show's crucial plot-twist, Brooke's stepsister, because it threatens the opposition by which they define themselves.

Significantly, the original plan for the show was to cast comparatively unattractive young women in the roles of Sam, Lily and Carmen, but the WB vetoed this approach. The idea that Sam and the others are in bad faith in their self-perception as oppositional to the popular clique was a useful creative response to this change of plan. Other changes by the network included making the stepsister theme central from the beginning rather than, as originally planned, playing out the hostility between the groups for weeks before having Brooke and Sam find themselves sharing a bathroom and a kitchen. This is one of many occasions on which television executives have been right for the wrong reasons – another is the replacement of the mediocre plump Riff Regan as Willow in *Buffy the Vampire Slayer* by the more talented, and skinny, Alyson Hannigan.

Both of these groups have satellite boys – and part of the point of the series' plot is that the boys are less stuck in social roles than the girls, but under equal pressure to conform. When the football player Josh tries to break free of expectation by appearing in the school musical, it damages his relationship with Brooke, whose status as half of the school's golden couple is threatened. It damages his friendship with the overweight Sugar Daddy, who sees his place on the football team as contingent on Josh; it gets the school's drama teacher fired for industrial espionage. It also precipitates the break-up of Josh's parents.

The pressures on Harrison, the boy associated with Lily, Carmen and Sam, are rather subtler. He wants to be seen as a sexual being – he is attracted to both Sam and Brooke – but his physical slightness and social association with girls makes this harder, especially when it becomes known that his mother is a lesbian in a settled relationship. It is only gradually that he develops a friendship with Josh and Sugar Daddy that enables him to perform masculinity more plausibly.

His skinniness turns out to be actual frailty – in the second season he develops leukaemia and nearly dies, saved, in one of the show's moments of complexity, by a marrow donation from Nicole. He then discovers, in a Christmas episode that directly references *It's a Wonderful Life* (1946), that he has been the moral centre of the group, that without him the others would be dead, disgraced or psychically wounded. (In the previous season's equivalent episode, the rebarbative Nicole becomes the centre of a version of *A Christmas Carol* and for a while manages to be less obnoxious to those around her – see an extended discussion of this in the next chapter, 'The Canon as Teen Dream'.)

Obviously, the internal group dynamics of the characters of an episodic television show intended to run for years are going to be different to, and more complex than, the purer dynamics of a similar group in a film. *Popular*'s title announces it as a consideration of the same themes as *Heathers* – Veronica, you will recall, refers to the Heathers as being 'like people I work with and our job is being popular and shit' – and the films which directly echo it.

Similar themes occur elsewhere in television, and not merely in shows aimed primarily at a teen audience, and are presented through a *Heathers*-derived vocabulary. In the early seasons of the mother-daughter show *The Gilmore Girls* (2000), the teenager Rory is seen as a threat, and intermittently persecuted, by the equally bright Paris, who has a small clique of her own at the private school Rory starts to attend. Here there is the interesting complexity that Paris's predominance is based partly on family connections and partly on her sheer intelligence, in spite of the fact that her two disciples are considerably less clever. Part of the long-term dynamic of the show was always that Rory and Paris would end up uneasy friends rather than enemies – at college, they find themselves being room-mates.

When *The X-Files* (1993–2002) wanted to deal with the issue of teenage girls manifesting poltergeist activity and accusing everyone around them, and ultimately each other, of Satanic cult membership, in the third-season episode 'Syzygy', it is significant that the (very funny) episode drew on *Heathers* as much as on *Carrie* (1976). The two girls who serve as that episode's 'Monster of the Week' are cheerleaders and, somewhat anachronistically in the mid 1990s, have hairstyles that recall those of Heather Chandler and Heather McNamara, and the way they dispose of their enemies – whenever they say 'hate him, wouldn't want to date him' you know someone is going to die – has a heartless comedy reminiscent of *Heathers*.

The film *Buffy the Vampire Slayer* (1992) positioned its heroine as part of a clique somewhere between the social aggression of the Heathers and the fluffy likeability of the central group in *Clueless*. It is only gradually that Buffy accepts that she cannot be the Chosen saviour of humanity from vampires and socially acceptable to flutter-brained teenagers at the same time. The ally and eventually boyfriend that Buffy finds in the film, Pike, is in a very mild way from the same stable as J.D. in *Heathers* – he is mildly alienated and slightly sardonic. It is in the two vampire boyfriends of the television show that derived from the film – Angel especially when he returns to evil and becomes Angelus, and Spike whether he is good or bad or the various points in between that he touches in six seasons – that J.D. is most obviously echoed. It goes almost without saying that liminal bad boys smoke, ride motorbikes and wear black leather dusters.

The television series gives Buffy this insight more or less from the beginning – on her first day at Sunnydale High, she is given a choice between the two social pariahs, Xander and Willow, who will become the friends of her heart and her allies in the fight against evil, or the clique dominated by Cordelia. Buffy makes the right choice almost without having to think. Later attempts to be a cheerleader or Homecoming Queen end in comic supernatural disasters like a witch's curse or demons hunting her. It is only at the prom at the end of her school career that she is acknowledged as something more important, the Class Protector who has kept her schoolfellows alive to graduate.

There is a sense of course in which Buffy, in both film and television show, is a development of some of the themes of *Heathers*. Like Veronica, she has had a phase of her life in which her job was 'being popular and shit' and has acquired power and liminality, in her case literally rising from the dead, several times, where Veronica only metaphorically did so, and moved on.

What is rather more interesting in some ways is the show's portrayal of Cordelia, who dominates a clique, the Cordettes, as Heather Chandler did hers, but who gradually moves away from the Cordettes to become something of a saviour herself. As early as the first season, we learn that she is not happy with her social role and she gradually becomes Buffy's ally as well as an exemplar of the road she did not take. Even in the first season, she accepts a measure of moral responsibility in a crisis – rescuing Willow and the computer teacher/technopagan Ms. Calendar from vampires and driving her car with them into the school and its library to escape.

In due course, but only after ceasing to be a teenager, Cordelia becomes a heroine in her own right and her own show – for its first three seasons, *Angel* is almost as much about her as it is about its eponymous lead. She becomes first a martyr to her circumstances, then a seer whose clairvoyant powers give her pain, then fully liminal when she allows her nature to be changed to become part demon so that she can continue to survive her visions. This ends badly: her takeover by an amoral Power that uses her as its murderous vehicle is signalled by a brief return, through misjudged magic, to her original shallow cheerleader persona. In an epilogue to her story arc, she returns briefly from the dead to give Angel a message – she is now fully angelic, fully transcended from the person she once was, and yet still has the same trademark verbal aggression. Her sarcasm is more than mere bitchiness – on two occasions it serves to defeat powerful super-natural entities.

The Cordettes are a hierarchical group and Cordelia's control of them is only ever contingent and provisional. Her lieutenant, Harmony – the equivalent in the show of Heather Duke – mounts a coup against her when she affronts the group's internal ethic by dating an unfashionable boy, Xander, and then again when, a season later, Cordelia finds out that he has betrayed her. Harmony never grows up – she is killed and turned at the climax of the third season of *Buffy* and becomes that most pathetic of creatures, an incompetent vampire. Since vampirism is seen in both shows as a condition in which hierarchical organization regularly recurs,

Harmony's constant failed search for an undead clique to belong to can be seen as a continuation of this theme into the adult world. Interestingly, it is seen as an entirely amoral search – Harmony is almost as liable to latch onto groups that do good as ones that do evil, but is incapable of consistency or proper loyalty.

Many of the films that attempted imitation of *Heathers* start off with more or less entertaining premises and characters, but lack its overall coherence and control. Darren Stein's 1999 *Jawbreaker* is a good example of this with its quasi-murderous popular group and its plot full of makeovers, humiliations and blackmail. Courtney, Marcie and Julie accidentally kill their best friend Liz on her birthday when a prank goes wrong and decide to cover it up with a fake rape-murder. The unpopular Fern walks in on them doing this, and is bribed into helping with the cover-up by being made-over into the glamorous Vylette. When she proves too popular for Courtney's taste, Courtney breaks her; Julie and Vylette engineer the revelation of Courtney's involvement in Liz's death during her coronation as prom queen.

Some of this is entertaining enough – Julie Benz is entertainingly dim as the sidekick Marcie though she was really far too old by 1999 to be playing a teenager with any hope of plausibility and Rose McGowan has some splendid moments of lascivious nastiness as Courtney. The blossoming of Vylette as a more over-the-top version of a popular girl is spookily plausible and Judy Greer gives her gawky charm both as Fern and Vylette. On the other hand, Rebecca Gayheart as Julie and Chad Christ as her boyfriend Zack confuse virtue with being lachrymose; Gayheart's big vulnerable eyes are exploited here in all the wrong ways.

The film is also morally incoherent – the same crowd that humiliates Vylette when she is exposed as Fern also humiliates Courtney over her involvement in Liz's death. It is shown as an evil vindictive crowd at one moment and a voice of justice at the next – actually, it is an unpleasant mob on both occasions. Courtney keeps announcing that Julie is no longer popular because they have ceased to be friends, but we never really perceive this; we do not see the mechanism of Julie's social destruction the way we do the creation and destruction of Vylette. Also, the idea that no one in a school is aware of Fern's change of identity, and that the entire school turns on her when it is revealed, is inherently implausible even by the standards of the rest of the plot. *Jawbreaker* is primarily worth remembering as a demonstration of how hard it is to get these things entirely right.

One way to reinvigorate the exploration of the post-*Heathers* tropes – the popular clique that rules by aggression and snobbery, the public humiliation, the plots of the underdog – is to turn them on their heads. Melanie Mayron's 2002 *Slap Her… She's French* reverses expectations in a number of ways, not the least of which is our gradual realization that our centre of emotional focus is the bimbo cheerleader Starla (Jane McGregor) and not the foreign exchange student, Genevieve (Piper Perabo), whom she so remorselessly patronizes.

Gradually, but faster than Starla, we realize that Genevieve is not in fact the fish-out-of-water ingénue that she appears, and that the gradual crumbling of Starla's perfect life is something that has been carefully engineered and orchestrated. Starla is in many ways the perfect target, the arrogant high school queen riding for a fall. She is a cheerleader who dates a jock, she has a posse of the like-minded, which she rules through mockery and the dispensing of favours, she is callous to outsiders unless someone is watching whom she needs to impress with her charitable instincts.

Yet there is little conscious malice in her, just callow insensitivity and a worryingly naked ambition to become a news anchorwoman. Since we know from the beginning that she is heading for a prison cell, we start to anticipate her fall, and become aware that we are not necessarily going to relish it, this time around. One of the reasons for this is that Jane McGregor gives Starla just enough innocence that we see her as fool rather than monster, and she makes the most of occasional pieces of attractive verbal aggression: 'What does not kill me is going to wish she had when I mail her sorry ass back to Skank Central.'

Starla has problems with her grades – and if she fails French she will lose her cheerleading spot; Genevieve offers to tutor her and teaches her by rote what sounds like a sexual proposition to the French teacher. Genevieve offers to take over her cheerleading spot – and proves vastly better at it, and distinctly more sexual in her dancing, than Starla ever was. Suddenly Genevieve has her boyfriend, and is going hunting with her father, and has managed to alienate Starla's friends from her. Soon she has spiked Starla's morning smoothie and railroaded her to jail – she even imitates Starla's drunken mother in order to keep her there overnight and steal her spot in a Junior Anchorwoman competition. This is all the standard mean stuff and we see it, this time, from the victim's point of view.

What goes wrong for Genevieve is that adversity is good for Starla – it makes her reassess some of her values and notice that the Yankee school newspaper editor Edwin is considerably more interesting than the jock Kyle. What also goes wrong for her is that she ignores the smartest member of Starla's family – her little brother Randolph. Starla is far from quick-witted, but a few hours in jail concentrates her mind to the point where she realizes that Genevieve is not all she seems – part of the joke is that, to any audience more sophisticated than Starla and her family, Genevieve's accent is always obviously fake.

Genevieve is not French – she is an American caricature of a Frenchwoman with a deeply inauthentic accent, an implausibly tragic back story and a knack for making mild dowdiness look effortlessly chic. She is, in fact, a former friend whom Starla humiliated when they were both five, who has spent over a decade plotting revenge. Piper Perabo makes her a powerful comic turn, only gradually revealing the vindictive nastiness that lies behind the innocent façade.

In a table-turning final confrontation, Starla reveals this and then makes great play with forgiving her enemy – there is a nice edge of cynicism to this film's assumption that someone like Starla can change for the better but not all the way. Genevieve forgets to take off her microphone when she disparages their native town, giving Starla an excuse to hit her, and look good for doing so. Neither of them wins the competition, of course, but Starla no longer even cares. She is outside in the corridor kissing Edwin, when the victory of the sentimental liberal Doreen is announced. The film does not even let us feel sorry for the defeated Genevieve, whom we see in an epilogue turning up in Paris as an American exchange student, named Starla, with a Texas accent as phoney as her French one had been...

None of this is ever quite insightful or funny enough to be truly memorable – most of the minor characters, including Starla's friends/rivals, never come interestingly to life in the way quite minor characters do in *Heathers* or in *Mean Girls*. Some of the jokes at the expense of Texas are cheap shots about the cattle industry – hard to believe, but nonetheless true – and yet there is hardly any sense of the real dark side of the Lone Star State; the film has no satirical edge beyond disapproving of schoolyard malice. *Slap Her... She's French* is a modest little entertainment with some interesting comic ideas and a couple of fine performances.

The versatility of these post-*Heathers* tropes is best demonstrated by Brian Dannelly's 2004 film *Saved!* which relies on them heavily to make gently damning satirical points about fundamentalist Christianity. Some critics have seen its quiet questioning and teasing as an overly soft-centred approach to a set of beliefs and community structures which are a deep threat to liberal civil society. Such critics ignore both the practicalities of film-making and the fact that, by for example not ultimately questioning the importance of faith in many people's lives, *Saved!* is a more complex and interesting film than would have been the case had its satire been more swingeing.

Simply by using the *Heathers* plot template, *Saved!* sets up a valid criticism of a particular sort of ostentatious piety, both in terms of its creation of hypocrisy and the damage it wreaks on both hypocrites and those who surround them. The school girl-band Christian Jewels is as much a clique as a group of purely social elitists, or cheerleaders, and the will to power exercised by Hilary Faye (Mandy Moore) over her close associates is as self-centred as Heather Chandler's.

The school's principal and pastor Skip (Martin Donovan) is self-deluded and self-torturing. He is at times a figure of fun – cart-wheeling onto the school stage as if school assembly were a rock concert and trying desperately to say cool things – and at times a man tortured by the consequences and inconsistencies of his belief. Compared to, say, the adolescent-hating principals in John Hughes' films, he is admirable, but he is shown here as nonetheless deeply flawed – not least by his complete failure to see through Hilary Faye.

From her first appearance, Hilary Faye is revealed as stupidly callow – when her paraplegic brother Roland (Macaulay Culkin) suggests that the billboard Christ she and Mary (Jena Malone) have erected during the summer break perhaps should not be white, she snaps at him that he must be retarded. Hilary Faye cannot share centre-stage – when pastor Skip's son Patrick compliments Mary on her keyboard playing, Hilary Faye points out that one of its main merits is that 'she complements my vocal stylings without overwhelming them…' When she and Mary quarrel, Hilary Faye treats badly both her imitator Tia – previously 'a wannabe with bad hair' – and the Asian girl Veronica, whom she patronizes for having been rescued from damnation by her adoptive parents. (Veronica's name is, of course, a specific *Heathers* reference.)

At the start of the film, Hilary Faye's best friend and loyal subordinate Mary is an unquestioning holy fool who, for example, believes absolutely in the rightness of picketing abortion clinics. 'I've been born again my whole life,' she says in the first line of the voiceover narration that dominates the film. When Mary's boyfriend Dean confides in her that he is gay, she decides, after hitting her head and mistaking the pool man who rescues her for a vision of Jesus, and after a conversation with Hilary Faye about spiritual virginity, to have sex with Dean to save him from damnation. His parents find out about his sexuality and ship him off to a Christian reprogramming institute, Mercy House. Mary believed, simplistically, that she had a deal with God and feels that he has betrayed her.

And then Mary finds out that she is pregnant. She has talked to her mother about Dean, and her mother Lillian has defended the decision to ship Dean off to Mercy House:

> Having a child is like owning a car … I can change the oil, take
> it to a carwash, but if the carburetor broke, I wouldn't have a clue
> how to fix it.

One of the film's secondary themes is just this – the way that evangelical Christianity encourages parents to see children as projects rather than as people. Hilary Faye is a product of this – when she was fat and spotty, her parents 'fixed' her with fat camp and antibiotics, making it clear that anything less than perfection was unlovable.

Mary goes to the outside of a church and looks up at the cross, trying out swearwords she has never used before – Jena Malone is quietly devastating in this scene. When she tries to share her spiritual crisis with her friends, Hilary Faye rejects her, removing her Christian Jewels pin and shoving her out of the door. At this point, Hilary Faye is as much self-deluded as hypocritical – she thinks she is rejecting Mary as a possible pollutant of the Christian Jewels, even though her real motive is rivalry with Mary over Skip's son Patrick.

Patrick (Patrick Fugit) is set up as an echo of *Heathers*' J.D. but also as very different. Fugit has the same sort of tousled good looks as the young Christian Slater and Patrick has the same capacity for seeing through fraud and bullying; at the same time, he is almost entirely without malice and his truth-telling has no nihilist agenda. And there is a sense in which someone first identified as a Christian skateboarder cannot be entirely cool.

It is worth stressing (because this is a point often missed in casual discussion of *Saved!*) that Hilary Faye's ostracism of Mary has nothing to do with a pregnancy that she does not know about until later – she is rejecting Mary for Mary's refusal to join in the self-serving irrelevancy of praying for Dean to be made heterosexual. Part of the contrast between them is that Mary tries, however stupidly, to do something for Dean that is not merely an occasion for ego-tripping and eventually accepts Dean and his boyfriend Mitch as part of her 'family' of the heart.

The moment of doubt outside the church aside, Mary never seriously ceases to be a sad true Christian; her instinctual rejection of Hilary Faye's perspective on the world is often phrased in terms that reveal her continued belief. When Hilary Faye and the other Christian Jewels try to abduct and exorcise her, Mary resists; Hilary Faye hurls a bible at her back shouting, 'I am filled with Christ's love.' Mary shouts back, 'It's not supposed to be a weapon.' No matter how desperate she is, Mary never contemplates abortion as a solution – the only character even to mention it is the school's single official non-Christian pupil, Cassandra, and she rejects it for the practical reason that it is too late.

Where in most teen films, the struggle between heroine and villainess over a cute boy is phrased in social terms, here both Mary and Hilary Faye are drawn to Patrick, who has quietly rejected his father's sectarianism for a religion of kindness and example. He never seriously considers being in love with anyone except Mary, and one of the first hints of the essential sadness of Hilary Faye's condition is that she is completely incapable of understanding why.

One of the beneficiaries of Hilary Faye's overbearing, ostentatious kindness-as-religious-duty is her brother Roland; another is the vaguely Goth wild child and Jew, Cassandra, for whose soul Hilary Faye constantly struggles. One of the complexities of the film is that Cassandra is, when we first meet her, genuinely troubled, automatically aggressive to everybody and sometimes out of control – she turns up drunk in the mall and while Hilary Faye tries to 'save her', Mary and Patrick simply get her home safely. Cassandra and Roland become girlfriend and boyfriend – the film is delicate and reticent about the extent of their physical relationship – and, after a few cynical comments, she becomes Mary's new best friend. She and Roland know by chance about the pregnancy, and volunteer to become her support system.

Just in case we think this is a simple opposition of good and evil, Cassandra and Roland retaliate against Hilary Faye in a number of ways in which Mary is effectively complicit and which are just as mean as anything Hilary Faye does. They use her credit card to buy Mary outfits to hide her pregnancy and they plant a photograph of Hilary Faye when she was still fat and spotty on the school's internal computer system. Since she is trying to get Cassandra expelled – by taping her threatening her for example and taking the tape to Pastor Skip – we don't feel this is especially excessive. It is clear that one reason she hates Cassandra is that Cassandra has robbed her of the chance constantly to demonstrate her piety by pushing her brother everywhere; another is that Cassandra has acquired the friendship of Mary, whom she wants ostracized.

Hilary Faye has a spiritual crisis over Pastor Skip's refusal to expel Cassandra for her threats. Like Mary before her, she prays to Jesus for a solution, and comes up with the idea of putting blasphemous graffiti all over the school. She assumes correctly that Skip will believe Cassandra to be the person responsible and search her and Mary's lockers, in which she has planted spray paint. This goes better than she could have imagined – the search reveals a sonogram of Mary's child, which she has been keeping at school for safety. (The frame-up and locker search is, of course, a stock device of teen films and television, obviously reflecting a genuine anxiety about the intrusion of authority figures into the private. The would-be male cheerleader Adam in *Popular* frames Brooke for example, and Veronica Mars, in the first episode of the show named after her, plants a dope pipe on her enemy Logan as part of an elaborate and complex scheme not even primarily aimed at him.)

What Hilary Faye does not know, and which makes her revenge all the more devastating in its consequences, is that Mary's mother Lillian and Pastor Skip have fallen in love. He does not believe in divorce and is separated from Patrick's mother; even the solitary kiss which is all we see and probably all there is has tortured him with a conviction of his own sinfulness. He suggests to Lillian that Mary's pregnancy is god's way of calling them to attention over their own 'sin'; he threatens to stop seeing Lillian altogether if she does not ship her daughter off to Mercy House. Skip has many of the functions of a villain, but he does much of his worst damage through trying to be good.

Lillian does plan to do this, though she repents before putting it into effect. Earlier, we have seen her and Mary bonding over programmes on the Christian channel; touchingly, Lillian's repentance is brought about by the quiz show she is watching by herself, in which one answer is that mother and child bond in the first three minutes. Prompted by this, she goes upstairs to talk to Mary, and misses the answer to the question 'What does Dorothy say when she clicks her magic red shoes?' The answer is, of course, that there is no place like home, which is something that neither she nor we need to have said aloud. Mary, though, is gone.

The film has followed the school year, and the course of a pregnancy, and, as Mary's labour becomes imminent, so does the school prom, which Hilary Faye has arranged as a triumph for herself, though without finding herself a date other than her two acolytes. Cassandra, Roland and Patrick have arranged a limousine and a tight red pregnancy-boasting dress for a double date at the prom from which Cassandra and Mary have been implicitly excluded, by being expelled from school. Roland for one knows that this will not pass off without incident.

Hilary Faye asks Pastor Skip to exclude them and he does not – in an earlier version of the script, he planned to have Mercy House collect Mary from the school, but this was cut as rendering him too unsympathetic and as complicating later events too much. In the slanging match that ensues, Roland reveals that the spray paint is listed on Hilary Faye's credit card bill and she responds with the claim that he must have billed it. Asked to swear her innocence, she pauses, tellingly, and then swears an oath that she did not buy the spray paint – at which point Tia turns on her and produces the credit card slip she found in the back of Hilary Faye's van.

Publicly humiliated and rejected by her acolytes and Pastor Skip, Hilary Faye storms out into the parking lot and careers around it in her van; she aims it at the billboard of Christ, repents, but skids and hits it anyway. His face falls off and lands looking at her reproachfully through the windscreen. One of the many ways this film avoids the obvious is that Roland and Cassandra come and look for her; Roland apologizes for ratting her out and he and Cassandra help her home. Moreover, broken, she lets them – our last sight of Hilary Faye is of someone who may have learned better, for whom there is hope past humiliation.

Meanwhile, Dean, his boyfriend Mitch and various other denizens of Mercy House have stolen its van and turned up for the prom they would have been at. Skip tries to stop them, and threatens them with arrest. 'There are no grey areas,' he says. Both Patrick and Mary rebuke him for his small, bounded vision of what God's will is: 'Why would God make everyone different if He wanted us all to be the same?' she asks – Jena Malone is heartbreaking here – and Skip has no answer. And in any case, Mary goes into labour on the spot.

The ambulance can only take one person with her – Patrick and Dean defer to each other, but then Lillian turns up and goes with her. The last scene has Lillian, Dean, Patrick, Mitch, Roland and Cassandra surrounding Mary and her child. Earlier Skip, ignoring Lillian's experience of widowhood, has claimed that a child needs a father and a mother and we see that Mary's child has all of that and more. Sadly, Skip cannot bring himself, yet, to join them; we last see him walking in anguish round and round the hospital car park. He has, however, brought flowers, that symbol of spiritual renewal, so there is hope for him, as for Hilary Faye.

Much of the film's humour consists of gentle teasing of the evangelical Christian sub-culture. 'I love these guys,' coos Hilary Faye about a boy band, 'they're so Christocentric.' One of its greatest and most beautiful ironies is that no one has ever told her about the dangers of spiritual pride. She and Mary both suffer from the delusion that God will protect them if they do the right thing, and originally identify the right thing with the simplistic codes their parents and Skip have taught them. And yet, there is always an ambiguity here – the decision to cast the singer Mandy Moore in the part means that Hilary Faye is genuinely talented. The version of the Beach Boys' 'God Only Knows' that she sings over the opening credits is as demonstrative of real religious feeling as anything Mary says.

Saved! sets up a telling distinction between that sort of virtue which is all about adhering to nominal pieties and that which is about the goodness of the heart – Mary, Patrick and Dean all rebuke Skip from their position as Christians. The *Heathers* template is an important part of what makes the film work, providing a useful genre shorthand that makes it possible to recognize Hilary Faye's power hunger for what it is. It is a delicate film and a sly one, underrated on its first appearance for its lack of belly laughs.

It was often contrasted unfavourably with a more commercially successful film that appeared at roughly the same time. *Mean Girls* has its origins partly in the post-*Heathers* sub-genre – it is worth stressing again that its director Mark Waters is the younger brother of Daniel Waters, *Heathers'* scriptwriter – and partly in Rosalind Wiseman's book *Queen Bees and Wannabes*, which looked at the question of female teen cliques from the point of view of anxious parents and concerned educators. Comedienne Tina Fey suggested this book to Paramount as a project and, after she had convinced them, faced up to the difficulties of actually adapting a book of sociological advice as a teen-oriented comedy. There was a precedent for this, of course, in the pre-genre days of the teen film and especially in the articles on which *Fast Times at Ridgemont High* were based.

Briefly, home-schooled Cady (Lindsay Lohan) starts attending high school and is recruited by her friend Janis (Lizzy Caplan) to infiltrate a popular clique, the Plastics. Cady becomes obsessed with her role to a point where she betrays Janis, and the friendly teacher Ms. Norbury (Tina Fey), as well as the Plastics' leader Regina (Rachel McAdams). Regina takes revenge for her humiliation and throws the whole school into turmoil – a chastened Cady makes her peace with everyone.

The various points in the film at which Ms. Norbury, the most sensitive and intelligent of the teaching staff and the part Tina Fey wrote for herself, explains to Cady and others the folly of their ways are the principal legacy of the Wiseman book. *Mean Girls* is a very funny film, but it is also a very preachy one, in which there is a constant tension between the anarchic comedy of bad behaviour and a desire to restore virtuous normality. Ms. Norbury's name sounds enough like Mayberry, the location of the homespun *Andy Griffith Show* (1960–1968), to have a resonance of common sense and decency that helps make her the film's moral centre, even though she is also made the victim of some routine slapstick, presumably intended to make the preachiness palatable.

Much of the film's sense of the interior workings of cliques derives from Wiseman (the map of clique tables in the cafeteria is based on hers), but equally from the acute sense of interpersonal politics that *Heathers* brought to bear – *Queen Bees…* is after all a post-*Heathers* book itself. It is, indeed, surprising that Wiseman never mentions the portrayal of teen cliques in television and film. Where Wiseman's book is an introduction to 'Girl World' – her phrase and one used by Fey's script – the film brings a naive protagonist into the thick of high school and has her explore her new milieu as if she were an anthropologist.

Cady has been in Africa with her parents, research zoologists. She is, accordingly, both a fish out of water and used to being one. From time to time, she observes her schoolfellows as if they were the animals of the African veldt and the fountain in the local mall were an actual water hole; at a crucial level, primate power struggles are seen as ruling. Her involvement in Janis's plot against Regina makes her a compromised observer, who misuses her skills and her objective observation to become part of what she is watching.

Her arrival at school walks her through a short but telling example of what I have elsewhere called the anthropology shot – she sees various cliques, which she has not identified, interacting with each other in a more or less hostile fashion. She witnesses more of the same in the classroom – the first girl she speaks to, later identified as one of the jocks, responds,

'Speak to me again and I'll kick your ass' – and in the cafeteria, where we
see the various groups that Janis later identifies for her: the cool Asian girls,
the band geeks, the burn-outs and so on. One of the economic virtues of
Tina Fey's script is that these groups, and their members, are individuated
just enough that when they, for example, turn up again at Cady's party, or
at the climax, we remember enough of who they are that they do not feel
like a simple horde of extras.

On her first day at school, Cady is almost entirely isolated – she ends
up taking her lunch into the girls' toilet to eat in a cubicle, in a scene that
is echoed, crudely but effectively, at the point where her intrigues have
placed her in a deserved isolation. On her second day, she is befriended by
the class pariahs, the arty Goth Janis and the plump camp student affairs
administrator Damian (Daniel Franzese), who start educating her in the
ways of school and point out the popular clique, the Plastics, and their
leader Regina George. Significantly, this happens while the three of them
are cutting a sex education class – this is, in a sense, Cady's real education
as opposed to the inaccurate scare stories about sex and death she would
have got from the hypocritical school coach.

This is a film in which names are important – Regina is first seen
being carried aloft by her admirers and her very name means queen,
just as her surname George is that of the king from whom America took
its independence. Janis Ian's name is that of a moderately distinguished
alternative pop entertainer, whereas Damian's name is ironic – in his genial,
caring way, he is the least bad seed imaginable. Cady's first name signals
a certain naivety and innocence, while her second name Heron indicates
both beauty and a certain capacity for predation.

Janis has already described Cady's looks as 'regulation hottie' – Wiseman
has several chapters on the social construction of acceptable teenage girl
body images – and Cady finds herself recruited almost instantly to Regina's
clique as a potential rival source of sexual power whom Regina needs to
control. Almost instantly, she finds herself caught up in Regina's little
ploys, such as praising Cady's bracelet and, when Cady responds, implying
that she is being vain. Regina is a queen of mixed messages – hopelessly
insecure herself and completely lacking insight into that insecurity. Rachel
McAdams brings to the role not only the right sort of near-anorexic good
looks, but the right febrile energy.

Cady is moderately hostile to the whole idea of hanging out with the
Plastics, but Janis persuades her that it would be fun to spy. For reasons that

it takes most of the film to make clear, Janis and Regina, who were once friends, hate each other passionately. Janis sees in Cady a possible means of getting her revenge without ever making clear to her what, save for Regina's general manipulation and intrigues, vengeance is being taken for.

We eventually learn, from Regina, that she announced suddenly that Janis was a lesbian and got her and Damian ostracized by doing so. Unusually, the accusation of homosexuality is here not merely a random piece of abuse, even though untrue; it has an embedded effect on the film's plot. Cady believes for a while that Janis is in love with her and this helps her gradual drift into being genuinely Regina's acolyte; her raising of the issue with Janis precipitates a total break between them until the film's climax.

In the end, of course, the question is handled in an anodyne way at any overt level – it turns out that what happened was that Regina (wilfully?) misunderstood Janis' self-description of herself as Lebanese. At a more subtextual level, of course, the presence of an overt imputation of lesbianism in the plot raises interesting questions about the intensely homosocial relationship between Regina, Cady and the other two Plastics, Karen and Gretchen.

When, after her near-fatal accident, Regina is reborn as a jock and hangs out with girls who are equally aggressive, and not afraid of her, there is a clear implication that she has found not only a social, but a sexual milieu, she finds congenial. During the trust exercises at the film's climax, Regina accuses Janis of wanting to be part of a big 'girl-pile' and that, when her friends pile on top of her after a successful goal at lacrosse, is exactly where we last see Regina. The film's origins in a parenting textbook is possibly the source of the slightly patronizing and pathologizing tone of this.

This interpretation is strengthened by the way that Regina treats Cady, first of all taking her under her wing and then subjecting her to deliberate cruelty to prove that she can, and that Cady will take it. When Cady expresses an interest in Aaron, Regina's ex, Regina arranges to start dating him again, perhaps out of spite and a desire to control, and perhaps, in part, because Cady has tried to find space in her emotional life for someone who is not Regina. Like all other heroines and heroes of teen films not specifically aimed at arguing for lesbian and gay equality, Cady remains almost entirely clueless about this subtext.

Cady is genuinely clever, and does her best to obscure the fact in order to pursue Aaron who is not – Ms. Norbury recognizes what is going on when Cady starts deliberately to fail her maths class in order to get Aaron to tutor her. Regina is far from being Cady's intellectual equal – she is so obsessed with popularity, glamour and control that it is genuinely hard to tell, save through such giveaways as her inability to see that cranberry cocktail has sugar in it, and is therefore not going to help her with weight loss – but it is significant that she has acquired as subordinates two girls who are stupid to a degree that takes the breath away.

Karen and Gretchen are a comic turn, but so well performed by Amanda Seyfried and Lacey Chabert as to come across as figures of genuine sweetness and pathos. It never occurs to them, for most of the film's length, that anything that happens as a result of their clique's dominance of the school is other than part of the natural order, or that the rules Regina has imposed on the Plastics – jeans on Fridays only, ponytails only one day a week – are other than completely arbitrary. They present no more of a challenge to Regina than does her over-friendly mother; Cady is her rival for looks and potentially in every other way, and Regina cannot resist the challenge of trying to break her to her will.

Regina's reacquisition of Aaron, however, gives Cady something to be angry about. She and Janis analyze the factors on which Regina's popularity is based and set out to take them away from her. One of these is Aaron; another is the loyalty of Karen and Gretchen; and the third is Regina's skinny body. The ruthlessness with which Cady sets out to take the last of these away is one of the points at which we realize that the title of the film refers as much to its notionally good characters as to its notional villainess – Cady has observed Regina's obtuseness about calorie-counting and persuades her to eat nutrition bars in the credulous belief that they are diet food. Regina accordingly wolfs more of the things the more she starts getting too big for her clothes – this is very funny, and like most cruel comedy it is also the stuff of nightmares.

One of Regina's favoured techniques for controlling her followers is the multiple-person phone call, which is not announced as such and is used to set Karen and Gretchen, and latterly Cady, off against each other. (In these conversations, and at no other point in the film, Waters makes competent but visually unexciting use of a split screen.) Cady turns this against her, and secures Gretchen's loyalty to her – Regina has become complacent and fails to use the carrot as well as the stick. It is never stated clearly, but the additional vulnerability that Gretchen feels as a woman of colour in a clique otherwise consisting of two very pale blondes is exploited here. (Interestingly, and in a way that is not pathologizing,

Gretchen is recruited by the film's end to be the one non-Asian girl in the clique of cool East Asians; to some extent, she finds the role of semi-outsider congenial.)

One of Cady's successful bids for power is the result of genuine competence. At the Christmas talent show, the Plastics perform 'Jinglebell Rock' – as they have for so many years that the choreography was originally devised by Janis in the days of their friendship with her. Regina decides, at the last moment, to show favouritism towards Cady by putting her nearest her in the line-up, and, unrehearsed, this leads to catastrophe as the cassette player that is providing them with a soundtrack is kicked into the audience.

Cady retrieves the situation by starting to sing, and Ms. Norbury scurries to the piano to play an accompaniment. Something that could have rendered the Plastics a laughing stock becomes a triumph for them, and Regina has nothing to do with it. The fact that this triumph is intrinsically tawdry, and involves reducing themselves to highly sexualized puppets, is a reminder that Cady has become obsessed with her role to a point that means she has lost her way.

There is a nice piece of genre-coding here. The point at which Cady stops merely being a spy and starts actively intriguing against Regina comes at Aaron's Halloween party, where she misreads the social code and attends in a fright costume, as a zombie bride, rather than in the highly sexualized cute-animal costumes adopted by the other Plastics. Regina exploits this to demean her to Aaron as a sad little stalker.

Tearstained after observing Regina and Aaron kissing, Cady turns up in the room where Janis and Damian are consoling themselves for social pariahhood by watching a zombie movie, and scares them into showering popcorn everywhere. A zombie of course is someone who has become monstrous as a result of being reborn as the instrument of someone else's will. This is what has happened to Cady, when she lets herself be persuaded to be the instrument of Janis's vengeance, and Janis has forgotten the usual fate in horror of those who, like Frankenstein, turn other people into their tools.

Her attempts at exposing Regina's constant infidelities to her relationship with him to Aaron are the subject of mildly amusing farce. Each attempt to trick Aaron into discovering Regina and her other boyfriend in a projector room leads to unintended consequences, such as the exposing of the relationship between the school coach, whose sex education sessions are moralistic and prurient, as a hypocrite who is sleeping with one of the East Asian girls. The sheer amateurishness of Cady's plots at this point softens the nastiness of her sabotage of Regina's diet.

One of the ironies of Cady's situation is that she has got caught up in obsessions that are intrinsically boring and trivial, at the expense of the relationships that are worthwhile and the things she is good at. She finds herself spewing out what she calls 'word vomit' – expressions of her love-hate relationship with Regina and with every fine nuance of what Regina has done, is doing or will do. She cannot hold a conversation on any other subject – though Cady is coded in the film as entirely heterosexual, her relationship with Regina has many of the attributes of an unhappy love affair.

She successfully marginalizes Regina from her own group – Regina cannot fit into her clothes and so has to wear sweatpants to school. Accordingly, she is rebuffed from lunching with the Plastics by the rigid imposition of her own rules – Karen and Gretchen turn on her as she has always had them turn on other people. Significantly, in this cafeteria scene, Cady says nothing, just sits looking sweet as Regina is first rebuffed by her friends and then mocked by others – Regina has taught her well. There is a real cruelty here and a real sense that Cady has willingly corrupted her own will.

She proceeds to do something worse. She opts out of a trip with her parents using Janis's art show as an excuse – significantly, the trip was to see Ladysmith Black Mambazo, a group moralizingly portrayed as part of her essential identity, and clearly more authentic than the ghastly boy bands that the Plastics listen to. She throws what is intended to be a small soirée for herself, Karen, Gretchen – and Aaron and a few of his friends. As always happens, both in films and in Rosalind Wiseman's book, the party turns into a colossal and overpopulated scrimmage at which she has to rush around stopping people destroying her parents' African objets d'art or having sex in the bedrooms.

She gets to express her feelings to Aaron and in the process reveals that she has deceived him about her ability at maths, and talks endlessly about Regina. She also literally vomits over him. She has betrayed herself, her real friends, her parents – and has got nothing worth having for it except the loyalty of two idiotic girls whom she more or less despises. Outside, in the street, Janis tells her that she has become entirely corrupted, that she has, in fact, become Plastic for real in a reversal of the Pygmalion myth.

Janis throws a canvas at her – a group portrait of Cady, Janis and Damian – indicating that the friendship the painting celebrates is over.

With excellent economy, it is also in the aftermath of the party that Regina is tipped off by her footballer boyfriend that she has been eating weight-gain food, not diet food. She sets out to retaliate against Cady and her other former friends by using against them one of the central objects of the Plastics' friendship rituals – the Burn Book. In this they have inscribed their bitchiest comments, worst libels and most malicious pieces of gossip at the expense of every other girl and female in the school.

Fey and Waters make the Burn Book central to the portrayal of Cady's corruption – part of her initiation into the Plastics consists of writing in it a piece of Janis's banter at Damian's expense, the description of him as 'too gay to function', and realizing as she does it that some jokes are only all right when made by your friends. She does far worse than this before she is through. When Ms. Norbury pressures her over her falling grades, she distorts Ms. Norbury's remarks into a confession of being a drug pusher, rather than someone who pushes failing students. This is pure malice at the expense of someone who is trying to help her, and the worst single thing that Cady does.

Regina places her own photo in the Burn Book with hostile comments appended and then takes it into Principal Duval's office, claiming that she has nothing to do with it – a claim which even the mildly clueless Duval realizes is almost certainly a lie. While he is grilling the other Plastics in his office, Regina scatters Xeroxes of its juiciest pages throughout the school, precipitating a riot as, for example, the coach's teen paramour discovers he is also sleeping with her best friend. (This aspect of the plot is, very loosely speaking, an echo of the exposure of Kathryn Merteuil at the end of *Cruel Intentions* via the publication of her stepbrother's journal.) It is during this sequence that the care that has gone into individuating a large number of the cast pays dividends – this is an effectively choreographed scene of chaos which works so well because it builds on material established throughout the film.

The succeeding scene, a seminar in which Ms. Norbury explains to all the girls why abusive remarks about each other are wrong, is, by contrast, irritatingly ma-wkish and soft-centred – there are fine things in Tina Fey's script and performance but this moralistic harangue is not one of them. She encourages each and every one of them to express their anger and resentment and insecurity before falling backwards in a trust exercise to be supported by her classmates – in a wonderful sad little joke the dim Karen falls backwards and is caught by nobody but Gretchen, the only person she can actually trust.

When Janis appears on stage, Regina taunts her over her alleged sexuality and Janis responds by spelling out the full extent of her successful plot against Regina and the depths of Cady's betrayal. Regina rushes from the room, ignoring Cady's attempts to explain herself to her, and walks under the school bus that almost crushed Cady on her first day at the school. This is an accident, and not explicitly a suicide attempt; it is also a very funny dark joke about the consequences of schoolyard malice – not least in the way that it becomes widely believed that Cady pushed her.

It is also the one exception, and a very successful one, that points to the difference between *Mean Girls* and *Heathers*. The earlier, and better, film had done exaggerated melodrama so well and so successfully that *Mean Girls* generally avoids extremes for things that might actually happen in a classroom. It makes its effects by tight plotting and manipulation of expectation rather than by Gothic gestures. The utter blandness of the film's notional hero, Aaron, is part of the downside of this – Cady as good girl, in an uncomplicated relationship, is just a lot less interesting.

The rest of the film is a restoration of normality – Cady is briefly ostracized, and then takes the step of making a full confession of everything she has done. She apologizes to Ms. Norbury and tells the police – who are investigating the maths teacher for drugs pushing that what she said was a malicious lie. Ms. Norbury makes her appear for the school in a Matheletes competition – social death for a Plastic – before attending the Spring Fling.

Implausibly, given that she was ostracized mere days before, Cady is voted Fling Queen and graciously breaks up her plastic crown giving fragments of it to Regina, Gretchen and Janis, whom she has beaten for her title, and slinging further pieces out into the crowd. It says a lot about the charm of Lindsay Lohan's performance that this potentially deeply mawkish moment comes off as well as it does.

What both *Saved!* and *Mean Girls* demonstrate though is that the principal contribution of *Heathers* to the teen genre has been a set of very effective comedic gestures rather than its deeply subversive spirit. At the end of *Heathers*, Veronica has gone through a night journey which leaves her with the kind of dark wisdom that makes it impossible to fit into normal suburban life any more. She has achieved personal autonomy at the cost for her, and at the expense, of the two most important influences in her life, both of whom wanted to control her. She has become an uncomfortable *unheimlich* being who has transcended conventional rules about appearance – the smuts on her face and the raggedness of her clothes – and the standard social rules of high school.

Even the best of *Heathers'* imitators lack that sheer darkness of perception. Where Heather Chandler dies in agony, Regina does not have to die for her influence to be broken – indeed, the setting up of a near-death and rebirth in a different social clique for her is ultimately an aggressive refusal of that particular trope. Hilary Faye's future is left more ambiguous – her absence from the final scene of Mary's 'family' though may be less an artistic decision about her storyline than to do with the availability of Mandy Moore for shooting.[1]

Similarly, the sorts of wisdom gained by Mary and Cady are of a radically different kind to that gained by Veronica. Cady's wisdom is indeed mostly handed to her on a plate by Ms. Norbury and has to do with self-respect and accepting that happiness is not a zero-sum game in which humiliating others makes us stronger. This is all very admirable, but hardly profound or subversive. Mary's wisdom is subversive in a sense, but only in the context of *Saved!*'s refusal to confront Evangelical Christianity in a hostile way and instead to suggest a way in which it could be truer to itself by abandoning its strict sexual mores and the temptation to spiritual pride they involve. This is an intelligent and ethical artistic choice – and a film in which Mary rejected her upbringing and family altogether would never have been made in the social climate of 2004 – but it is hardly a subversive one.

Note

1. The DVD commentary is ambiguous on this point but seems to imply as much.

The Canon as Teen Dream

Clueless
and others

*T*o take a canonical text, a so-called classic, and to recast it in accord-
ance with a set of genre rules, can be seen, if we choose to adopt a
Manichaean model of clear distinctions, as either to lower the classic to
the gutter, or to dignify the low genre by association. It can also, more rationally, be seen as starting a dialogue between what is already accepted as
canonical and what is not yet so accepted. When, in *Joseph Andrews*, Henry
Fielding fits heroic similes of the sort we would expect to find in epic poetry into a farcical account of below-stairs life, he is asserting the dignity of
the novel through burlesque, yes, but also starting such a dialogue. He is
also asserting the right of the novel's audience to know about epic.

   The eventual rise of the novel in the course of the eighteenth century
into a status where it is automatically included in our sense of things which
might be canonical was hindered by the assumption that it was a 'low'
form with which lesser mortals – notably women – might waste their time.
The establishment of a dialogue with 'higher' forms is part of the process
whereby the canon is expanded, and also, as a general rule, whereby the
'low' audience is brought to a higher status as a part of the audience for
what has become canon art.

A significant part of the history of the teen movie genre is the creation of works solidly within that genre which adapt classic novels, Shakespeare's plays or, indeed, material from films in genres already taken seriously. When a type of film or television show that is automatically undervalued as less important, more commercial and less worthy of consideration as art, engages with adaptation of works from the literary canon, something similar to the process whereby the novel moved from 'low' form to serious mode of artistic creation is perhaps taking place. (At the point where SF movies start to be considered seriously, *Forbidden Planet* (1956) adapts *The Tempest*.) At the very least, some individual works, created in such moments, are respected on their own merits even though the genre they are part of continues to be thought of as abject.

One of the reasons why such works change the way in which the genre in which they are rooted is thought of is that they demonstrate the preparedness of their assumed ideal audience to recognize and cope with the element of adaptation, to the references being made. Often such reference is free-standing – *Clueless* at no point underlines the fact that it has drawn for much of its plot and characters on Jane Austen's *Emma*.

Sometimes the game of reference is part of the point of the film or television show. The teen TV show *Popular* was pitched at a hip teen audience that would, for example, recognize such a reference. When a pram with a doll inside falls down a school staircase – to the Odessa Steps sequence of Eisenstein's *Battleship Potemkin* (1925) either directly or through the reference to it made in Brian de Palma's gangster drama *The Untouchables* (1987).

In another episode, the stepsister rivals Brooke and Sam enact scenes from Robert Aldrich's camp Grand Guignol, *What Ever Happened to Baby Jane?* (1962), with each at different times taking the role of oppressing sister and victim sister. The show's cancellation after two seasons implied that it overestimated the sophistication of its audience; its continued post-cancellation popularity indicates that it did not.

One particular episode from the first season – 'Fall on Your Knees' (1.10) – is a comprehensive adaptation of one of the most populist of Victorian novels, Charles Dickens' *A Christmas Carol*. The novel has, of course, often been filmed – including a version by the Muppets – and Bill Murray's *Scrooged* (1988) is a contemporary adaptation, about as faithful and unfaithful as the *Popular* episode. Briefly summarized, the ultra-bitchy cheer leader Nicole goes through the experiences of Scrooge and is temporarily softened by them to the point of allowing Carmen, whom she despises, to become a cheerleader.

I would argue that the presence of many lines directly taken from Dickens indicates that 'Fall on Your Knees' is as much an adaptation as a burlesque or a mere reference. When the invisible Nicole attends her schoolfellows' Christmas feast, the decision to include her in the toast 'for the day's sake' works emotionally in terms of these characters, but is directly taken from Dickens and is profoundly nineteenth-century in its feel.

Many of the adaptations are ingenious to the point of brilliance. Jacob Marley is replaced with Marley Jacobs, a cheerleader who died of anorexia; the plump Carmen has broken her ankle at dance practice in order to give her Tiny Tim's crutch. When, in the vision of Christmas Yet-to-Come, the episode needs Carmen to be as dead as the future Tim, the improbability of her dying of this injury is shrugged off with an elegant 'gangrene can be awfully fast'.

Some of the comedy of the episode comes from these elegances, some from sheer incongruity. The Ghost of Christmas Present, for example, is replaced by the idiot Texan cheerleader Mary Cherry – Leslie Grossman's grotesque caricature of a Southern accent in which every vowel becomes a surreal trill of diphthongs is wonderfully maladapted to verbatim chunks of Dickens. Nicole is shown Ignorance and Want crouched behind the Spirit's skirts and Grossman makes of the exhortation 'Beware' ('BeeWhayUh') a thing of glory.

Some of the episode's preoccupations are ones present in Dickens by implication but foregrounded in a modern version. Up to this point, Nicole has been shown, in Tammy Lynn Michael's performance, as a creature of motiveless malignity. Here we get her back story, as we get Scrooge's in the original. We learn explicitly that she is a victim who has become a bully as a way of taking revenge on the world, and in order to be accepted as first peer of, then replacement for, Marley Jacobs in the school's hierarchy of the popular and successful. Michaels manages to give her bitch queen moments of real pathos while still relishing, and making plausible, her condemnations of Christmas and kindness as 'humbug'. She is also excellent as the (briefly) repentant Nicole, whose moments of gift-giving graciousness are as scary to her former victims as Scrooge's must have been.

At the same time, some aspects of 'Fall on Your Knees' are less successful. The episode does not escape Christmas kitsch in its shots of carol-singing waifs – the show's secondary cast of genuinely unpopular characters – and the final visit to the monstrous Glass sisters. Some of this saccharine is sardonic and knowing – thick snow in Southern California is a miracle of heavenly grace in *Buffy the Vampire Slayer*'s Christmas episode, 'Amends' (3.10), and here is just a surreal joke that has not entirely been earned. In the second season of *Popular*, the Christmas episode was – what else? – an adaptation of Frank Capra's *It's a Wonderful Life* and the kitsch element took over rather more.

Still, 'Fall on Your Knees' demonstrates in its forty minutes some of the possibilities of adaptation. It takes from its classic original a handy way of doing some character work that the show needed in order to deepen the portrayal of its villainess; it has great fun with both ingenuity and incongruity. It is a way of displaying show-runner and scriptwriter Ryan Murphy's technical virtuosity – it also demonstrates that the rules of the teen genre are a solid enough piece of engineering to stand up under the weight of significance that the Dickens original brings to the episode. The three films we will now consider demonstrate the same strengths at greater length.

In spite of being described by Jane Austen as 'a heroine whom no one but myself will much like', Emma has always been one of the most popular of her heroines. Charming, rich and intelligent, she manages to do comparatively little mischief in the lives of the people in whose lives she meddles, and manages to marry a man from whom she will learn the good sense she occasionally lacks. It is amusing to contemplate just what Austen would have thought of *Clueless*, Amy Heckerling's 1995 film which draws, in crucial respects, on Austen's *Emma* for its central character and key parts of its plot.

The focus of Heckerling's film is her heroine, Cher Horowitz (Alicia Silverstone), coming to terms with the fact that she, rather than the people around her, is clueless, that she does not understand her own motivations or the world. A majority of the good teen movies are about outsiders who try and fail to fit into the world of the popular kids, but some of the best and funniest are those which turn their attention to the popular kids and look at how things work for them.

Like Emma, Cher is 'handsome, clever, and rich, with a comfortable home and happy disposition … with very little to distress or vex her'. As her name indicates, she is dear to the world and to herself. She has also, like Emma, the habits of getting her own way and of thinking too well of herself. When her stepbrother Josh (Paul Rudd) asks her, 'What makes you think you can get teachers to change your grades?' Cher replies, 'The fact that I've done it every other semester.' The reason her failure to pass her driving test and her fear that Josh will mock her for it are so significant in her narrative arc is just this – she finds herself in a situation where charm and the exercise of will cannot get her out of trouble.

She is significantly younger than Emma – sixteen rather than twenty – and yet lives a life in Beverly Hills that has some of the same upper-class trappings. Alicia Silverstone is almost perfect in the part, as she has been in very few roles since;[1] Heckerling used such felicitous accidentals as Silverstone's inability to pronounce the word 'Haitian' to give the characterization of Cher additional points of humour.

While Mr Horowitz (Dan Hedaya), Cher's father, is a workaholic rather than an obsessive hypochondriac like Austen's Mr Woodhouse, she constantly takes care of him and of his health. Like a woman of an earlier time, she is responsible for ensuring that the family servants run the house smoothly – at a point when she is most self-doubting, her father points this out to her. The fact that she is capable of crassly offending the El Salvadorian housekeeper by speaking to her as if she were Mexican is never seen as more than a venial fault – she realizes she has caused offence and asks Josh why. Like Emma, she lost her mother while young, and the slightly black joke about its having been due to an accident 'during a routine liposuctioning', does not diminish the pain.

Cher is not one to admit vulnerability, though, and the film is full of her attempts to manage everyone around her, as well as of her belief that charm will secure her everything she wants. She is not entirely wrong in this assumption. She match-makes her debate teacher Mr Hall (the always excellent Wallace Shawn) with her socially committed Bohemian teacher Miss Geist (Twink Caplan). Although this starts off as part of a campaign to make Mr Hall happier so that he will raise her grades, she and her friend Dionne (Stacey Dash) become genuinely concerned with these two lonely people's happiness.

Mr Horowitz has always taught Cher to negotiate – he is a successful, and scary, lawyer – and she is genuinely effective at such moments. We also note, with interest, that Mr Hall's original low mark for Cher's debating skills is unfair and based on a sterile academic sense of what debating is. Cher's two speeches may express themselves through a vapid airheaded vocabulary but, in both cases, her impeccably progressive arguments (for a generous asylum policy and for uncensored media) cut to the quick. In the former case, her closing remark – 'There is no RSVP on the Statue of Liberty' – is an effective piece of rhetoric. These scenes usefully make the point that Cher is nowhere near as much of an airhead as she thinks she is.

The central thrust of the plot, and one taken directly from Austen, is her patronizing attempt to make over the life of a new girl at the school, Tai (Brittany Murphy), whom Cher and Dionne decide to adopt as part of their popular clique. Tai, who is clearly something of a stoner, is drawn instantly to the skateboarding class clown Travis (Breckin Meyer) – in Cher's world, this is social death and she tries to match-make Tai with the almost entirely worthless, but apparently cool, Elton (Jeremy Sisto). There is genuine kindness in the way Cher takes Tai on as a project – and yet there is also a fundamental lack of respect. Cher is someone who selects her own outfits by using a computerized dress-up doll of herself, so it could hardly be expected that she would entirely acknowledge another person's autonomy.

She fundamentally misreads the situation with Elton – who flirts with Tai purely as a way of getting close to Cher, and who, when she rebuffs him, puts her in genuine jeopardy by driving off and leaving her. When Tai announces that she is over Elton, and gets Cher to help her dispose of souvenirs, she is appalled to realize that Tai has turned her attention to Josh and at first reacts with real snobbery, for which Tai justifiably jumps on her. However, the film lets her off the hook in an important respect – her snubbing of Travis has actually encouraged him to turn his life around by going to a 12-step meeting for his drug use. He is still a skateboarding idiot, but he is now good at being a skateboarding idiot and he and Tai are clearly going to be strangely, dopily happy together. Cher's meddling has not done any lasting damage.

Cher and Dionne are a little clique all of their own. The reason why I have not dealt with them already in the chapter on the Heirs of Heather is that the pair of them are so entirely without malice that they serve, in a sense, as Heckerling's riposte to the *Mean Girls* trope. Clearly their treatment of Tai has disturbing elements – they make over her look and try to find her a boyfriend they consider socially acceptable – but there is no conscious malice to the pair of them. Indeed, the closest thing to an enemy Cher has, Amber (Elisa Donovan), resents her far more than Cher deigns to notice the fact. Cher only vaguely acknowledges that anyone might resent her and says, of Dionne, 'She's my friend because we both know what it's like for people to be jealous of us.'

The closest that either of them come to Heather Chandler bitchiness is a remark Dionne makes to Amber during tennis practice:

Amber:	Ms. Stoeger, my plastic surgeon, doesn't want me doing any activity where balls fly at my nose.
Dionne:	Well, there goes your social life.

Most of Amber's resentment comes from the fact that Cher has no concept of playing by the rules – she complains to Mr Hall that Cher has not done the assignment properly and merely looks whiney for doing so. Cher is manipulative, shallow and insufficiently respectful of other people's selfhood, but that is the worst you can say of her. She is genuinely popular without especially working at it. Like the movie that contains her, she has charm.

Where Austen's focus is on Emma's finding the husband who will minimize her faults, Heckerling's film is, though tactfully so, about Cher's considered selection of the boy to whom she will give her virginity. When, in the final scene, she wins money for Josh and the film's other two suitor figures, Murray (Donald Faison) and Travis, by securing Miss Geist's bouquet, we are not meant to assume that the sixteen-year-old Cher is about to get married.

Virginity is an important issue in this film, as generally in the teen genre, but not in a way that would have other than appalled Austen. Loss of virginity is a rite of passage, and it is important that it be managed with a minimum of risk and a maximum of pleasure: Cher says, on this subject, 'You see how picky I am about my shoes and they only go on my feet.' She responds to Elton's pass with horror not because she has an issue with passes being made, but because she is not interested in him; earlier, she shoves a groper away with a dismissive 'As if'.

Loss of virginity is not for her a moral issue – she mentions at one point, almost in passing, that Dionne's virginity has gone from technical to non-existent – and she is concerned that people will think her naive because still a virgin. The cruellest thing anyone says in the film is when Tai says, 'Why am I even listening to you? You're a virgin, who can't drive.' She subsequently withdraws a 'way harsh' comment that Cher is genuinely hurt by, but she is absolutely on the money in the way she equates sexual knowledge with the ability to drive; in the Los Angeles she and Cher inhabit, both are essential tools to navigation.

At the same time, the decision to make this issue, as far as the film's heroine goes, somewhat less than explicit is one of many examples of the way in which Hollywood often skirted the issue of virginity during the two decades of the teen film's existence as a genre. These were, after all, years in which sexual abstinence, as opposed to sex education, moved back onto the public agenda, largely as a consequence of the growing political influence of the Christian Right and the reluctance of many liberals directly to confront them. Yet it remained the elephant in the room for the teen movie, as one of the most important rites of passage experienced by its audience.

Even the *American Pie* films treat loss of virginity as an important issue, if only as the prize of male status competitions. Those films in which it is an explicit theme – *Heathers* and *Saved!* being the obvious examples – are very keen to show it as something which is never free of consequence. One of the many wicked lies told by the Moral Right – whose selective reading of the Commandments never seems to extend to the one about bearing false witness – is that Hollywood standardly preached to the young a gospel of sex without consequences.

When Buffy the Vampire Slayer finally sleeps with her Byronic vampire boyfriend Angel, he loses his soul and nearly destroys the world. The otherwise not especially interesting teen horror film *Cherry Falls* experiments with a reversal whereby the serial killer targets virgins, prompting the pupils at the local high school to decide that losing virginity is a life or death issue. Ironically, it is the very creative constraints experienced by American directors making films aimed at a young audience that stopped their examination of these issues being as mature as those in the films of a European director like Lukas Moodyson, say.

In *Clueless*, the important thing about affairs is that they be reasonably serious and committed. Dionne and her boyfriend Murray have, under her airhead fashion-victim aspect and his remorseless pursuit of gangsta style, a real consideration for each other. They are in each other's lives to the extent that, when he decides to shave his head at a party, she pulls out a mobile phone and threatens to ring his mother on the spot. In spite of vague hints of his infidelity – Dionne finds a hair extension in the back of his car and points out that it cannot be hers as she would never wear polyester – there is no implication of their relationship's ever being seriously at risk.

The reason why Cher realizes that the one she loves is her stepbrother Josh is that he will give her what she needs – a more profound appreciation of the political world and the life of the mind – and that she can treat him as a project, quietly improving his self-presentation. It is not that she needs to stop managing, just that she needs someone who is as prepared to manage her as they are to be managed by her. Josh fits this bill – part of the plot of the film is her gradual realization that his criticisms of her are in part motivated by deep affection.

There is, of course, a complexity here – it is stressed that Josh is not a blood relative of Cher, but rather the son of one of her father's ex-wives by an earlier marriage. He is living with the Horowitzes in Beverly Hills partly as a way of interning in Mr Horowitz's law practice and partly because his stepfather is one of the few people who actually cares what happens to him. Josh is at exactly an age such that a mother busy moving onto a third (or later) husband does not want him around as a reminder of her own age.

Nonetheless, the relationship between Josh and Cher has a quasi-incestuous aspect that gives the film a slight edginess here. The semi-familial ties between them are, of course, a parallel between Cher's relationship with Josh and Emma's with Knightley, who is, in a different way, connected to the Woodhouses by marriage, the elder brother of the husband of Emma's elder sister. Again, this is not incest or what the Anglican church regards as prohibited degrees of kinship, but close enough for a frisson.

It also explains why Cher for so long ignores Josh as a potential partner, until she faces the possibility of losing him to Tai. She thinks of him as her brother, in some sense, even though he is not, and mocks him like a kid sister: 'Wow, your face is catching up with your mouth.' He is protective of her, and she expects it of him, calling him up when Elton maroons her in the middle of nowhere for refusing him sexual favours and she has been robbed at gunpoint. This familial relationship leads to a physical ease between them – they slouch on a sofa watching movies and eating popcorn, that contrasts with the relationship she has with young men she thinks of as potential partners.

There is, for example, always an extreme awkwardness between her and Christian (Justin Walker), *Clueless*'s very loose equivalent of Austen's Frank Churchill. When she lies on a bed with him to watch his selection of films, she clumsily falls off the side. She is prepared to be ignorant in front of Josh, asking him why and how she has offended the housekeeper, whereas with

Christian she feigns knowledge and makes a fool of herself; he plays her Billie Holiday and she assumes, from the name, that the singer is a man.

She entirely fails to notice what is more or less obvious to, for example, Murray, which is that Christian is gay. He takes his whole retro look from James Dean, for example, and the first and only book we see him reading is by William Burroughs. Heckerling gives us no sense of Christian's inner life – one can conceive of very good reasons why, at an American high school, a young gay man might choose to date a popular good-looking girl like Cher, as a beard to protect himself from obvious comments and bullying.

Austen's Frank Churchill uses Emma as a front for his wooing of her friend, and is far more culpable – it is, after all, perfectly possible that Christian assumes all along that Cher knows about his sexuality. Showing her, as he does, one of the notably homoerotic scenes between Laurence Olivier and Tony Curtis in Stanley Kubrick's *Spartacus* (1960) might, for example, be taken as a clue.

Christian's sexuality is Heckerling's way of demonstrating that Cher is not seriously pursuing love so much as the social status of having a boyfriend, partly because, as we realize before she does, her heart is already taken by Josh. It is also a useful way of defusing the at least homosocial aspects of the relationship between Cher and Tai, or at least pointing up the fact that Cher's cluelessness extends to being blissfully unaware of them.

Her brief relationship with Christian helps demonstrate her father's fierce protectiveness of her. He mocks Christian's pretentious image-building – 'What's with you, kid? You think the death of Sammy Davis left an opening in the Rat Pack?' – and warns him of the consequences of upsetting his daughter: 'Anything happens to my daughter, I got a .45 and a shovel, I doubt anybody would miss you.' Mel Horowitz's passionate regard for the daughter he sometimes seems to neglect for work, and on whom he relies to ensure he eats properly, helps define our sense of her as a worthwhile person and also, without being creepy, to point to her likely eventual happiness with someone who at least through aspiring to imitate her father, is like him.

Part of Cher's charm rests in her idiolect. The idea of teen speech as a particularly fertile area in which coinages and happy inventions are constant is one of the minor delights of the teen genre. There is no especial hint of this in the John Hughes films and, as so often, the idea was crystallized in *Heathers*. Some of the examples of teenspeak in *Clueless* are foreshadowed in the earlier film – Cher's 'As if' is paralleled by Veronica's equally terse

'Not even'. The culmination of this trope is the constant verbal invention of *Buffy the Vampire Slayer* on television (Michael Adams' *Slayer Slang* (OUP, 2003) is the standard work on this).

Some of Cher's idiosyncrasies take the form of a warped version of euphemism – 'Do you prefer "fashion victim" or "ensembly challenged"?' Others are merely a matter of adopting cants like fashion tradespeak into normal conversation, as when Dionne accuses her of skinning a collie to make her fake fur backpack, and Cher replies 'It's faux.' She uses 'totally' as her standard emphatic – this is a tic which has totally become the standard way of representing teenspeak ever since.

Nor is it Cher alone who has verbal charm in this movie. Travis is scarily articulate, in a way that recapitulates and parodies standard media speak, even when he is stoned. Told by a teacher that he has the most demerits for lateness of anyone in the class, Travis gives a charming acceptance speech parodying the standard tropes of Oscar Night:

> I would like to say this. Tardiness is not something you can do on your own. Many, many people contributed to my tardiness. I would like to thank my parents for never giving me a ride to school, the LA city bus driver who took a chance on an unknown kid and last but not least, the wonderful crew from McDonalds who spend hours making those egg McMuffins without which I'd never be tardy.

Heckerling has learned from both Austen and her own earlier work on *Fast Times at Ridgemont High* that convincingly imagined worlds are those in which more characters than the central ones say interesting things. *Clueless* works because it is not just about its heroine, but about her world.

10 Things I Hate About You achieves the interesting feat not only of transferring *The Taming of the Shrew* to an American High School and its senior year rituals, but of replacing most of its misogyny with a sympathetic view of the principal heroine's feminism in the process. It is a modernization of its source material whose games with intertextuality are at times ideological in nature without being heavy-handed.

Inventively, it manages to find equivalents not only for Bianca's suitors, and Petruchio's roughness, but for such other features of the play as Baptista's insistence that Katarina wed before her sister and a Renaissance attitude to virginity. Rather less inventively, it relies on some fairly simple transferences of names, so that Padua is the name of the High School the adolescent characters attend and Verona is the surname rather than the hometown of Patrick (Petruchio). Kat (Katarina) and Bianca have the same names as their equivalents in the original, but are given Stratford as a surname, one of the film's several slightly overdone references to Shakespeare himself. (Others include the sonnet read by Mr Morgan in class with a rap-like urgency and the use of a shared obsession with Shakespeare in the wooing of Michael and Katarina's friend Mandella and Cameron's occasional implausible collapses into a Shakespearian idiom – 'I burn, I pine, I perish.')

Morgan's reading of the sonnet is effective in itself, but is mostly there to set up an exercise in sonnet-writing that he sets. The resulting poem by Kat which gives the film its title is an equivalent of Katarina's speech of capitulation, yet manages to be very different in its affect. The major area for which there is no equivalent in the film is the 'fourth wall' material about Christopher Sly the tailor, for which, on the whole, thanks. Generally speaking then, the allusiveness to the original is considerably more overt than that to 'Emma' in *Clueless* and, unnecessarily, more apologetic.

Kat Stratford (Julia Stiles) turns out to have good reasons for the misandry that makes her notorious and unpopular with her schoolmates, where Katarina in the original is merely a humour whose shrewishness is a comic given. Before the scene in which she spells these reasons out, she is shown to enjoy, like Katarina, the chance her anger gives her to rail at all her schoolfellows male and female (her father asks her, 'Hello, Katarina. Make anybody cry today?' and she replies cheerily, 'Sadly, no. But it's only 4.30.'), and to mock her younger, and apparently more superficial, sister Bianca.

Bianca (Larisa Oleynik) is originally shown as an airhead along the lines of Cher in *Clueless* and she and her friend Chastity (Gabrielle Union) – whose name is clearly ironic – are given little establishing conversations very much in the *Clueless* manner:

| Chastity: | I know you can be under-whelmed, and you can be overwhelmed, but can you ever just be, like, whelmed? |
| Bianca: | I think you can in Europe. |

She is capable of patronizing bitchiness, telling Cameron (Joseph Gordon-Levitt) that he is cute for asking her out. Yet we gradually realize that she is nicer than she seems and has more character. One of the early signs of this is actually the fact that she knows how automatic some of Kat's rants are, and calls her on them, and that she is as effective as her sister in mocking their father's eccentricities.

Sent, for the umpteenth time, to the guidance counsellor Ms. Perky (Allison Janney – of whom there is nowhere near enough in this film once she has been used to establish several of the core characters), Kat talks of herself as 'tempestuous' and is told by the teacher that the standard description of her is 'heinous bitch'. Ms. Perky also mentions that one of Kat's victims has had a successful operation for the retrieval of his testicle. Ms. Perky, with her constantly rewritten novel of torrid passion for which she neglects her pupils, is never specifically set up as the slightly mad and frustrated middle-aged woman Kat might become, but some such thought may be there.

Kat's taste for riot girl bands and her capacity for violence prompt Cameron at one point to ask Bianca whether her sister is 'a k.d. lang fan'. Bianca responds that she did worry for a while that her sister might be engaged in same-sex relationships but, she says, 'I found a photo of Jared Leto' in her drawer. More recently one of the companions in Oliver Stone's *Alexander* (2004), Jared Leto had an iconic role in the teen TV drama *My So-Called Life* as the beautiful but dumb Jordan whom Angela intermittently pursues.

This discussion aside, *10 Things I Hate About You* has less queer subtext than any other major teen movie. The successful heterosexual pairings at the end are the result of genuine growth and change by six of the principals and the excluded villain is coded as straight in spite of his 'unmanly' obsession with good looks which are, at least temporarily, taken away from him. The closest any of the males come to subtext is vague homosexual panic when someone speaks verse near them.

Kat is verbally violent and physically aggressive – boys who stare at her on the sports field are liable to find a soccer ball bounced off their head. She has a running fight with her African-American English Literature teacher Mr Morgan (Daryl Mitchell) over her desire to have a more woman-centred curriculum. He is shown as having some right on his side when he mocks her feminism:

> I know how difficult it must be to overcome all those years of
> upper-middle-class suburban oppression. Must be tough. But the

next time you storm the PTA crusading for better … lunch meat,
or whatever you white girls complain about, ask them WHY they
can't buy a book written by a black man!

On the other hand, much of what she says about the canon in her replies
to him is both pithy and accurate – 'Hemingway? He was an abusive,
alcoholic misogynist who squandered half of his life hanging around
Picasso trying to nail his leftovers.'

At the same time, Kat is shown as often self-indulgent – her fondness
for that suicide's handbook *The Bell Jar* is an indicator of mild morbidity
as well as feminism – and not entirely honest. She is trying to protect
her sister from the world without telling her important truths about, for
example, the repellently slick Joey Donner (Andrew Keegan), for whom
Bianca is in danger of falling as she did. (It is rumoured that, in an earlier
version of Karen Lutz and Kirsten Smith's script, Joey actually date-
raped Kat rather than merely dumping her when she slept with him once
and decided against a repeat performance. The alteration, based on test
screenings, weakens this and leaves Bianca's eventual violent attack on Joey
marginally less sympathetic. On the other hand, it renders Kat's silence less
culpable.) She resents her father's attempts to impose innocence on both of
them, but her insulting protectiveness towards her younger sister is more
like his behaviour than she is prepared to admit.

Walter Stratford (Larry Miller) is a control freak gynaecologist obsessed
with keeping his daughters from joining all the other teen pregnancy cases
with which he deals every day. His wife is either dead, or missing – the
film is deliberately ambiguous as to which, allowing us to wonder whether
he is blaming himself for his deficiencies as doctor or as man. In order not
to seem unreasonable, while maintaining his obsession – which extends
to making his daughters wear a pregnancy belt to remind them what nine
months of childbearing will feel like – he switches his absolute ban on
dating to a demand that Bianca only date when Kat does.

What makes Walter a comic character is that his daughters entirely have
his number:

Walter:	I delivered a set of twins to a fifteen-year-old girl today, and you know what she said to me?
Bianca:	'I'm a crack-whore who should have made my sleazy boyfriend wear a condom'?

Walter: Close. She said, 'I should have listened to my
                            father.'

Walter suffers from the delusion that he understands teenagers – the scene
where he tries to demonstrate his command of slang is a standard joke
– see Jim's Dad in the *American Pie* films – but done especially well by
Larry Miller:

> I'm down, I've got the 411, and you are not going out and
> getting jiggy with some boy, I don't care how dope his ride is. My
> mama didn't raise no foo'!

Bianca tells one of her suitors, the slight charming Cameron, about her
father's rules, and he and his wily adviser Michael (David Krumholtz)
decide that the only way to proceed is to find a man brave enough to take
on the job of wooing Kat. A brief selection process among the daft and
desperate demonstrates to them that they need to find someone who will
do the job for pay, and that they don't have nearly enough money. Their
first attempt to recruit Patrick (Heath Ledger) ends in his living up to his
myth as someone not to be trifled with by drilling a hole in Cameron's
textbook – without the point being stressed, we realize that Patrick is
doing vocational courses in his final year.

The script sets up some widely held beliefs among his fellow-students
about Patrick. He is variously held to have set a state trooper on fire,
to have been a porn star and to have sold his liver. The source of these
rumours turns out to be his extended absence the previous year – in fact, as
we eventually learn, he was helping to nurse his dying grandfather. (Heath
Ledger's pronounced Australian accent is explained away by Patrick's
having lived there for some years as a child.)

Accordingly, and ironically given his past with Kat, of which they are
unaware, Michael and Cameron suggest their scheme to the more affluent
Joey, a cool bully who casually draws a penis on Michael's face as they
talk. This incident helps establish that Joey is more than merely a vapid
bore obsessed with his own good looks and modelling career – there is an
imaginative nastiness to him about which we gradually learn more.

Cameron, an army brat who has never had a chance to settle, proceeds
to woo Bianca by offering to tutor her in French, a subject in which,
we eventually realize, his attainments are less even than hers. Bianca is

originally shown as superficial, and preferring Joey's good looks and status to Cameron, who has been relegated to the ranks of the uncool by being given the nerdy Michael as his guide by the school authorities.

Michael has his own agenda – he has been ostracized by his original social group, the boys who intend to attend business school. (Early in the film, with the pretext of showing Cameron around, he leads us through a fairly standard anthropology shot which includes would-be white Rastas and the MBA crowd as well as more standard stoners and popular kids.) He and Cameron need a party so that Cameron can ask Bianca to it – so they obtain the invitations to the MBA crowd's little Saturday soirée and forge them into a general invitation which they throw into the school stairwell. The fact that this also reduces the genteel evening of Michael's former friends to rubble is merely a bonus.

Both Cameron and Michael have a ruthless streak that is not entirely sympathetic. The film addresses this issue, which is integral to the setting up of the plot, by showing Cameron as physically frail and allowing him to be genuinely hurt by Bianca's original preference for Joey. They are responsible for plots for which the vicious Joey lacks the brains, but because he victimizes them both, he ends up being the villain of the piece. It also helps that Michael's wooing of the slightly fey Mandella (Susan May Pratt) makes a touching use of her literary tastes and love of romantic mystery.

Joey goes to the party with Bianca, who has been allowed to attend because Kat is going with Patrick. He proceeds unwittingly to blow his chances with her by endless conceited boasting about his modelling career – we start to realize that Bianca is more complicated than she appears, because she has enough good taste to realize how little she actually likes Joey once she is dating him. Meanwhile, Patrick sees Cameron sulking and tells him not to think he is less good than anyone else – this is one of several moments at which the morally equivocal Patrick nonetheless acts as one of the film's moral centres:

Cameron:	She never wanted me. She wanted Joey the whole time.
Patrick:	Cameron, do you like the girl?
Cameron:	Yeah.
Patrick:	Yeah, and is she worth all this trouble?
Cameron:	Well, I thought she was, but you know.
Patrick:	Well, she is or she isn't. See first of all, Joey

is not half the man you are. Secondly, don't
let anyone ever make you feel like you don't
deserve what you want. Go for it.

His advice starts the process whereby Cameron and Michael manipulate
people less and act straightforwardly instead – there is a clear link here
between manipulation and lack of self-respect. His advice is also the
moment at which he moves from being Cameron's pawn to being
something like his friend – this is something that reflects well on both
of them given their original bad start. Patrick, Cameron and Michael are
all three of them outsiders – Cameron as the new boy, Michael as a nerd
and Patrick because of his unsavoury reputation – and they come to see
themselves as allies accordingly.

Joey asks Bianca to break her curfew and go off with him somewhere
else – she refuses and has to get a lift with Cameron. He tells her off for
exploiting his good will, and she spontaneously kisses him. One of the
reasons why we forgive Cameron his Machiavellian scheming is that he
actually voices his resentment; one of the reasons we start to like Bianca
is that kiss. She has stopped thinking in terms of what will be appropriate
to her pursuit of status and reacted to someone who has demonstrated she
can hurt him. Cameron's sheer joy as she walks away from him, and stops
and looks back, is particularly attractive – Joseph Gordon-Levitt manages
to make this young schemer more sympathetic than the script does.

Meanwhile, Patrick's wooing of Kat succeeds, up to a point, by sheer
persistence; it helps, as we subsequently realize, that in his rough and ready
manners and craggy face he is practically the anti-Joey. The main reason
she agrees to go to the party with him is because she is irritated with her
father, who is threatening to withhold the financial support that would
enable her to attend a college away from home, and because Bianca begs
her to. She gets very drunk when she sees her sister with Joey and does a
sexy dance on top of a table – we realize that there is more to Kat than
meets the eye. However, once she is sober, she starts to suspect that Patrick
has an ulterior motive for asking her out – she does not guess what it is,
but she rejects him on the mere suspicion.

Offered considerably more money by Joey, whom he has started to
detest, in order to take Kat to the prom (and developing feelings for her
that he is not yet prepared to acknowledge), Patrick takes advice from
Cameron, who in turn takes it from Bianca, who legitimizes the scheming

to some degree by taking part in it. The continuing moral ambiguity of this is acknowledged by the scene where she shows Cameron Kat's room so that he can search out clues that will help Patrick's wooing. When Cameron asks to see her room, so that he can know her heart, she refuses on the grounds that a girl's room is private.

Patrick woos Kat in part by affecting an interest in the things that matter to her – he turns up in the small venues where she listens to angsty girl bands and affects, to some degree develops, a taste for the same music. He even prowls the women's studies section of the local bookstore. More inventively, he wins the chance of a hearing from her by bribing the sports field audio tech and the school marching band so that he can serenade her with 'You're Just Too Good to be True (Can't Take My Eyes Off of You)'. This scene almost certainly derives from a similarly anarchic moment in John Hughes' *Ferris Bueller's Day Off*, but it is nonetheless a wonderful comic moment in which Heath Ledger's Patrick evolves from a grumpy thug into a lord of misrule.

He is given detention for this – it is not entirely clear under what rubric of school rules – and Bianca enables his escape by monopolizing the attention of the coach, who is in charge of it. She gabbles about tactics at an upcoming women's soccer match and then distracts the coach altogether by flashing her breasts at him. Kat has moved from an aggressive asexuality to an aggressive use of femaleness. Significantly, the idyllic afternoon she spends with Patrick goofing off school may start with them boating in the harbour, but rapidly graduates to their going paintballing.

Kat's eventual decision to attend the prom has as much to do with her improved relationship with Bianca as it does with her growing feelings for Patrick. By rejecting Joey for the less obviously attractive and popular Cameron, Bianca has demonstrated maturity in Kat's eyes, so that Kat confides in her the truth about her own earlier relationship with Joey. Joey, meanwhile, has simply assumed that Bianca will be going to the prom with him and turns up at the Stratford house to collect her long after she has left with Cameron.

What follows is standard teen movie plotting, albeit managed efficiently. As a piece of gratuitous cruelty, Joey reveals in front of Kat that he paid Patrick to date her, causing her to leave feeling betrayed. (It is a standard piece of teen movie morality that heroes who compromise themselves by scheming are always vindictively exposed by their partner in crime – a classic example of this is the sub-Pygmalion arrangement in *She's All That* where Freddy Prinz, rejected by his girlfriend, bets his friends that he can turn the plainest girl in the school into a winning candidate for prom queen. Of course he falls in love with her. Of course the bet is revealed by his former best friend.)

Joey, finally aware that he has been deceived, knocks Cameron down with a punch, only to be comprehensively demolished himself, by Bianca, whom he has threatened as part of his ongoing rant. 'That's for making my boyfriend bleed,' says Bianca – breaking his nose – 'and that's for my sister' – blacking his eyes – 'and that's for me' – kneeing him in the balls. Insofar as this is a film as much about Bianca as it is about Kat, Bianca moves from a conventional popular girly style of womanhood to a capacity for aggression which equals her sister's. She is protective of the physically slight Cameron, who is clearly not in any sense a fighter.

There follows a chastened interlude in which everyone is trying to be nice to Kat. Her father tells her that he is paying for her to go to Sarah Lawrence. Bianca and Cameron suggest that she go out with them – Cameron is not shown as explicitly taking responsibility for her misery, but he is at least obviously abashed by it.

There follows the finale – Mr Morgan's class and Kat's reading of her poem. This is a moment at which the entire effect of the film could crumble – Julia Stiles is exemplary throughout but never more so than here, gradually moving from scorn to near breakdown and tears. The poem is worth printing in full, simply because it is such an improbable climax for what we expect from a Hollywood movie aimed at teenagers:

> I hate the way you talk to me, and the way you cut your hair.
> I hate the way you drive my car. I hate it when you stare.
> I hate your big dumb combat boots, and the way you read my
>   mind.
> I hate you so much it makes me sick; it even makes me rhyme.
> I hate it, I hate the way you're always right. I hate it when you lie.
> I hate it when you make me laugh, even worse when you make
>   me cry.
> I hate it that you're not around, and the fact that you didn't call.
> But mostly I hate the way I don't hate you. Not even close, not
>   even a little bit, not even at all.

Interestingly, there are somewhat more than ten things here.

She rushes from the classroom, only to find a particularly fine guitar in the seat of her car. Patrick has used Joey's money to buy her one of the things she most wants – given the male associations of guitars in rock, he is indicating that he accepts her desire to claim areas of male privilege. Certain things cannot be apologized for verbally – the guitar is a far more effective symbol of apology than any words could be. Verbally, he is terse to the point of near brusqueness; she is almost as terse in her expression of acceptance and forgiveness:

Patrick:	Some asshole paid me to take out this really great girl.
Kat :	Is that right?
Patrick:	Yeah, but I screwed up. I fell for her.

They kiss and the film ends with a pull back from them to the vast chateau-like school and the ocean beyond it. There is nothing more to say, and they disappear into the world, like all happy couples.

Perhaps the very best of the teen films which adapt literary classics is *Cruel Intentions*, which is an adaptation of the often filmed *Les Liaisons Dangereuses* by Choderlos de Laclos – in the credits, it is described as 'suggested by'. Rather than allowing himself to be overly influenced by such classics as the version starring Alain Delon, or the comparatively recent Stephen Frears film of Christopher Hampton's stage adaptation, writer/director Roger Kumble went straight back to his source.

There are advantages to his decision to remake this often-filmed novel as a teen movie. For one thing, the genre conventions of the teen film make social ostracism a plausible fear on the part of the protagonists. When Sebastian (Ryan Philippe) tells Kathryn (Sarah Michelle Gellar) that he is in love with Annette (Reece Witherspoon), she manipulates him into breaking up with Annette, by suggesting that he will turn from a prep school legend to a joke if he does this. The social ostracism that is Kathryn's fate at the end of the film is plausible in a school context – as it was in the aristocratic society of the eighteenth century for her equivalent, Madame de Meurteuil, in de Laclos's original – and nowhere else in modern society.

Only in a teen context is the obsession with virginity a live issue in the late twentieth and early twenty-first centuries. Sebastian decides to seduce Annette without even knowing her, simply because she has published an article in a women's magazine about her desire to remain a virgin until married. This film is one of the few – *Saved!* is another – and certainly the earliest to pick up on the religious campaign in favour of abstinence as a counter to teen pregnancy and disease.

Setting the story among the children of old, rich families makes plausible a certain impunity. Early in the film, Sebastian parks his car in front of the apartment block where his family lives, cheerily ignoring the policeman who tells him not to, waving himself past the doorman. De Laclos assumes a society based on privilege and on extralegal penalties for transgression; Kumble finds in the teen movie a precise equivalent. The centrality of a wager to the plot of *Les Liaisons Dangereuses* is similarly something that is plausible in the teen movie where it is a trope (see, for example, *She's All That*).

The central characters, all with close equivalents in the de Laclos novel, are also conveniently drawn from the stock characters of the teen movie. Sebastian in particular is closely analogous to the almost equally posh Steff, James Spader's character in John Hughes' *Pretty in Pink* and, in his capacity for redemption and weakness in the face of social pressure, to Steff's friend Blane in the same movie. His stepsister Kathryn is the most popular girl in school, a position she maintains by utter social ruthlessness, if more subtly so than such princess figures as Heather Chandler in *Heathers*. The two ingénues, Annette and Cecile (Selma Blair), who end up engineering Kathryn's downfall, have much in common with the virtuous heroines of John Hughes' films in their original naivety, something in common with Veronica in *Heathers* in their eventual growth into agency.

Kumble changed a lot more than the ages of the protagonists. De Laclos's novel is a piece of polemic aimed at the doomed French aristocracy of which the writer was part, and Kumble realized that the things which were shocking to an eighteenth-century audience were not necessarily going to shock a late twentieth-century one. He deliberately ups the ante to include homosexuality male and female, drug taking and date rape. The wager between Kathryn and Sebastian (that she will allow him sexual favours if he helps debauch Cecile for her and succeeds in wooing the chaste Annette) is made more shocking by the fact that they are stepsiblings rather than cousins. He also includes race as a replacement for the fine distinctions of class in the original. Kathryn exploits Ronald's race several times, first by playing on the racism of Cecile's mother, then, in a scene that was deleted in the final cut, adding alleged racial slurs to the seduction of Cecile in her goading of Ronald (Sean Patrick Thomas) to attack Sebastian.

(To summarize, Kathryn exposes Cecile's thus far chaste relationship with her music teacher Ronald and then suggests that she and Sebastian be their go-betweens. Sebastian uses this to seduce Cecile; Kathryn seduces Ronald. Meanwhile Sebastian seduces Annette, and falls in love with her. He breaks with her as Kathryn demands and Kathryn then announces that she has won their wager, by manipulating him into doing this. Sebastian gives Annette his journals before encountering Ronald, who attacks him. Annette intervenes and falls in front of a taxi; Sebastian saves her life at the cost of his own. Annette and Cecile use the journals to destroy Kathryn.)

The other principal change, a really significant one, in Kumble's film from de Laclos's novel is that he makes Annette and Cecile the agents of Kathryn's destruction. They survive and prosper where their equivalents are destroyed.

The sheer youth of these characters – Sebastian and Kathryn are about to start their senior year at the private school where Kathryn is head of the student body – also makes them both shocking – they are teenagers who are aged in sin and diabolical in their successful temptation of their victims. In such scenes as the one when the unfortunate music teacher Ronald arrives to ask for their help, and a door opens to reveal them standing there in identical dark glasses, Ryan Philippe and Sarah Michelle Gellar manage to convey a sense of utter damnableness. They almost always wear dark clothes – when Annette rises up on an escalator and finds Sebastian waiting for her at the top wearing a bright blue shirt it is a symbol of his moral regeneration.

The difference between the stepsiblings is one enforced by a double standard as true in 1999 as it had been two centuries earlier – Sebastian can afford, up to a point, to have a bad reputation whereas Kathryn has to be an accomplished hypocrite to succeed. Again, this is more plausible in a private school with a clergyman as headmaster than it would be otherwise. She reassures Cecile's mother about her probity, claiming that she always turns to God for help – as indeed she does, as we see when she snorts cocaine seconds later from a phial contained in the silver crucifix she always wears. Kathryn is an accomplished hypocrite, which makes it ironic when Sebastian accuses Annette of being one.

This is a post-*Heathers* adaptation of the original. Kathryn and Sebastian, when talking to each other, use a vigorous verbal violence that has much in common with the earlier film. A mood of aggression is established in exchanges like:

Kathryn:	The parental units called while you were out.
Sebastian:	How IS your gold-digging whore of a mother enjoying Bali?
Kathryn:	She suspects your impotent, alcoholic father is diddling the maid.

This also confirms their precise relationship as quasi-incestuous rather than actually so. Their unhealthy and destructive relationship is, it should be noted, based on the same degree of kinship as the rather cuddly one between Cher and Josh in *Clueless* with the sole distinction being that there is no significant age gap between them as there is in the other couple. Clearly the shock of incest in teen movies is a matter of relativities.

An early version of the script involved Annette using Sebastian's journal to control Kathryn rather than to destroy her. The existing scene in which they meet (for the first time) in a restroom where Kathryn is preparing herself, with a snort, for her role at the memorial assembly for Sebastian has them dressed in precisely the same degree of formality in their school uniforms. Shots of Annette planning her coup as she drives around and putting on a pair of sunglasses similar to those worn by Sebastian make her resemble Kathryn in all but hair colour. In the course of their restroom conversation, Annette echoes Kathryn's earlier speech about her reliance on Jesus. Clearly, since she was not present during it – it was uttered in the presence of Cecile and her mother – she has learned of it from Sebastian's journals, or from Cecile.

There is a vague echo in all of this of the scene at the end of *Heathers* when Veronica seizes the red rosette hair scrunchee that has been the Heathers' insignia of leadership. The ending is still somewhat ambiguous – has contact with Sebastian Valmont and his stepsister changed Annette for the better, by making her more knowing, or for the worse? Perhaps the only indicator, and that not a strong one, that she is still virtuous, though no longer innocent, is that in the film's last moments she is driving away from New York, that city of evil, whereas in the opening ones Sebastian was driving towards it.

The final version of the film is constructed in a way that, except for this vague subtext, presents Annette in a positive light. She is shown driving moodily around what is supposed to be the countryside near New York, even though the constraints of reshooting mean that the countryside is clearly that of Southern California. This is part of a general pattern of softening which seems to have been imposed on Kumble by the studio. Also, the aerial shot of her route omits the graveyard we saw Sebastian pass and which prefigured his end. Of course, this may have to do with the fact that the city she is driving away from is not actually New York, but Culver City in California. Sometimes the financial exigencies of film-making can give the appearance of telling symbolism.

In some of the deleted scenes (present on the DVD), Sebastian is significantly nastier and more manipulative even than he is in the final cut. For example, in the scene where he blackmails Annette's friend Greg (Eric Mabius), whose seduction by his friend Blaine (Joshua Jackson) he has commissioned, he originally asked Greg to prove his sincerity by giving him a blowjob, only to reject him when Blaine complies. This sequence nearly got Kumble fired from the movie – it was seen as making Sebastian far too unpleasant. If we see this as an odd commentary on late twentieth-century mores – the studio were worried at the possible imputation of bisexuality to a character who earlier seduces a young woman, and traduces her on the Internet, in order to get back at her mother, his therapist, at whom he also makes a pass – that is our right.

One of the film's strengths is that the relationship between Sebastian and Annette is genuinely romantic – the chemistry between Reece Witherspoon and Ryan Philippe reflected the fact that in private life they were husband and wife. When Annette asks Sebastian to leave her alone because she cannot trust herself with him, we believe in the deep sexual longing the line conveys.

Even in de Laclos's fairly cynical original, the character arc of Sebastian is a redemptive one, though not to the extent of his dying to save Annette. The scene where he breaks with her is deeply upsetting, if not quite the equal of the equivalent scene in the Stephen Frears film – Ryan Philippe gives one of the best performances of his career here, but he is no John Malkovich.

Sarah Michelle Gellar is quite remarkable in this film. She was, at this point, some years into her role as Buffy on television and chose to play against type in what is still vastly the best thing she has done on film. (Her performances as Daphne in the Scooby Doo movies are perfectly competent in entirely worthless material.) She demonstrates a capacity for real lascivious suggestiveness in her remark to Sebastian that, should he win the bet, he can 'put it anywhere'. Gellar displays something of the same capacity for sexual aggression when, playing Buffy-possessed-by-Faith, she propositions Riley in the episode 'This Year's Girl' (4.15) but without quite the edge of manipulative nastiness she manages here. She is also very good in the scene of Kathryn's exposure and humiliation – Gellar is known to be able to cry to order and uses this skill very effectively to release a single damning tear.

I have praised the chemistry of Philippe's scenes with Witherspoon – the chemistry between Philippe and Gellar is often equally remarkable. The scene where he arrives to claim her and is rejected has a script drawn for the most part directly from de Laclos, save in a deliberate coarseness of language at certain points that reminds us that these are adolescents playing successfully at evil. The scene is wonderfully lit – Kathryn's blue and gold boudoir has its curtains slightly drawn, for the first time, making it a more liminal space, posed between daylight and enclosure on the cusp of both characters' entire destruction by her wilfulness.

His fingering of the champagne bottle is a crude but effective piece of phallicism which reminds us of what is at stake here – she verbally castrates him as she sips the wine and tells him that it tastes good:

> You were very much in love with her. And you're still in love
> with her. But it amused me to make you ashamed of it. You
> gave up on the first person you ever loved because I threatened
> your reputation. Don't you get it? You're just a toy, Sebastian. A
> little toy I like to play with. And now you've completely blown
> it with her. I think it's the saddest thing I've ever heard. [Drinks
> champagne] Tastes good. So I assume you've come here to make
> arrangements, but unfortunately, I don't fuck losers.

Gellar is icy and imperious here, while Philippe is grinding his teeth with humiliation. Earlier, when he rejects her advances because of a genuine ambivalence, she is kittenish and he brusque. At all times, we believe in the sexual games between them as deeply plausible and deeply unhealthy for reasons that have nothing to do with their purely technical kinship.

All of the cast have praised Kumble – a first-time director – for his capacity to tell them what he needed them to do, a skill he attributes to the fact he was having to make up directing as he went along. He gets as finely judged a performance out of the first-timer Selma Blair as he does out of the seasoned professionals – Louise Fletcher, for example, or Swoosie Kurtz – who play the film's rarely appearing adults. Blair was significantly older than Cecile, yet manages to convey admirably the character's slightly clownish naivety when manipulated by Kathryn, a manipulation which includes lesbian quasi-seduction under the guise of kissing lessons. It is important that Sebastian's qualms about debauching a young and innocent girl be more than token so that we are angry with him when he eventually does so – and for this to be the case we have to believe in Cecile's utter innocence.

Christine Baranski, as Cecile's mother, Bunny Caldwell, is a wonderful monster of snobbery and hypocritical probity. Her viciousness towards the entirely virtuous Ronald demonstrates both snobbery and racism, which entirely undercuts her right to the moral high ground from which she warns Annette against Sebastian. Kumble's writing at this point is classically sharp:

Bunny Caldwell:	How dare you treat me with such disrespect! I got you off the streets and this is how you repay me?
Ronald Clifford:	Got me off the streets? I live on 59th and Park!
Bunny Caldwell:	Whatever!

and:

Ronald:	I would like to think that in these times someone of your stature could look beyond racial lines.
Bunny Caldwell:	Oh, don't give me any of that racist crap! My husband and I gave money to Colin Powell!
Ronald:	I guess that puts me in my place.

Bunny's idiotic description of his plea for equality as 'racist' when racism is the thing of which he is accusing her is particularly and effectively repellent. Her presence in the last scene at the side of the headmaster when he reaches out for, and is given, Kathryn's crucifix/coke phial, is a signifier of the moral ambiguity of the film's resolution.

The other major strength of this film comes from the decision of Kumble and his cinematographer, the far more experienced Theo van der Sande, to create a feel in the lighting, the design and the music that alluded to the eighteenth-century original while remaining plausibly contemporary. This is the only one of the teen movies based on a literary original to go for this particular sort of homage to the source's period. It works well here, partly because it enables the writer/director to make a plausible point about the timelessness of the wealthy and their cruelty.

It appears that, when they interviewed the costume designer Heather Zeegan, the production designer Jon Gary Steele and the art director David S. Lazan, they recruited them in part on the basis of each of these having suggested something of the sort spontaneously. The DVD commentary has a useful documentary about how this period-ambiguous look was achieved. To mention but one thing, Sebastian's long dark coat is based on an eighteenth-century frock coat design, while cut to hang in a more modern way. Similarly, at the film's climax, Kathryn's humiliation takes place with the heavy string sonorities of the Verve's 'Bitter Sweet Symphony' on the soundtrack, itself a particularly effective blend of the old and the new.

Not all teen movies that derive from literary originals are as successful as these three. *Get Over It* (2001) has the advantage of Kirsten Dunst at her most charming and a wonderful early sequence in which the hero, rejected by the love of his life, walks down a suburban street oblivious to the carnivalesque troupe of eccentrics which gradually accumulates behind him. It has a coarse but effective running gag about the accident-prone girl who, for example, entirely destroys a sushi restaurant to which he takes her. What does not work is the interpolated performance of *A Midsummer Night's Dream*, or the crude analogy between his pursuit of the girl who deserted him for a singer in a boy band, and his eventual realization that he loves Dunst's character, and the performances of these four as the lovers in the play. What especially does not work is the doubling up of the play's technical crew and their miniaturized fairy equivalents and Martin Short's bizarre performance as a campy director.

'O' (2001), in which a young black basketball player finds himself recapitulating the self-destruction of Othello, is similarly unsatisfactory. The problem here is that the white-on-black racism of Shakespeare's time maps poorly over contemporary racism. There is a limit to what ingenuity can do with historical analogy.

Worth mentioning here, though, I would argue, essentially not a teen movie at all, is Baz Luhrmann's *Romeo+Juliet* (1996) which is not an adaptation of a classic text, but rather a modern-dress performance of it. It shares with the adaptations some ingenuity of transposition – the street gangs who have replaced the warring families carry guns whose brand name is Rapier, and an express freight company which delivers a message is called, like the command to deliver, Post Haste. Some of its embellishments are simply Luhrmann's trademark wilfulness – Mercutio spends much of the film in drag for no more particular reason than that he thus looks ornamental. (Oliver Morton has suggested to me, ingeniously, that the costuming signifies his liminal status as a member of neither family.)

Clearly it was sensible to reconfigure Romeo and Juliet as teenagers in the face of a stage tradition which far too often treats them as a star-crossed couple of rather more mature years. Claire Danes is excellent as Juliet, bringing to the role the combination of beauty and gawky confusion which she trade-marked in *My So-Called Life* on television, Leonardo DiCaprio rather less interesting. And yet Luhrmann's film is, rightly, far more in the end about a damaged society than it is about the adolescents who become its victims and its cure. In the end, it is not a teen movie because it is not, centrally, about its teenagers and because it has no interest in the body of tropes and stock characters that the teen movie had accumulated.

Note

1.   An exception can be made for *Blast from the Past* (1999), in which she plays
      the modern woman who copes with the noble savage played by Brendan
      Fraser when he emerges from his parents' bomb shelter into what he assumes
      will be the radioactive rubble of LA.

The Trouble with Boys

*O*ne of the transgressive pleasures of twentieth and twenty-first century western adolescence has always been seeing films that you are not supposed to. Adolescents have always tried to see 'adult' films as a rite of passage, especially adolescent boys who have more opportunity to do so and are less likely to find themselves stigmatized as sluts for being interested. Given the steadily increasing spending power of adolescents in the 1970s and early 1980s, it was inevitable that Hollywood would perceive this as a niche market. Given the extension of what was acceptable in films teenagers would see, it was inevitable that Hollywood would make bawdy films aimed specifically at the teenage boy market – the three *Porky's* films in the 1980s are good examples of this, though of no particular interest in themselves. Any account of the teen film in the 1990s and 2000s has to take on board what happened to the teen sex comedy in those decades.

The generation that came of age then, and started making films, had a more complex attitude to masculinity and male sexuality than the generation which preceded it. Though it is very easy to see *American Pie* and its two successors as lineal descendants of *Porky's*, they are far more complex films. A default bawdiness that relies on jokes about bodily fluids and physical functions is constantly undercut by some (comparatively) rather more radical thinking about what this sort of thing means in an age of at least theoretical gender equality. The same is, if anything, even more true of the underrated *The Girl Next Door* (2004), which was marketed with a teaser slogan that probably put off more people than it drew in – 'Matt never saw her coming – but all his friends had.'

This thoughtfulness is partly a matter of the educational backgrounds of later film-makers – it was hard to get through film school in the 1990s without taking at least one course on gender representation – and partly a function of the greater thoughtfulness that was one of the things that John Hughes and the makers of *Heathers* brought to the teen movie. It was also a function of the desire to make these films to some degree 'date' films, so that the adolescent girls and women in the audience would not feel themselves insulted to the point of alienation by the sexual humour. Indeed, some of the time, but not all of it, the films avoid standard sexism to the point of being vaguely misandric.

There is a fundamental internal paradox to all three of the *American Pie* movies, and it is this. They are films which portray the coming of age of a group of young American men in terms of their full acceptance of the sensual and sexual equality of their female partners. This coming of age takes the shape of their various explorations of behaviour, much of it thoughtless or otherwise negative. They are comically punished for each and every one of their experiments which can be seen in a negative, sexist light, including their failure to understand that the girls and women in their lives are at least as much sexual beings as they are. And yet the comedy which derives from those punishments is aimed very precisely at a section of the movie audience more interested in the physical comedy and farce than in its ethical component, the younger equivalent of the movie audience which liked earlier teen sex comedies, like the *Porky's* trilogy, which had no ethical concerns whatever.

There is an interesting respect in which the *American Pie* films (*American Pie* (1999), *American Pie 2* (2001) and *American Wedding*, aka *American Pie – The Wedding* (2003)), only one of which, strictly speaking, deals with its central characters as teenagers, are the only films for this market which actually did something that John Hughes hoped to do when he made *The Breakfast Club*. They deal with ageing, and with the ways in which the friendships of teenagers can have consequences for their adult lives, in a way that is only possible on film with a series and with sequels. Some television shows – notably *Buffy the Vampire Slayer* and *Dawson's Creek*

– have survived long enough to do this. (Most others – the much-loved *Popular, Freaks and Geeks* and *My So-Called Life* – only managed to run for a season or two.)

Specifically, the fact that the series' main protagonist Jim (Jason Biggs) chooses Michelle (Alyson Hannigan) as his prom date, her acceptance of him, and the sexual humiliations that led to those choices, lead directly to their eventual marriage. While there is no especial sense in which this can have been planned – clearly many of the plot developments in the later films were dependent on which of the stars of *American Pie* were available – the films succeed in feeling like a trilogy. Specifically, the extent to which the third film focuses as much on Stifler, a secondary figure in the earlier films, as on Jim and Michelle – to an extent that means it could be subtitled 'The Redemption of Stifler' as truthfully as 'The Wedding' – has to do with the talents and availability of Seann William Scott who plays him.

The central given of the plot of the first movie is essentially a wrong-headed decision by its four principals. Under the (mistaken) impression that even their fairly gauche friend Sherman has lost his virginity at a party, Oz, Kevin, Paul Finch and Jim make a pact that they will all four of them lose their virginities by the time they graduate from high school. This pact is phrased in extravagant terms – 'masters of our destiny' – that indicate the absurdity of the deadline they have imposed on themselves and each of them learns, in a sense, that the important thing is for sexual intercourse to take place in the context of an actual relationship. The *American Pie* films have their cake and eat it – they play around with an ethic of mere sexual point-scoring before settling down into a more or less moral conclusion.

All four of them are allowed moments of grace – we never get any sense of them being sexist buffoons like their friends Stifler and Sherman. Sherman (Chris Owen) is the less harmful, save for the lie about losing his virginity with the girl he spends the night talking to, and who humiliates him at the prom by telling the truth. He has a geekish routine about being the Sherminator, a sex robot sent back in time – the implication is that he thinks this is cool, but also that he sees love-making as a set of soul-less routines. It is a way of ensuring sexual failure in advance so that such questions as his attractiveness do not come into play. In the second film, this in turn gets transformed into a moment of grace, of which more below.

Stifler does service throughout the trilogy, straightforwardly so in the first two films, as a representative of the ids of the four less unsavoury protagonists. He is a useful plot device – the popular jock who has both a house and a lakeside house at which he can throw large parties because of his young, beautiful and permissive mother. (In the third film, when accusing Jim of ingratitude, he describes himself as a 'grand facilitator', and this is more or less true, though more ambiguously than he allows himself to realize.)

He is also the voice of completely unregenerate sexism – he has the role of tempter and adversary in the lives of his friends by constantly trying to drag them down to his level. Seann William Scott has tremendous brio in the role – and in the third film manages to do rather more with it. He added improvisatory material to the script at his original audition and by the third film Adam Herz, the writer, had developed a degree of symbiosis with Scott such that he was allowed ever more leeway with improvisation. (The other actors, including the older ones, were given a fair bit of leeway too, but in the commentaries on the unrated DVD it is clear that Scott improvises more than the others.) Stifler, with his mugging and leers, is at the same time deeply unlikeable at a conscious and also vaguely endearing, like a large smelly dog. We never find ourselves especially questioning that his more thoughtful friends choose to continue to know him.

It has, however, to be noted that there seems never to have been any question of encouraging the actresses playing female characters – even the eccentrics Nadia (Shannon Elizabeth) and Michelle who are the characters we take away from these films – to improvise in anything like the same way. We remember Michelle either for some heavily scripted lines, quirkily delivered by Alyson Hannigan, or by the intense facial expressions, happy or sad, for which she was already well known. The films indulge Seann William Scott more than his male co-stars, and infinitely more than his female ones. There are, in the end, limits to the egalitarian ethic of these films: they are fine when it comes to autonomous female desire, less so when it comes to women having any measure of creative input or control.

Periodically, he is the butt of particularly gross jokes by the screenwriters, most of which are specific punishments for specific acts, but all of which are also punishments for being Stifler, punishments he will only eventually escape by in a very real sense becoming a different person. Many of these jokes have to do with his sheer obnoxious physicality and the prurience that goes with it. He is the person most likely to come into unwitting contact with other men's bodily fluids as when he inadvertently drinks a beer, pilfered from the girl he is trying to seduce, which has been contaminated with Kevin's semen. The callowly homophobic Stifler spends some considerable time hawking over a toilet – it is clear that he feels contaminated, irrationally. In the second film, expecting a girl to pour champagne on him, he is instead urinated on by John, the Asian youth who wanders through all three films as a plot function with a sidekick – if the sidekick has a name, no one ever calls him by it.

In the second film, it is Stifler who becomes obsessed with the idea that two women whose house the five are painting as part of their summer job are lesbians, and goes scouting in their absence looking for evidence of this. He almost dies of pleasure on discovering a dildo among their possessions – Jim and Finch go into the house after him, but get embroiled in his voyeurism. Caught by the two women, the three young men are offered a deal – the women will perform sexually in front of them, if they do the same for the women. Jim and Finch will participate in kissing and buttock-fondling, but draw the line – as Stifler does not – at giving him a hand-job. All of this is picked up on walkie-talkies all over town, but there is no particular shame for them in this. The adult and young men who hear them regard a little bit of homosexual behaviour as apparently a reasonable price to pay for watching a little lesbian action… This is, of course, a joke, but quite a good one; a particularly masculine trucker who is listening in starts reminiscing about two transvestites he picked up once.

Finch (Eddie Kaye Thomas), who spends most of the film practising tantric meditation in preparation for his older paramour's return, says that he is comfortable in his sexuality at the point when the kissing starts. Actually, obnoxious as he is, Stifler is at least as much so – and it is him that the two women end up with when they turn up at the climactic party. 'We didn't say we were lesbians,' they announce and we last see them both in bed with Stifler. The films' attitude to him is more complex than at first appears, something which becomes more important in the third film, which focuses on him as much as on Jim and rather more than it does on Finch.

Of the four principals, Kevin (Thomas Ian Nicholas) already has a girlfriend, Vicki (Tara Reid), with whom he has not yet had sex. We know what he does not, which is that Vicki is discussing the situation with her more experienced friend Jessica (Natasha Lyonne). Jessica makes a point of debunking sexual mystique – 'It's not a space shuttle launch, it's sex' – and is one of the film's foci of good sense and sexual expertise. Kevin has working for him another source of information – a book, containing generations of hints on, for example, oral sex, which is bequeathed to him by his brother – and against him his inability to lie. He will only say that he loves Vicki when he genuinely feels that he does, by which time rationality has taken over for her.

They have sex on the night of their senior prom, and she points out to him in the afterglow that they are going to different colleges a significant distance apart – and that their relationship is probably doomed. The relationship between Kevin and Vicki is generally seen in positive terms – his original weak behaviour is taking somewhat for granted that they will eventually have intercourse and he redeems himself in her eyes by performing cunnilingus on her with an expertise derived from the book. Significantly, he needs to be prompted to do so by Jessica, who has previously ascertained that Vicki has never in fact had an orgasm, even from masturbation, and takes it upon herself to give Kevin sterling advice.

Though it is Kevin who is most pompous and pretentious in the pact scene, the relationship between him and Vicki is generally seen in idealized terms as what high school romances are supposed to be like. There is one dirty joke at their expense, but it is a very mild one – the orgasming Vicki moans, 'I'm coming, I'm coming' and this prevents their being discovered having sex in her unlocked room by her father who has come up to tell her supper is ready. Good sex is a precaution against humiliation, where bad sex is almost always punished by it.

'Oz' Oestereicher (Chris Klein) is a jock with a heart who decides that the way to get himself a girlfriend is to explore talents he has not previously developed and move into social scenes where he can meet new people. He takes up Jazz Choir and is mocked for this by jock friends like Stifler, and discovers a capacity in himself for musical excellence, which brings him almost automatically the interest of the equally gifted Heather (Mena Suvari), with whom he performs duets that are chastely erotic. She asks him to be her prom partner, only to break with him when she sees his lacrosse buddies react to news of their date in a mode of bawdy camaraderie that she finds demeaning and for complicity in which she blames him. We see the mockery from her point of view and a distance, so that it is genuinely unclear to what extent Oz lets himself be persuaded into participating in it.

She refuses to talk to him outside of their artistic collaboration – he only wins her back by walking off the field in an important game in order to make a concert at which they are supposed to perform together. In a nice touch, he listens to the pep talk from the coach and interprets it for himself – the coach is talking about doing the thing that matters most to you, and

Oz decides that sports is no longer that thing, as far as he is concerned. He demonstrates his withdrawal from the male camaraderie which has nearly ended their relationship in the most dramatic way possible.

Oz and Heather do not have sexual intercourse on prom night – they are seriously sexually involved but don't in the event feel that they are ready. Oz has learned to put this potentially important relationship ahead not only of his sports prowess, but of the egocentric pact he formed with his friends. One of the attractive things about the final scene is that when he makes this clear to them, they are entirely respectful of his decision. In a sense, though, and this is a point picked up in the relationship between Jim and Michelle in the second film, shared musical performance is seen here as an intimacy at least as good as semi-competent sexual intercourse – certainly the scenes in which Oz and Heather duet are genuinely affecting.

Paul Finch is an eccentric and something of an exquisite, who cannot bear, for example, to use the toilets at school, and always runs home whenever he needs to and who brings mochaccino to school in a vacuum cup. His intellectual and artistic interests – and his high level of pretentiousness – make him an unobvious friend for Kevin and Oz, and make him a target for hostility from Stifler, the comically obnoxious sexist and male sexual facilitator who is the butt of many of the film's sexual humiliations. Their antagonism has a sexual edge to it which can be decoded in a number of ways, including unacknowledged homoerotic feeling.

Finch's plan for losing his virginity is more elaborate than any that occurs to the other three and only gradually emerges – they never entirely work it out for themselves. Essentially, Finch bribes Jessica to start rumours about his sexual prowess, the size of his genitals, his intimate tattoos and so on which spread like wildfire through the school and are deliberately at odds with his quiet, intense image. Suddenly, a variety of young women are intrigued by, and attracted to, him – one woman asked for a prom date explains that she is holding out for the possibility of a date with Finch. Others ask his mystified friends if the rumours are true…

Stifler orchestrates the destruction of this scheme and Finch's humiliation in one of the 'gross-out' scenes for which the film is famous – he feeds Finch laxatives and misdirects him into the female washroom. A group of young women who, as it happens, are fascinated by the Finch of legend are confronted with the real thing, suffering from extreme flatulence and diarrhoea – his reputation never recovers. At the prom, Jessica, who has also gone alone, refunds part of his bribe in the shape of a hipflask of liquor, while also making it clear that she has spent the bulk of his money on earrings and that he does not stand a chance with her. (In the second film, which has far less of her than the first, there is a similar moment when, at the final party, she and Stifler look at each other, clearly contemplating the awful possibility of sex between them, and then shake themselves awake from it.)

And so Finch appears to be punished for his presumption and scheming by absolute humiliation. At Stifler's post-prom party, he wanders off into the billiards room by himself while the others are exploring their bedrooms. There he meets Stifler's famously young and attractive mother and their conversation strays rapidly into innuendo as she offers him Scotch, he asks for single malt, and she says, 'Aged eighteen years, the way I like it.'

The slightly overdone suaveness that renders Finch bizarre to his contemporaries comes across to an older woman with a taste for the young as more charming than otherwise – we catch the end of an anecdote in which he identifies a picture as a Piero Della Francesca – and then he glances over to the billiard table. She drags him to his feet and the last thing we hear, over the strains of Simon and Garfunkel's 'Mrs Robinson', is balls going into a pocket. The song refers of course to the iconic film *The Graduate* (1967), in which a very young Dustin Hoffmann is seduced by Anne Bancroft, the mother of his girlfriend, as does their exchange: 'Mr Finch, are you trying to seduce me?' 'Yes Ma'am.' This, of course, reverses the *Graduate* seduction line. Nor is Stifler spared the sight of his loathed enemy naked in the arms of his mother.

This relationship becomes one of the series' running jokes, but one with a slightly sour edge. Alone of the group, Finch never ends up with a partner his own age, ending the other two films in temporary short-term trysts with his older mistress. He says, early in the second film, that none of his younger lovers compare to Stifler's Mom, who is a goddess. A part of the joke, moreover, is that we never get very much sense of the relationship he has with Stifler's Mom, whose name, Janine, we only learn towards the close of the second movie; she simply turns up from time to time and drags Finch off to bed. Perversely, even after she has told Finch her name, she insists on his calling her Stifler's Mom while they are making love. She turns up at the end of the third film after Finch has definitively lost a battle of wills with Stifler over Michelle's younger sister Cadence (January Jones), a battle, moreover, in which these two old enemies adopt each other's personal styles as a tactic.

There are some dark sides to this. Part of the joke lies in the assumption that Stifler is humiliated by his friend's sexual access to his mother, an assumption which does not bear much unpacking. In the second film, he fails to pass on a message from his mother that she will be coming to see Finch, while allowing Finch to believe that the arrival of the obnoxious younger Stifler brother was the object of the calls. Stifler ends up providing a test of Finch's commitment, when he merely meant to hurt and humiliate.

Earlier in *American Pie*, John and his sidekick, whose principal defining characteristic in each film is behaving badly, shout, a propos of Stifler's mother, 'MILF – mothers I'd like to fuck,' in a way that leaves a bad taste in the mouth. In the third film, we are left with their fascinated gaze as a final image, as they spy on Finch performing oral sex on Stifler's mother in a bubble bath. Clearly they are in some sense not merely plot functions but representatives of the unregenerate element in the audience.

Overall though, the crucial lesson that Finch learns is the same one that his friends do – in sexual matters, women have a will which has to be respected. He is punished for trying to seduce himself a woman by deceit – he loses his virginity by being himself. The lesson he and his friends learn is that learned by Chaucer's Gawaine in 'The Wife of Bath's Tale' – that women desire sovereignty.

This is the lesson that Jim eventually learns and even, in the second film, Sherman and, in the third, Stifler. The central figure of the films is Jim, who even more than the other three members of the pact, has to learn better and does so. Many of the humiliations inflicted on Jim have to do with his father, played by the excellent Eugene Levy in all three films, the problem about whom is his more or less remorseless desire to be helpful and under-standing to his son. Jim does not know what he wants from his father, but acceptance of him as a sexual being is something that he finds deeply prob-lematic. His father brings him pornography and tries to talk him through the various ways in which female anatomy is portrayed in centrefolds; his father tries to talk to him sensibly about masturbation and contraception.

When his father catches him masturbating into a warm apple pie, his father simply says that they will have to tell Jim's mother that they ate it. Acceptance could hardly go further or be more embarrassing – except that this acceptance becomes one of the series' running jokes and Jim has several more such moments to come. In the second film, for example, his parents turn up in his dorm room, his father planning to bond with him, and walk in on him having sex; later he has to help Jim at the hospital when Jim accidentally superglues his penis to his hand. As the films wear on, we come to accept, as does Jim, that there are many worse things in life than a deeply understanding father.

The apple pie scene, which in part gives the film its name, can be seen as implying that Jim is very mildly autistic, since it derives from his failure to see as metaphorical a description of 'third base' by his friends as being like sticking your fingers into warm apple pie. It certainly demonstrates that for Jim at this point, sexual intercourse is something that is desired not as intimacy with a person but as a comfort zone of pleasurable sensation in the abstract. His father's speech that compares masturbation to throwing a ball against a wall, perfectly good in its way, but not as good as an actual game with someone else, to this extent falls on deaf ears.

Eugene Levy becomes the focus for the intense sentimentality that progressively forms a part of what makes these films work. When, in the third film, he arrives in the restaurant with the engagement ring Jim has left at home, only to find his son, as he gradually realizes, in the throes of orgasm from an under-the-table blow job from Michelle, he stands patiently by while his son proposes and boasts to the shocked bystanders, 'That's my son.' Levy's slightly busy-bodyish portrayal of fatherhood is used to underline the film's sex-positive message – even when it appears, in the third film, that Jim is involved in four-way congress between a cake-smeared Stifler and two dogs, he contents himself with a firm 'Back away from the dog, Jim,' at a point where Michelle's more prudish parents are having hysterics.

One of the reasons we enjoy as comic the humiliations heaped on Jim and the others is that they are deserved consequences of thoughtless humiliation of the women they are involved with. Jim treats the sweet-natured exotic exchange student Nadia (Shannon Elizabeth) badly, and the consequences for her are, through his carelessness, far worse than could have been expected: she is sent back to Czechoslovakia in disgrace overnight, not to reappear until the second film. The fact that there are also consequences for him is the only thing that makes him other than hateful.

Nadia asks if she can come round to his parents' house to study after ballet class – she will need to change her clothes there, she says. Almost immediately, Jim allows himself to be persuaded to let his friends spy on her via his web camera, which will be left turned on – he even dashes out of the house and over to Kevin's house in order to spy on her himself. This would be bad enough a breach of trust even were the broadcast not being accidentally sent to everyone on the local computer network.

He and his friends get more than they bargain for – they have set Nadia up to be viewed as a sexual object, and they discover from spying on her that Nadia has sexual desires of her own. She finds the pornography stash in Jim's bedroom drawer and starts using it to masturbate. When Jim turns up, hoping to have intercourse with her after she has primed herself in this way, she makes him strip for her. When she proposes that they have sex, Jim experiences premature ejaculation, twice. His discovery that this humiliation has been broadcast to the world, and is quite specifically known to just about every woman he might have hoped to ask to the prom, is entirely appropriate. He has treated Nadia as the subject of sexual objectification and discovers that he too is the victim of the pornographic gaze.

In this state of abjection, he is reduced to asking to the prom someone he regards as equally abject in her way – Michelle, who is despised by Jim and everyone else for her obsessional chatter full of anecdotes about what she did at band camp. (It is one of the givens of teen film that certain extracurricular pursuits like sport and cheerleading are socially acceptable and others – mathlete competitions in *Mean Girls*, chess in the television show *Popular*, jazz choir and band here – are hopelessly uncool. Why this should be so is one of those great mysteries.) In order to spend time with Michelle, who is surprisingly willing to go to the prom with him, Jim has to be prepared to listen to her, and to her anecdotes. He has, in other words, to put her and her interests ahead of himself and what he thinks of as cool.

Alyson Hannigan was offered far larger parts in *American Pie* – her star was in the ascendant as a result of her TV role as the much-loved Willow in *Buffy the Vampire Slayer* – and chose to play Michelle instead. This was a very smart move – the part is a dopier, and in the end sexier, role than Jessica, say – and in the event she ended up reprising the part of Michelle in the later *American Pie* movies.

The joke is that Michelle is at least as much of a sexual being as any of the other women in the film with the possible exception of Stifler's Mom. The string of more or less cosy anecdotes about band camp culminates, at the post-prom party, in one about how she used her flute to masturbate, and the remark that, of course, one of the principal points of band camp is having a lot of sex – she is keen to get Jim up to their room, because she is getting antsy in her eagerness to get on with it.

Jim has assumed that she is prepared to go to prom with him because she is enough out of the loop that she has not seen the webcast – in fact, the whole point is that she has seen it, and liked what she saw. She provides Jim with two condoms – it is important that he be desensitized so that there is no repetition of his earlier sexual malfunction – and works her wicked way with him in a role-reversing sexual encounter in which she spends much of the time on top and calls him her bitch.

Jim has been the victim of regular and deserved sexual misfortune – here he finds himself instructed by someone who is considerably more experienced than he is, and who likes him anyway. He wakes up cuddling what proves to be not Michelle but an inflated plastic shark – we are, I think, supposed to see this as a comment on Michelle's exploitative nature rather than as relating to the sexist slur that refers to women as 'fish'. He finds himself alone and says, memorably, 'I've been used. She used me. Coool!'

The film's final scene places all four in a diner discussing their situations – they toast the next step. The second film, which takes place during the first summer vacation of their college career shows them taking such steps, though not necessarily quite in the ways they plan. (When, in the third film, Kevin tries to toast the next step again, Finch and Jim shut him up.) All of them have fantasies of a wild summer in which they have a lot of sex – in the event, most of them don't. Finch spends the summer practising Tai Chi and tantric meditation in order to prepare himself for a woman who may never show up. Oz is cheerfully celibate – Heather is abroad and, between her roommates and Stifler, they never get an uninterrupted occasion even for phone sex. Kevin is foolishly hopeful that he and Vicki will get back together – even though she has made it clear that all she is offering him is friendship. The lesson he learns over the summer is that if he wants to have Vicki as a friend – which he does – he has to accept that she has moved on. This is in fact rather touching – Kevin at the same time experiences real pain and behaves with reasonable manners to Vicki's date.

Jim also spends the summer waiting – Nadia has returned to America and plans to turn up in Michigan for the gang's end-of-summer party at the beach house they have hired for the summer. He worries that his sexual accomplishments are not enough for her – especially after he has asked Michelle for a frank review of his performance on prom night and she has said, as nicely as possible, that he sucked. Over the summer, he takes advice from Michelle, breaking into band camp in order to do so.

In one of those moments of unamusing tastelessness which are these films' major flaw – as opposed, that is, to the genuinely funny tastelessness which produces some of their funniest moments – he impersonates Petey (Jesse Heiman), a trombone player with learning difficulties. Jim does not set out to do this in the first instance – he is concussed in an accident and is wearing a band camp outfit as disguise, and is shoved on to the stage with a trombone in his hand before he quite knows what is happening or who he is supposed to be. He waves his instrument around and makes appalling noises with it, and gradually starts doing so with a measure of bravado, while Michelle looks embarrassed. If there is an excuse for this sequence, it has to be that it is an extended sexual metaphor about another sort of performance at which, according to Michelle, he sucks.

Jim injures his penis as a result of one of those humiliations which ensue when he listens to Stifler, who has provided him with pornography and lubricant; earlier Jim has superglued a broken bedside lamp and, in the heat of excitement, glues one hand to his penis and the other to the pornographic video. Unable to open the bedroom door, even with his teeth, he is arrested when he climbs out of the window, more or less naked, and is seen by neighbours – he ends up in the emergency room with his father, who is as understanding as always. The comic chemistry between Eugene Levy and Jason Biggs in this scene is particularly admirable; when Jim's Dad says that they had better keep this episode from Jim's mother, who, let it be remembered, has earlier walked in on Jim having sex in his dorm room, his quiet seriousness is achingly funny.

Then Nadia turns up several days early, expecting to pick up with Jim where they failed to start up a year and more earlier. Jim wants nothing more than to oblige, but his pride will not let him admit what has happened. Michelle concocts a scheme whereby she will pretend to be his mildly jealous girlfriend and break up with him before the party, by which time his penile damage will have healed, using their time together to teach him areas of sexual technique like removing a girl's bra non-clumsily. (She makes him practise with a pillow.)

There is real cruelty here – Nadia's feelings for Jim are being tested and she has no idea why. Further, Jim has entirely failed to consider the possibility – indeed the probability – that Michelle has feelings for him herself, and that this is why she suggests the arrangement in the first place. Alyson Hannigan manages to make this convincing – as played by her, Michelle is weird enough to be capable of almost anything – and it is only after their feigned break-up, when she is alone in her car, that the audience is let in on her secret. Admirers of Hannigan's performance as Willow in *Buffy* know only too well her capacity to break our hearts with a sorrowful glance.

During the party, and significantly after spending some time on the beach with the other two, listening to Kevin's slightly overextended speeches about the mutability of emotional life, Jim faces up to his true feelings and responsibility. (The scene with Kevin is overlong in the final film – in a deleted scene, he went on to drag the others back to high school, show them the niche where the book of sexual advice is kept and talk about wanting to go on knowing them all – touching but, at this stage in the film, beside the point.) Nadia persuades him to walk with her to a lighthouse further along the beach, and there he confesses his feelings for Michelle and his hope that she will find someone better. Nadia is entirely gracious about it. (The symbolism here is a little, shall we say, overt – a lighthouse is a phallic object which sheds light and prevents danger – can we say duhhh?)

Jim races off to band camp, where Michelle is performing a flute solo; he announces his presence by recapitulating his performance, as Petey, on the trombone, punctuating her elegant twirls with raucous abstract noise. She responds with delight and they end up on stage kissing to tumultuous applause, most of it from people who still confuse Jim with Petey; rather charmingly, the reunited pair take a bow. Given the original sexual anecdote about the flute, the earlier trombone scene with its pregnant symbolism, and not forgetting either Oz and Heather's duet and the scene where, as part of his sexual education, Michelle anally penetrates Jim with the mouthpiece of a trumpet, the linkage of music and sex in the first two films can be seen as pretty much proven by this point.

Meanwhile, Nadia, who has graciously told Jim to go and find his geek, proceeds to go on the prowl for a geek of her own. One of the charming things about these films is that Nadia, caricatured in *Not Another Teen Movie* merely as an exchange student airhead who wanders around in few or no clothes, does combine her extreme good looks with a slight awkwardness that has nothing necessarily to do with her being a foreigner with imperfect English. Hanging around disconsolately, she is approached by Sherman, who tries his stale old routine on her – Nadia, because the film is newer to her, is utterly charmed and drags him off to bed. These films present a universe in which there is a right person for everybody.

The third film has as significant elements in its plot fairly conventional romcom material about Jim's attempts to ingratiate himself with Michelle's somewhat hostile parents, and to provide her with the romantic wedding of her dreams. Much of the plot's tension comes from the fact that, on the one hand, neither he nor Michelle want Stifler, and the complications he brings with him, at the wedding and, on the other hand, that, knowing this, he makes himself essential to Jim's success. Nothing too dreadful happens to Jim in this film: he is caught having oral sex and his shaved pubic hair ruins a wedding cake. (One writes that sentence and realizes how these films redefine one's sense of 'nothing too dreadful' so as to naturalize extreme sexual embarrassment as standard.)

Stifler teaches Jim how to dance, and the mild frisson of sexual ambiguity that one might expect from two nervously homophobic men dancing is, needless to say, played with. This is played with further in a scene when the four principals are searching Chicago's bars for the dressmaker Michelle wants for her dress. Stifler ends up in a gay bar, and manages to cause endless offence; he and the others are about to be unceremoniously ejected when he challenges the most vocal man present, Bear, to a dance contest. As happens with the scenes in the earlier films that use musical duets, notably the one between Oz and Heather, we learn that there is an intimacy in competent performance that transcends sex. On the dance floor, he and Bear compete, and hostility turns into genuine friendship – it is one of the first real indications that there is more to Stifler than we have previously seen.

Michelle's sister Cadence arrives for the wedding, and almost at once Stifler and Finch start competing for her affections. Earlier Jim had pointed out to Stifler that he needs to change, to be less himself – 'Impolite would be an improvement.' Stifler adopts a persona which is almost a caricature of Finch, referring to himself by his first name – Stephen – instead of as, for example, the Stiffmeister, and affecting a higher voice, a sissyish delight in flowers and chocolate, and real consideration for the feelings of Mrs Flaherty, Cadence and Michelle's mother. In some scenes he does this, while pulling faces at his friends appropriate to his actual personality while standing behind the Flahertys. Finch retaliates by adopting a persona which is a less extreme version of Stifler's normal one and for a long time Cadence is genuinely torn between the two of them, before opting for Stifler, in spite of Michelle's warnings about him.

One of the problems with these three films is that the DVD versions include extra material that plays to the prurience of part of their audience.

This is never more the case than with the – admittedly often achingly funny – material dealing with the bachelor party the other three organize for Jim without his knowledge. He has told Stifler to surprise him, and not thought of the possible consequences of this, and then gone ahead with a private dinner for Michelle's parents, who arrive with him at his parents' house as the orgy the others have set going is under way.

When this is bawdy farce, it is admirable, as Jim tries frantically to conceal from his future in-laws Kevin (gagged and tied to a chair) and Finch (semi-naked and covered in chocolate sauce), as well as explaining away Bear (posing as a sommelier hired to serve them wine, but wearing leather chaps that leave his buttocks exposed) and two strippers, one dressed as a French maid and the other as a policewoman. Stifler makes things worse by refusing to break character and concocting a bizarre story about an attempt to demonstrate Jim's courage to them that results in Mrs Flaherty appointing him best man and giving him the wedding ring.

Some of the material, though, is deeply offensive even by the standards of bawdy. A shot of Stifler using the vagina of a blow-up sex doll as a repository for his beer is one of those moments that almost incline one to stop making excuses for these films, or looking for significance in them. This is far too revealing a moment about what the character thinks about women – it is genuinely unclear whether this is meant to make this point, or merely demonstrates that Scott and Herz have a dark side to their sense of humour which periodically gets out of control.

Stifler cannot resist boasting to Finch about Cadence's offer to sleep with him, and does so in insulting terms that, overheard by Cadence, put paid to her illusions about him. When, later on, it turns out that he has accidentally destroyed the flowers for the wedding, Jim unceremoniously sends him away. Stifler manages to retrieve the situation by assembling the team he coaches and putting them to work rebuilding the floral decorations he has destroyed – he placates his friends by demonstrating ingenuity and teamwork and leadership. In other words, he turns his persona as 'the grand facilitator' to productive ends.

He even manages to apologize to Cadence when she gives him a chance to, asking him whether he did all this to make the wedding work, or to have sex with her. He acknowledges that both are true, an answer she can accept as an honest one. He leaves to get on with his task, and then dashes back, shoves a rose in her hand, pecks her on the cheek and leaves. Earlier, Michelle had regarded Jim's belief that Stifler has a more sensitive side as evidence that masturbation has rotted his brain; now she says, 'Steve Stifler just gave a girl a flower, and meant it. This is awesome. It's like watching monkeys using tools for the first time.' This chapter has commented regularly on the charm of Alyson Hannigan's performance in these films – the glee she gives these lines is exceptionally charming even for her. There is not enough of her in this third film – her commitments to *Buffy* limited her availability – but what is there is delightful.

The film is not done with humiliating Stifler, even though he has started to improve and the material grows ever more problematic. He loses the ring which is swallowed by the smaller of the Flahertys' dogs. Inevitably – in these films at least – the dog turd containing it is mistaken for a chocolate truffle by Mrs Flaherty and Stifler has greedily to eat it to remain in character as 'Stephen' and prevent her collaring it. Later, Cadence fails to turn up on time for their tryst in a dark closet and Stifler instead makes love to Jim's obnoxious grandmother, who has been dumped there by John, who had been lumbered with pushing her wheelchair.

Grandmother Levinstein (Angela Paton) has been appalled by the fact that Michelle is a gentile and has generally thrown a damper on the proceedings – in an early version of the script, she was known to be dying and the wedding had been rushed through to ensure her presence. Sex with Stifler puts a smile on her face and makes her cooperate with the proceedings. This ought to be as offensive a moment as the sex-doll beer-holder, and yet somehow it is not quite. Part of what softens it from the merely pornographic into the comic is that she is genuinely enthusiastic about sex with a much younger man – 'Focus, focus' she shouts at him when they are discovered and her identity revealed; the sex is clearly consensual on her part even if the result of a misapprehension on his. Part is the way that the incident gets built into the ongoing, and increasingly friendly, relationship between Stifler and Finch, teasing each other as 'motherfucker' and 'grandmother fucker'. My suspicion is that the scene demonstrates how the controlling hand of the Weitz brothers, director and producer of the first film, producers of the second and only executive producers on this one, kept Herz's more problematic side under control.

In the end, this incident serves as a handy touchstone for the complexity of a reasoned critical response to these three films. It stretches the sense of what is acceptable humour and has a certain degree of sentimentality to it that is itself a source of unease. The popularity of the *American Pie* sequence says something quite unsettling about the attitudes of their target audience to sex, gender and sexual etiquette. They are neither wholly sexist – though often straying wholeheartedly into offensive territory – nor more than marginally progressive – though having a cheerfully sex-positive attitude that is often rather delightful and sometimes genuinely subversive. At their best they have the honest vulgarity of the old British seaside postcards of Donald McGill; at their worst they are genuinely unpleasant in their sadistic humiliation of the films' comic butts.

The mismatch between the *American Pie* trilogy's tastelessness and its thoughtfulness, between its sentimentality and its intermittent gross sexism, is perhaps best understood if we look at the comparative commercial failure of a rather more coherent and nuanced film, Luke Greenfield's *The Girl Next Door*. This is a quietly bawdy farce whose heart is even more clearly in the right place, and whose script, by Stuart Blumberg, David T. Wagner and Brent Goldberg, is considerably more elegant. (Interestingly, the project was at first conceived and sold as something more like an *American Pie* film, and evolved into its present state.)

To synopsize briefly, Matthew (Emile Hirsch) is Student Body President at his high school, 'a straight A overachiever' with political ambitions, when he meets, and falls in love with, Danielle (Elisha Cuthbert), the niece of a neighbour. When he discovers from his friends that she has been a porn star, he treats her with contempt, and loses her. Realizing that he loves her, he follows her to an Adult Film convention to win her back with fervent apologies and does so. Her manager/lover/pimp Kelly (Timothy Olyphant) takes revenge by stealing money for which Matthew is responsible and by spiking him with Ecstasy before Matthew is due to give a speech on which a scholarship depends. With Danielle's help, and that of his close friends, Matthew uses the school prom to shoot what we take to be a porn film. Kelly steals it and shows it to Matthew's parents and headmaster – it turns out to be a highly sexual, but good, sex education film. This not only pays back the money Kelly stole, but pays for Matthew and Danielle's college education. Matthew has come of age and earned the woman he loves on terms acceptable to both of them.

One of the strengths of this film is that it is not frightened of the deeply unlikeable sides that Matthew shows at various points. When his porn-ob-sessed movie geek friend Eli (Chris Marquette) shows him one of Danielle's videos, he starts to see her every movement as potentially pornographic. For example, her quiet conversations with her parents are suddenly staged in his head as the prelude to seductions of them – and he treats her with a quietly salacious aggression that she recognizes only too well. She does not have to be told that he has found out what she did not find a way to tell him about herself to recognize that he is treating her as meat, and that her hope of regaining innocence is wrecked. The fact that he is also sexually incompetent, relying on the half-baked sexual notions of Eli as to how a seduction should proceed, merely makes the scene more painful.

The scholarship Matthew is trying to win is based on the possession of moral fibre and when he is confronted with a serious test of it, for the first time in his life, he fails. He fails further when Kelly drags him off to a strip club where he masks his discomfort by trying to imitate a man who is leading him, with cigars and lap dancers, to make an ever greater ass of himself. Kelly is demonstrating to Danielle that all men, even this nice boy, are pigs, and so she might as well stick with the devil she knows. Timothy Olyphant is suitably Mephisthophelean in the way he manipulates both young lovers in these scenes.

Matthew spends the rest of the film making up for his behaviour. First, he humbles himself to appeal to Danielle to pay him attention in a press conference full of her slavering fans, of whom he could so readily be seen to be one. Then he deals with the consequences for both of them in her accepting his apologies and walking away from her life a second time.

One of Matthew's follies is that he suffers from the delusion that Kelly is a reasonable man, rather than someone whose superficial charm can slip over in a second to near-psychotic violence. Riding in Kelly's car, he offers to make up any financial losses Kelly has incurred, over time, and Kelly asks him for a blowjob, as proof of sincerity, before slugging him around the face and head in a temper tantrum. Kelly asks him to steal an award from a former business partner, Hugo (James Remar), and then calls the police on him – it is only Matthew's presence of mind which stops him being arrested and mauled by Hugo's watch-parrot.

Then, of course, he has to deal with making his scholarship speech while stoned out of his mind. Hirsch is admirable in this well written sentimental scene and convinces us that Matthew is someone capable of being formidable. He discards his deeply conventional speech – one of the other contenders has in any case already used his prized quotation from JFK – and speaks from the heart. Moral fibre, he says, is something he has just come to understand, and it is doing whatever is necessary to get the thing on which you have set your heart. Is the juice worth the squeeze, Kelly has contemptuously asked him, and Matthew answers him in his absence; yes, he says, to the slight confusion of all his hearers save Danielle, the juice is worth the squeeze.

The audience are moved by his sincerity – he gets considerably more applause than the boring Brian, who actually gets the scholarship. In a scene cut from the final movie, he almost loses Danielle all over again when he subsides into self-pitying regret from this moment of real commitment, only to win her back when he goes to her rather than to his parents or the authorities when he discovers Kelly has stolen the money. The studio felt it was a mistake to make him unsympathetic all over again, and the studio, for once, clearly had a case.

If the film has a weakness, however, it is the sense that Danielle's arc is over at this point and that she and Matthew have only to solve their practical problems to achieve their final relationship. The question of whether boy and girl have got each other is pretty much resolved by the end of the second act. The fake issue of whether or not Matthew stars in his own film – in the event, the subject of the condom-putting-on scene is his friend Klitz (Paul Dano), in a fencing mask to preserve his anonymity – and whether this would be infidelity – Matthew makes his decision not to participate when Danielle comes into the room where they are shooting – is no substitute for real drama at its later point, especially when, as we discover, the issue is totally spurious in any case.

More pertinently, Danielle, who has walked away from pornography and the fringes of prostitution twice, the first time for reasons that have nothing whatever to do with Matthew, is hardly shown to have any agency at all, even though she clearly has a fair measure of it. She exercises it a little in her teasing pursuit of Matthew, making him apologize for spying on her undressing by making him strip naked for her in the street, and by dragging him to a party where he is forced to declare himself unequivocally or lose her to jock bullies. From what we know about the experiences some women have had on attempting to quit the sex industry, and from what we are shown of Kelly's capacity for vindictiveness and violence, she shows real moral courage, and we are not shown it. This is a film about Matthew and his choices, whereas it ought to be a film about both of them.

The film is extremely insightful on both the dark and positive sides of male friendship. Everything I have said elsewhere about the homoerotic component in adolescent male friendship as portrayed in teen film is borne out here. Eli in particular is obsessed with Matthew's sexual success with Danielle. 'I swear I'll kill myself if you don't fuck her,' he shouts across the school quad. 'Fuck her for me.' At the same time, he and the third of their group, Klitz, will drop everything to help Matthew when he is in trouble – the sex education film is a calling card for Eli's entry to the film industry, but it is also a serious risk for him to take.

This sense of the complexity of male bonding is also true of the relationship between Matthew and his adversary Kelly. At a point when Matthew is filled with self-contempt over how he behaved when making a pass at Danielle, Kelly leads him to a nightclub, arranges for an older man to buy him a lap dance, and encourages him to act like a punter. (Significantly, Kelly does not pay for the lap dance himself; when Matthew recognizes one of his parents' friends, Kelly sets this up as a humiliation of both squares.) When Matthew pretends to a bank clerk that this strange bearded hipster is his student adviser, the film is setting up Kelly's later theft; it is also telling us something quite crucial about their relationship. In a very real sense, Kelly is Matthew's mentor, far more of one than he intends to be.

Kelly resents Matthew's innocence, which is the thing that has made it possible, as he sees it, for Matthew to take Danielle away from him – Kelly is very keen on telling Matthew to respect Danielle's choices, but never does so himself. Accordingly, he sets out to destroy it, by framing him for crimes, by seeing if Matthew is prepared to have sex with him to protect Danielle and by trying to destroy his dream of the scholarship.

By dragging Matthew into his world of vengeance and point-scoring, rather than letting things be, Kelly loses by overreaching – one of Hollywood's favourite villain clichés. In order to make plausible his attempt to frame Matthew for burgling Hugo's house, Kelly tells him about the idea Hugo stole from him for filming porn in real settings. There is a piece of justice here: he steals from Matthew and Matthew puts things right by stealing this idea all over again. Matthew has also learned something of which Kelly is more or less incapable and he is gracious in victory: he sends Kelly a box of cigars as a present, with a note that says, echoing Kelly's own earlier sexist line, 'The juice was worth the squeeze.' We can see this as Matthew still operating some of the time in Kelly's belief system rather than his own, or, more plausibly, as Matthew trying to communicate with Kelly in terms he can understand.

Quite often, in Hollywood films, the female part is there because there needs to be something that explains why two very good-looking men are not displaying even a bat's squeak of interest in each other. Martin

Scorsese's *Gangs of New York* (2002) is a good example here – Daniel Day Lewis and Leonardo DiCaprio have far more chemistry with each other than either has with Cameron Diaz, whom the script short-changes. That is not the whole of the problem here. Elisha Cuthbert has real charm, and is beautiful in both her wholesome and her porn-star incarnations, but she shows no especial sign here, or in her other best-known role, in *24*, of being able to show much in the way of emotional depth.

Olyphant and Hirsch on the other hand are one of the reasons why this film is good – they have a chemistry together which inevitably suggests sexual subtext as well as the adversary and mentor relationships they have in text. It is this sexual edge between them that makes it brave of the film to make it overt, even momentarily; you do believe that, gay or straight, Kelly would seduce Matthew sexually as well as in other ways if he thought there was profit in it, or merely for mischief. And at the point when this happens, Matthew still thinks Kelly is a man with whom deals can be done. Greenfield links this aspect of the film to *Something Wild* (1986) and, in this respect, *The Girl Next Door* goes further than that excellent adult comedy – Timothy Olyphant has a degree of bisexual menace that Ray Liotta does not.

In his DVD commentary, Luke Greenfield argues that this is not a teen film, that the issues in it are too serious to be pigeon-holed in what he sees as a lightweight genre. Certainly there are things here which stretch the idea of teen comedy – Matthew is at various points in serious jeopardy. (Keith in *Some Kind of Wonderful* or the teenagers in *Adventures in Babysitting* are in at least as much physical danger, but we feel it less intensely.)

However, *The Girl Next Door* has many of the surface tropes of a teen movie. Its whole opening sequence, when a variety of types – girl soccer player, drunken jock, mathlete, grind – soliloquize their memories of high school as they will appear in the yearbook, as a prelude to Matthew's realization that he has nothing he cares to put in, is a version of the anthropology shot. The major authority figure, his relationship with whom is threatened by Danielle – both early on when they skinny dip in his pool, and later by the sex education video – is the high school principal, who has always regarded Matthew as the ideal student.

The entire film happens in the last weeks before graduation from high school – the jocks and stoners keep cutting class to go to the beach, while Matthew and his friends go to class. When Matthew considers doing so seriously, he is prevented by his nervousness about consequences. When he has further such apprehensions, which always take the shape of threatening daydreams that are only taken back later, they usually involve school rather than the dangerous real-world figures he is finding himself coping with. His relationship with Danielle brings him across the threshold into the adult world, but only gradually – significantly she is capable of persuading him to cut class, and equally, the film's membership of the teen genre is demonstrated by this.

Matthew's entire relationship with Danielle has an element, as public performance, of dream revenge on the jocks and bullies who despise him. She even uses this to force him to commit to her properly for the first time. When they turn up at the prom together, with Eli and Klitz squiring her friends April and Ferrara, there is a wish fulfilment aspect to the situation that precisely parallels the display element of Gary and Wyatt's relationship with Lisa in *Weird Science*. Further, they persuade a couple of the jocks to participate in the film, turning down the one who earlier tried to eject them from a party; faced with threatening adult women, the jocks prove impotent, which is why Klitz has to step up to the mark.

The film always skirts the issue of Danielle's exact age – she is clearly somewhat older than Matthew, but we are never told how much. When he asks her to the prom, she is thrilled because, as she says in one of the film's few references to her back story, she never got to go to hers. This is another way in which *The Girl Next Door* both is and is not a teen movie: it defines a second chance of innocence for someone who has been out in the world as getting the chance to go back to the end experience of high school.

It is also worth pointing out that the film's title implies its relationship with the *American Pie* franchise. *The Girl Next Door* is a film about regaining, or keeping, or preserving, innocence that takes its title from one of the great American clichés – Danielle is, originally, only the girl next door because of physical location, but she gets to be that thing again as a result of her and Matthew's adventures. The other great cliché about innocence and home cooking is of course apple pie – the whole arc of Jim's life, and of his dialogue with his father (in the third film, and also Michelle's dialogue, when she asks Jim's Dad for help in defining her vows), is about taking traditional pieties and redefining them while keeping their essence. Jim's masturbation into the pie becomes a way for him and his father to find a space to talk – home cooking still has a purpose, just a different one.

In the end, teen sex comedies are teen movies in that they deal with coming of age, and redefining identities, which, we have already implicitly seen, are crucial themes of the genre. Sex and its discontents are always, especially perhaps in films with teen male protagonists, a way of talking about personal integrity and personal growth. One of the reasons why senior prom is so important to teen movies is that it is a precisely defined rite of passage, a liminal moment between adolescence and responsibility. There is a Capra-esque aspect to high school and its discontents and its high points – it is seen as a test. The trouble with boys, in teen movies, both the boys who are characters in them and the adult boys who make many of them, is that such tests are seen in terms of particular ritual moments rather than as the consequence of ongoing lived experience.

On Being Good
at Things

Female competence
and sexuality

N othing that has been said thus far in this book should be taken as implying that the contemporary American teen genre film is necessarily a secondary form of comparatively little importance. The formal near-perfection and charm of *Clueless* and the dark mordancy of *Heathers* and *Cruel Intentions* rule out such an interpretation, for one thing; working within the genre has enabled the making of thoroughly good films, always an important test of a genre's intrinsic worth. Also, the genre teen movie is as capable as the non-genre movie about teenagers of dealing, in a light-hearted way, with moderately serious issues. It would perhaps be useful in order to make these points more absolutely to compare a film that is definitely part of the American teen movie genre with a film which, though superficially similar in most ways, is equally clearly not.

The American film *Bring It On* (2000) which was clearly created and marketed with the audience for teen genre movies in mind, and the British film *Bend It Like Beckham* (2002) which was aimed at various markets including a British Asian one but made no particular gestures to a teen audience save the age of its two protagonists, have a surprising amount in common. Both of them deal with a quasi-romantic friendship (at an overt level, and at the very least) between two young women from radically different backgrounds, whose bonding is based on shared excellence at a skill central to their sense of personal identity. In both films, questions of ethnicity and of cross-ethnic appropriation are addressed in a complex fashion; in both films there is a romantic heterosexual subplot which only partly defuses romantic chemistry between the two female principals.

One of the major differences between the films is of course that in *Bend It Like Beckham*, questions of ethnicity are central to the film, whereas in *Bring It On* they are at a literal level placed at one remove. The film centres on the mostly white cheerleading team, the Toros, rather than on the impoverished urban black team, the Clovers.

The Toros win national cheerleading competitions that the Clovers are too poor to enter; for some years the Toros' former captain Big Red has been plagiarizing the Clovers' routines. Their new captain Torrance (Kirsten Dunst) is told about this by her new friend Missy (Eliza Dushku). She is at first persuaded by peer pressure to continue the theft, and then commissions a choreographer, who has double-sold his routines. Only then does she trust her judgement and develop routines of the Toros' own with which they come a close second to the Clovers in competition.

Identity, ethnic and otherwise, is complex here – the urbanite of European extraction Missy Pantone is constructed as an exotic in a way that the East Asian Whitney is not. In a moment none the less effective for being corny as hell, the teacher who introduces Missy's brother, Cliff Pantone (Jesse Bradford), to his new class finds his name difficult to pronounce. Dushku's sultry South European looks and bad girl style do not, though, make her African-American, though they do position her as able to act as advocate of and go-between to the Clovers. The particular way she braids her hair on her first appearance indicates that she is prepared to be influenced by black style; she also struts around in tight dark jeans with keys jangling from her right hip that indicate the difference of another type of style altogether, a queer one. She and her brother Cliff are hip in a way that Torrance (Kirsten Dunst) is not – in a way that goes back to Norman Mailer's essay 'The White Negro' (1957), hipness is positioned as a bridge between races. When the issue at stake is appropriation of black style and talent, this is a problematic procedure.

The film starts out from the standard mythology of cheerleaders in teen movies and exploitation movies. In his commentary, Peyton Reed acknowledges that he and scriptwriter Jessica Bendinger determined that they had to include every single one of the clichés present in sexual exploitation films about cheerleaders as well as those in teen movies. Thus we have a semi-nude locker-room scene, a potential cat fight between the film's two principals and the deliberately cheesy car-washing scene.

The locker-room scene is set up in an interesting single long take that indicates many of the tensions of power among the cheerleaders – there is a longer version which is even more effective. Both this and the car-wash scene are examples of the way this film tries to have its cake and eat it – to reference the sexually objectifying cliché in an ironic way is still to inhabit it. Nor is the cliché entirely defused by shooting the car-wash from the viewpoint of the gay male cheerleader, Les.

The film's opening minutes lay out the cheerleader clichés of teen movies and television in a thoroughly witty manner, performed in a way that owes as much to Busby Berkeley as to actual cheerleading:

> The Toros: I'm bitchin', great hair,
> The boys all love to stare,
> I'm wanted, I'm hot,
> I'm everything you're not,
> I'm pretty, I'm cool,
> I dominate the school,
> Who am I? Just guess,
> Guys wanna touch my chest,
> I'm rockin', I smile,
> And many think I'm vile,
> I'm flyin', I jump,
> You can look but don't you hump,
> Whoo
> I'm major, I roar,
> I swear I'm not a whore,
> We cheer and we lead,
> We act like we're on speed,
> You hate us 'cause we're beautiful,
> Well we don't like you either,
> We're cheerleaders.

The film's date places it after *Heathers*, after the run of *Popular* and after the high school years of *Buffy the Vampire Slayer*. It is a revisionist response to the standard portrayal of cheerleaders, which directly alludes to that mythology in order to suggest a new and more nuanced perception. Even the name of the school where it takes place – Rancho Carne – alludes to the standard perception of cheerleaders as complete sexual objects – meat, as it were, on the hoof.

This routine turns out to be a dream sequence at the culmination of which Torrance is announced as the new squad leader only to discover that she is publicly naked. In the course of the film, she discovers that much of what she believes to be the case in her perfect little life is untrue. Her boyfriend does not love her or think her good enough to be squad leader. The victory of the squad in championships during the years that her role model Big Red was in charge are based on plagiarism, lies and implicit racism. Some of her easy friendships inside the squad are not to be relied on when the chips are down. The nakedness in her dream is symbolic of a lot of unacknowledged fears, and among them is the fear that the thing to which she devotes herself is as trivial as her parents think it is.

One of the major strengths of this film is simply this – Kirsten Dunst gives a performance of real subtlety and charm. Torrance is a character almost entirely without nuance – she is conscious of not being an intellectual and worried that she is not creative. One of the reasons why she speaks so movingly about cheerleading as a valid form of endeavour is that she has at every moment to persuade herself of this. Kirsten Dunst gives her an evangelical fervour at such moments. She lets us know that Torrance is not nearly as shallow as she thinks she is, and makes us love her for her insecurity.

In the end, this is a film about Torrance and her choices. She inherits the captaincy of the squad after a vote, but primarily as appointed by Big Red; she has never thought about what leadership means because she is trained in cheerleading, not leading cheerleaders. Her first attempt at exercising control leads to her crippling one of the squad by getting them to do a difficult manoeuvre. This is an economical piece of plotting – it means that the squad needs a new member and it also strengthens the possible threat of Whitney and Courtney to Torrance's leadership.

If cheerleading is to be taken seriously – when Missy tells her that 'it's only cheerleading', Torrance replies, and it is not a joke, 'I *am* only cheerleading' – then nepotism and plagiarism are as wrong as they would be in any other field of serious endeavour. To choose Whitney's moderately talented younger sister as a member of the squad over the far more talented, but more difficult, Missy, would be to take the easy path of popularity with rivals for leadership. To continue to use the Clovers' stolen cheers is to devalue any victory in competition – when Torrance agrees to continue with the Clovers' cheers rather than face a leadership challenge from Whitney and Courtney, it is a failure of nerve for which we know she will be punished with further humiliations.

Part of Torrance's problem is that she relies on the advice of her entirely unsatisfactory boyfriend Aaron – the audience knows, and she does not, that he is already cheating on her at college. She lets him advise her to hire a choreographer, Sparky – technically against the rules, but, as he points out, everyone does it. As indeed they do – the choreographer turns out to have sold his awful disco routine to several teams. Again, Torrance fails by not following her own best instincts: at the regional competition, the Toros are only allowed through to the nationals on the basis of earlier victories.

This sequence is effective partly because it is very funny, even though it goes on for rather a long time. The sub-Fosse work of the awful Sparky is an aching parody of what we fear cheerleading is all about. His angry rhetoric – he is clearly a disappointed man – has a relationship with every drill sergeant in every army film, and is all the funnier for its incongruity here:

> I am a choreographer. That's what I do. You are cheerleaders.
> Cheerleaders are dancers who have gone retarded. What you
> do is a tiny, pathetic subset of dancing. I will attempt to turn
> your robotic routines into poetry, written with the human body.
> Follow me, or perish, sweater monkeys.

In terms of Torrance's internal drama, he externalizes all her fears about the second-rateness of what she does. His brutal risk-taking nearly causes Missy a potentially fatal accident – Torrance has something else to lose.

There is also a certain knowing irony here – this is after all a film whose cast had had to be sent to cheerleading camp to learn cheerleading skills from scratch. If the film is especially successful in its ensemble performances, that is partly because most of the female cast had been through a crash course in bonding.

Torrance moves from a minimalist version of personal honour to something rather more admirable. She realizes that to participate in a competition from which the Clovers were barred by economic considerations would be to win a hollow victory. Torrance's instinct here is sound and she is right to offer the Clovers the money that will enable them to compete, just as Isis, their captain, is right to refuse it. This is Torrance's film, but Isis has a character arc too – at this point, she assumes that Torrance is trying to buy her silence, or assuage her guilt, and she is neither wholly wrong nor entirely fair in her assumptions.

Part of the point here is that Torrance has to learn that there are minimal requirements in this world and that you get no virtue points for ceasing to appropriate black culture. She has to learn that the universe is not all about her moral choices – it is important that she try to help the Clovers, but even more important that she respect their right to be treated as equals without receiving any favours from her. All Isis asks of her is that she compete on equal terms and without pity – the film's title refers primarily and literally to this equal competition.

One of the film's few real weaknesses is the additional layer of plot laid in to explain Torrance's fear of failure. She believes herself to be cursed – as the result of a dare by Big Red at cheerleading camp, she let the Spirit Stick fall to the ground. (The Spirit Stick, and the curse attached to it, is apparently a real piece of lore which Jessica Bendinger had encountered and decided to use.) It brings with it a semi-surreal flashback, which even in the cut form in the final cut, feels extraneous – this was one of those good ideas which might usefully have been discarded. About the only good thing about this sequence is the moment after the final where Missy mocks Torrance about it and allows her to feel that the curse is lifted – but it would have been better that it were not in the film to begin with…

At every step in her moral journey, Torrance is influenced by one or other of the Pantone siblings for the better. Cliff's tape of the music he has written when inspired by her triggers her realization in a dark night of the soul that the Toros are talented enough to come up with their own original routine in the short gap between the regional and national competitions. Missy provides her with support every step of the way and, while it is Cliff with whom Torrance ends up in a clinch as the body of the film ends, it is Missy to whom she turns the night before the final heat. 'Thank God you're here this season Missy,' she says, 'I couldn't have done it alone.' It is a highly charged emotional moment between them, not undercut by Missy's ironic remark 'Aww, tear' pointing to an invisible tear on her face.

One of the reasons why we read the friendship between Torrance and Missy as romantic, even more so than the relationship between Torrance and Cliff, is that the various threats to it are more crucial. The original bonding between Torrance and Cliff is a matter of her vague approval of the way he handles himself with the boys that bully him in class – when they call him a loser, affecting to sneeze the word, he tells them that the 'Loser sneeze' is out of date, even in Kentucky.

We also notice from the pre-existing relationship with Aaron that Torrance is used to low-intensity relationships with boys – it is significant that he is not committed to her even to the extent of waiting around to see whether she wins the vote for head cheerleader. He is coded – and the director's commentary confirms this quite specifically – as sexually neutral, as a glad-handing Archie character whose infidelities to Torrance at college happen to be heterosexual, but could have gone either way. Crucially, he betrays her in the crunch, trying to persuade her that she is not captain material, and going behind her back to offer a joint captaincy to Whitney and Courtney.

Cliff never betrays Torrance like this, but he does not handle well even the faintest hint of rejection. Their relationship starts well, if bizarrely – they competitively clean their teeth at each other in a scene that is at once charming and slightly childish and certainly not very sexual. He walks out on her when he discovers Aaron's existence – and this at a point when she really needs him. He goes into a sulk with her that lasts almost until the end of the film when he turns up to watch the finals and is there to congratulate her – in a back-handed way that nonetheless acts as the culmination of her moral arc. 'So, second place,' he says, 'how does it feel?' Torrance replies with absolute sincerity 'It feels like first'. It is significant, though, that his major influence on all of this took place in his absence when she played his tape.

By comparison, from the very first, there is a bitter-sweet chemistry operating between Missy and Torrance; their relationship has all the fire and spark that Torrance's relationships with Aaron and even with Cliff lack. For one thing, it is a relationship which means she has to put herself on the line, something which Torrance is not used to doing. Missy becomes the battleground on which Torrance's captaincy will be threatened by Whitney and Courtney, who are not reconciled to her easy accession to the throne.

And the ground on which they choose to fight, absolutely from the beginning, is that of Missy's sexuality. Hardly has she walked into the gym where try-outs are taking place than they have accused her of parking a Harley outside, while telling her that cheerleaders are not allowed tattoos

– hers is fake and she sensually licks a finger to remove it. Various of the cheerleaders ask her to perform difficult gymnastics – no one else has been asked to do anything of the kind – and she performs them with ease. (The finely comic earlier part of the audition scene is reminiscent of nothing so much as the audition of the singing Hitlers in Mel Brooks' *The Producers* (1968).) Missy ignores their jibes and concentrates her considerable intensity on Torrance – she has come for the audition and she needs to be persuaded that it was not a complete mistake her doing so. Torrance gives her a cheer to do, and Missy responds with a laconic chant of 'Your school has no gymnastics team/This is my last resort,' before walking out to a final 'She looks like an überdyke' from Courtney. (It is worth noting, at this point, that Missy is the only one of the female Toros to have a feminine name – the others are all called by names we would more normally read as surnames or, if first names, male.)

Actors and actresses do have baggage, and it is worth remarking that, irrespective of her actual sexuality, Eliza Dushku has, for someone her age, more than most. She has been more or less typecast for sexual ambivalence on the back of her run as Faith in *Buffy the Vampire Slayer* and this has continued since *Bring It On*, which did nothing to change her image in this respect. She plays overtly bisexual characters in both the wretched horror film *Soul Survivors* (2001) and the self-indulgent Kevin Smith farrago *Jay and Silent Bob Strike Back* (2001). Peyton Reed knew exactly what he was doing when he cast her opposite Kirsten Dunst, a skinny blonde; at one point, the Clovers even refer to the Toros as 'Buffys' in case there was any doubt that we were meant to take Dushku's most famous role into account.

Torrance immediately chases after Missy not even waiting to change out of her cheerleading costume before heading off to the Pantone home. At the very least, she puts her instant loyalty to Missy as a potential asset to the squad ahead of all possible negative inferences that her rivals on the squad might draw. Torrance, it needs pointing out, is about the only person in the film who does not ever draw conclusions about other people's sex lives. Missy, for example, asks Torrance whether Whitney and Courtney are a couple ('Dykedelic?' she asks) and grills the heterosexual Jan and the gay Les. 'He's straight and I'm... controversial,' Les replies. As I remarked in the introduction, central characters' extreme cluelessness in the face of the blindingly obvious is one of the ways in which the teen movie regularly defuses seriously queer romantic chemistry.

The arguments in which Torrance convinces Missy that cheerleading is worthy of her would be taken as wooing were they of different genders, as would their confrontation over the plagiarism of the Clovers' routines. It matters to Torrance that Missy think well of her, even if it jeopardizes her captaincy by making her look weak in front of rivals who have clearly identified Missy as her Achilles Heel. Torrance chases after Missy a second time when Missy walks out after recognizing Clovers' routines, and the two of them square off as if for a fist fight in the school parking lot. There is chemistry between them, because there is the potential for real conflict – the title refers to their conflict as well as to the competition with the Clovers, and to that crucial extent it is a film about their relationship. There is also loyalty. Missy supports Torrance when, against their better judgement, the two of them are forced to capitulate to Courtney's demand that the team go on using the Clovers' routines. Torrance has successfully overruled Courtney and Whitney over Missy; she does not feel that her power base is strong enough to compete with them on this and she is clearly right. In the event, the Clovers turn up at the next game at which the Toros are cheering, and humiliate them with a parody of the stolen cheer – Courtney of course does not have to take any responsibility for a humiliation that is the result of a policy she pushed for.

When, after the humiliations of the choreographer, and the regional competition, and Aaron's betrayal, Whitney and Courtney mount their attempted coup, Torrance finally stands up definitively for her own ideas and her right to lead. Missy is the first to support her in this and it is from the Pantones' hipness that Torrance has learned enough of a sense of the richness of possible influences to concoct the eclectic routine that takes the Toros back into serious competition with the Clovers.

In his commentary on the DVD, Peyton Reed denies any specific intention of portraying the relationship between Torrance and Missy as romantic, but does so in a disingenuous way. When they share a bed at a sleepover, he mocks that part of the audience that was looking for girl-on-girl action. What he gives us though, is something quite complex in its own right, which is a pan and fade from Missy at one side of the bed to Torrance on the other to Cliff in his bed by himself in his own room. The deliberate eliding of the break of scene makes it clear that the relationship has three participants, not merely two. And, as Veronica Schanoes has pointed out, Missy may start the night facing away from Torrance, but in the morning she gazes at her.

Indeed, the film is open to the interpretation that Missy self-sacrificingly fosters her brother's relationship with her friend and does so in spite of feelings which are strongly implied. During the sleepover, for example, Torrance enters Cliff's room to watch him play his guitar and there is a shot over her shoulder of Missy watching her watching him which is clear in its implications. She advises Cliff not to give up on his hopes of Torrance just because of the existence of Aaron. When Cliff arrives in their hour of triumph, she smiles a bitter-sweet smile and announces her intention of leaving them alone to spend time with Les, who, it should be noted, has just met his own possible future partner.

The last thing Missy says in the film codes her as non-heterosexual – she has not, after all, gone off with a straight male cheerleader like Jan – and Dushku's patented ironic sultry smile is as much to do with our interpretation here as the actual words. Everything else in Torrance's life is reconciled – her parents and obnoxious little brother have turned up to watch her win – but there is this slight edge in respect of her best friend.

Peyton Reed's eventual choice of an ending indicates that he thought hard about where to take this film. One possible ending had Torrance mocking the audience for their prurient desire to see more flesh – this use of the fourth-wall trope gives Torrance more knowingness than it is right she possess. Another ending showed her a couple of years later at college with Cliff and Isis – significantly, given another deleted scene in which she argued with her parents about her choice of college, she is shown to be cheerleading at UCLA Berkley rather than at one of the Southern schools where she hoped to get a cheerleading scholarship.

She is clearly in a relationship with Cliff, and is mocked by Isis for a failure to focus wholeheartedly which will cost her the captaincy for which she and Isis are competing. Whereas in the version of the film that ends with her and Cliff in a clinch, the camera pans up from the heterosexual couple to the crowd, here Torrance leaves Cliff and goes off with Isis and the film ends with a pan of the two women going across a field to the rest of their squad to compete as equals. With the boy left behind. I can see why this ending was eventually rejected, but it says something interesting about what the film means – it is neither entirely about female bonding or entirely about race and appropriation, but about a blend of the two.

The Cliff and Torrance clinch, though, is not the last thing we see on screen, merely the end of the linear plot of the final cut. What follows, over the end titles, is something rather interesting – a sequence which combines a blooper reel with a video of 'Micky' in which the entire cast, especially the principals, mug frantically for the camera. No one in the dance is with any-one particular – everyone is with everybody, Clovers and Toros, boys and girls; Carter who was crippled in an early scene is dancing around gamely on her crutches. A film which is specifically about competence and ends with a sequence of mistakes is suddenly going carnivalesque on us – a film which has at a literal level enforced binaries of race and gender and sexuality ends in a Dionysiac romp in which they cease to be even slightly relevant.

Moreover, the song used in this sequence – apparently an innocent bit of fluff – is oddly relevant to a film which in one reading is about unstated emotional feelings and the cluelessness of the love object. 'Oh Mickey, what a pity, you don't understand,' the lyric goes, 'you take me by the heart when you take me by the hand.'

How seriously we take this depends in part on how knowing we take Peyton Reed to be. It is worth pointing out that he has a subversive sense of humour that extends to continuing his DVD commentary over the final end credits in which he attributes to himself the particular virtue of spelling everyone's names and titles correctly, and using a font that can be clearly read white on black. He is, in other words, a joker and a trickster who can be assumed to be at least as smart as any critic.

The 'Micky' sequence is one of the most obvious resemblances between *Bring It On* and the British film *Bend It Like Beckham*, which also has a combination of blooper reel and video playing over its end credits. The song 'Hot Hot Hot' combines Britpop and Bollywood influences in a way that make it appropriate for a film that celebrates both cultural diversity and the coming together of different cultures in interesting new blends. There may be no reference to the American teen movie intended in the British film, and no influence, but at the very least a similar solution is arrived at to a different but linked set of problems.

Like *Bring It On*, *Bend It Like Beckham* is a movie about two teenagers whose friendship is primarily centred on a shared obsession with competence. Jules (Keira Knightley) is a South London white girl whose working-class father has encouraged her to play football and whose aspiringly middle-class mother is worried about the tracksuits and trainers she wears all the time. The family of Jess Bhamra (Parminda Nagra) are Punjabi Sikhs who came to London after being expelled from East Africa – they are exiles twice over, whose inward-turning sense of family and community result in part from the experience of racism. They are obsessed with her sister's imminent marriage, with Jess's A-Level results and with continuing a traditional lifestyle so as to hold up their heads in a self-policing community. Jess's obsession with football is something they expect her to put away for university or marriage – they are appalled at her recruitment by Jules for a women's soccer team.

The two girls are both attracted to their coach Joe (Jonathan Rhys-Meyer), who prefers Jess – Jules's mother overhears a row between them and mistakes Jules's accusation of betrayal for clear evidence of a lesbian relationship between them. (Earlier in the film, a casual embrace between the two of them leads to the temporary cancellation of her sister's wedding when her groom's parents mistake the tall short-haired Jules for a boy and accuse Jess of public immorality.) Jess has to contend with her mother's fear that football will prevent her making a good marriage, her father's distrust of her relationship with Joe and resentment of his own lost sporting aspirations, as well as the practical problem that an upcoming final coincides with the wedding. Both Jess and Jules get to play; both win football scholarships to the USA and may play professionally.

There are a number of subplots that interact with all of this. One of the major ones is the story of Tony (Ameet Chana), Jess's best friend, who comes out to her as gay, and at one point offers to become engaged to her as a way of persuading her parents to accept her going to California. Another is the whole question of Joe's future – prevented from playing by a knee injury, he is torn between moving to coaching a male team or continuing with women's soccer; he also has a difficult relationship with his father.

We care quite significantly about Jess's sister, Pinky (Archie Panjabi), who wants all the things her sister does not – a standard marriage to a standard Indian boy – and alternately betrays and supports Jess as plot convenience dictates. The parallel of the dancing at her wedding – from which, with the connivance of their father, Jess sneaks away to play – and Jess and Jules's triumph on the football field is deliberately paralleled and cut between. The two sisters have a different set of ideas about personal fulfilment and different sources of ecstatic happiness and the film is in large part about the difference between them, without entirely privileging one over the other.

The story ends with Jess and Jules going off to California and Jess and Joe agreeing that they will get her parents used to the idea of a relationship between them – he is sticking with women's football. The film ends, significantly, somewhat later with Pinky heavily pregnant and with Mr Bhamra (Anupam Kher), Tony and Joe playing cricket together. This is a film that goes out of its way to ensure that everyone gets a happy ending.

Bend It Like Beckham is a film which centres on two teenagers and their problems, but there is a real sense in which it is not a generic teen movie, largely because so much of it is concerned to present a wider context in which Jess and Jules have to relate to their parents and the broader communities of which their parents are part. It is, though, a film that has more in common with American teen movies than one might expect. The trio of girls who are friends with Pinky, Jess's sister, are specifically described as being the Southall equivalent of Valley girls and are clearly a reference to the popular clique trope in teen movies. In the end, though, it is a film about issues as much as about having fun.

What these issues are is a matter of some controversy. It has been claimed, by director/writer Gurinder Chadha's friend and rival Nisha Ganitra, that the film was originally and explicitly scripted as a lesbian romance between Jules and Jess and that Gurinder Chadha and her collaborators 'chickened out' of the likely controversy in the Asian community in Britain and beyond. Chadha's other films include lesbian content, but in the context of relationships between British women; the controversy in India about *Fire* (1995) makes it clear that the issue is to do with Indian women being portrayed as lesbian as much as the issue of lesbianism itself.

Chadha has never directly confirmed or denied Ganitra's story. What she has done is discuss the issue as a matter of artistic byways she chose not to travel. She has described the film as:

> a story that encompasses sexuality to some degree but also
> transcends those boundaries, and talks about other things as
> well. Also I wanted to have fun with the idea of 'Oh, if you're
> a woman and you're into sports then you must be a lesbian.' It
> would have been sick I think, to kind of have this whole 'maybe I
> am a lesbian. What am I going to do?' storyline.

She decided, in other words, that she did not want to make the film a 'coming out' drama. A solid case can be made that, given the broader theme of women getting to do what they want in defiance of family and cultural expectations, her decision was the correct one. It is, after all, a decision which, as I have demonstrated implicitly throughout this book, teen movies almost always make for purely commercial reasons even without the additional issue of attitudes within ethnic minorities to confront.

The relationship between Jess and Joe is regarded as highly transgressive by all of the Bhamras – Pinky is as shocked as her parents at the idea of marrying a white boy. In a crucial scene, Jess tells Joe that they cannot have a relationship because persuading her parents to let her go to California is enough of a struggle; later, at the airport, she suggests that, in due course, she may be able to take them this extra step. The level of drama involved in even a heterosexual relationship across the racial divide is as much as the film can contain.

It has, however, to be added that Nisha Ganitra sees it otherwise, and sees the insertion of Joe as the equivalent of the regular insertion in Hollywood movies of a female character who is purely there to defuse sexual chemistry between male characters (an obvious example of which is Cameron Diaz's character in Martin Scorsese's *Gangs of New York*). In a sense, Chadha plays with this convention by having a row about Joe lead to Mrs Paxton's misapprehension that she has overheard a row between lovers.

At the same time, she gets to have her cake and eat it; Gurinder Chadha is not naïve. She knows that an audience that has watched, for example, *Bring It On* and noticed a bisexual subtext is going to read certain sequences in *Bend It Like Beckham* as indicating at the very least a romantic vibe between the two central characters. Jules first sees Jess when the other girl is playing football in the park and her glance is that of someone falling in love at first sight, whether that love is sexual or otherwise; admiration for competence and a desire to play alongside the best have an inherent romantic component. For a character represented as heterosexual, Keira Knightley's Jules gets to deliver a surprising number of long lingering glances at her co-star. If Chadha were concerned entirely to avoid a queer reading, she might have chosen to give her two central characters less monosyllabic, and, in the case of Jules at least, butch, nicknames. (Jess is short for Jesminder.)

The film is, in a sense, a coming out movie, but not in a sexual sense. Jess spends most of the film avoiding confrontation with her parents – wearing her football kit under a dressing gown when she pretends to be ill to avoid a trip to temple, claiming to have a job at HMV when she is practising, borrowing a pair of Mrs Paxton's shoes so that she can spend the money for her wedding shoes on football boots. Each time they catch her out, she pretends to comply with their wishes rather than stand up to them.

It is only when her father realizes that she will spend the entire wedding wishing she were somewhere else that he lets her go and play in the final. It is after that, when she knows that she has a chance of persuading him, that she insists on telling the whole story of what she wants, rather than covering it up via Tony's offer of marriage.

One of the reasons why the film has resonated so entirely with lesbian and gay viewers is that this sense of reluctance about commitment to a clear statement to family, and all the strategies for leading a double life, are only too familiar to us. Again, Gurinder Chadha's status as a straight woman closely involved through family and friends with a queer community has to be taken into account here.

Chadha gets a lot of comedy out of Mrs Paxton (Juliet Stevenson) who reads aspects of the relationship as indicating lesbian involvement; interestingly, Mr Paxton (Frank Harper) is not represented as not believing she is right, just as not caring one way or the other so long as his daughter is good at football. Mrs Paxton is there both to defuse queer readings by mocking them, and to make them overtly part of the final film. For the Sikh characters, the relationship between the two girls is not even an issue in this sense – when Mrs Paxton confronts her daughter's supposed seductress, one of the wedding guests says 'Lesbian? Her birthday's in March. I thought she was a Pisces.' Mr Bhamra brushes the accusation off, like the early mistake about the gender of the person Jess was holding at a bus stop, by remarking that girls have such short hair nowadays.

The two sets of parents are compared and contrasted. Mrs Paxton is as guilty as the Bhamras, with rather less excuse, of wanting her daughter to be an accessory to her life rather than a person in her own right. It is as if she feels her own feminine identity threatened by having a daughter who refuses to wear inflatable falsies and go out with boys. As stunningly portrayed by Juliet Stevenson, she is a vulgarian and yet oddly touching in her attempts to do the right thing – understand the offside rule as acted out by her husband ('The offside rule is when the French mustard has to be between the teriyaki sauce and the sea salt'), talk of how much she appreciates George Michael and Navratilova. Her husband is taciturn and long-suffering and deeply likeable.

The Bhamras are at the same time idealized and mocked. The film is dedicated to the memory of Gurinder Chadra's own father, and Mr Bhamra is seen as at once loving, admirable and potentially frightening. The deleted scenes include a telling one in which he originally refuses to accept the apology of Pinky's suitor for the breaking off of the match, obviously cut because it made him almost hateful. Anupam Kher is normally known for buffoon roles – he brings a warmth here that stops him being merely a heavy father.

Mrs Bhamra is portrayed with mockery and affection. According to Gurinder Chadha, she is the aspect of the film to which British Asian audiences most respond. Where Pinky knows what she wants and chooses it, Mrs Bhamra does not even begin to understand why anyone, let alone a daughter of hers, should want anything else. All of the family gaze from time to time at the benign countenance of their prophet Guru Nanak, who has pride of place on the living room wall – Jess even phrases her apologia, when she finally faces her parents directly, in terms of his having gifted her with her skills. It is Mrs Bhamra who is most entirely devout. And a part of her sense of devotion is cooking – faced with Jess's decision to go to California, she says, 'At least I taught her full Indian dinner. The rest is up to God.'

Mrs Bhamra is but one of an entire bevy of fearsome middle-aged and older women, the 'aunties', who act as the voice of traditional morality in Jess's life. When Jess makes the penalty shot that wins the final game, she sees the opposing team round whom she has to bend the kick as suddenly transformed into her mother and her friends. This is a film in which traditional models of Indian femininity are seen as an obstacle to the heroine's self-realization; Jules, the secondary heroine, is under far less serious pressure. The aunties and Mrs Bhamra are part of the point of the film here; it is as much about the community from which Jess springs as it is about her individualistic struggle. To recapitulate, it is in other words a movie with teenagers in it, rather than a teen movie.

Watching the Teen Detective

Veronica Mars

*B*y the middle of its twentieth year of full existence, the teen genre as I have tried to describe it had accumulated enough tropes of its own to sustain fertile cross-fertilization with other genres. This had to some extent been true as early as Joss Whedon's film and television series *Buffy the Vampire Slayer*: the series' first three seasons make a point of using the supernatural horror aspect of its plots as metaphorical commentary on adolescence in general and high school in particular. In 2005, it became even more radically true of the excellent Rob Thomas-created teen detective show *Veronica Mars*.

Shown belatedly in the UK, and in its second season subjected by the UPN network to constraints that gave rise to fears that its excellence might be compromised, the first season of *Veronica Mars* combined an intensely plotted season arc with new cases each week for Veronica and her private detective father Keith. Most of the individual cases Veronica takes on personally are to do with people who attend school with her, and explore teen movie tropes like accusations of drug use, sexual harassment, pranks, threats to personal sexual reputation, the kidnapping of team mascots and threats of violence. Some of course have to do with more standard criminal matters like a fraud perpetuated on high school students by college techies or an elaborate scheme to track down someone in witness protection.

At the start of the first season, Veronica has become a pariah at Neptune High School where she was formerly part of the in-crowd, the 09ers. This is a consequence of her father's investigation, when sheriff, of the murder of his daughter's best friend, Lilly. Keith suspected Lilly's father, software billionaire Jake Kane, because of inconsistencies in the alibis of all three surviving Kanes, and as a result lost his job in a snap election. Neither he nor Veronica believe in the guilt of Koontz, the man who confessed and is awaiting execution. In the aftermath of Lilly's murder, Veronica was fed a date-rape drug at a party and, at least, sexually molested; she and Keith were left by Veronica's mother, Lianne. Veronica, against the wishes of her father, is investigating Lilly's death, her own molestation and her mother's departure; solving these mysteries, he points out to her, will not take things back to how they were.

Veronica is stigmatized as a slut because of her behaviour under the date-rape drug and because she no longer has social power as Lilly's friend, consort of Lilly's brother Duncan, and the daughter of the sheriff. Asked how she bears being subjected to random everyday harassment, Veronica says, 'I got tough; I got even.' She sometimes abuses her special knowledge of people's lives – in 'You Think You Know Somebody' (1.5), Ashley mocks her and Veronica replies by talking to her about the imminent divorce of Ashley's parents over her father's infidelities. Her real cruelty generates even more hostility towards her – this incident is recalled by Pammy in 'Like a Virgin' (1.8) to justify her traducing of Veronica's reputation.

Further complicating the situation are such matters as the possibility that Veronica is not, genetically, Keith's daughter, but Jake's, Lilly's relationships with the obnoxious rich boy Logan and the dangerous biker Weevil, and the efforts of Jake's head of security to frustrate Veronica's investigations. Veronica used to date Lilly's brother Duncan and is appalled by the possibility that their, as she thinks, unconsummated relationship was incestuous; she finds herself increasingly attracted to Logan, especially after the suicide of his mother makes his vulnerability clear to her.

This central plot then is partly about the relationship of parents to children and partly about the extent to which nature trumps nurture, or the other way around. In a key episode, Veronica's computer adviser Mac is unhappy in the family where she was reared after a confusion of babies in the local hospital, which resulted a couple of years later in the parents taking a cash pay-off to keep the children where they were and avoid scandal. As the episode ends, her 'real' mother observes her from a distance with constant longing. Another of Veronica's clients discovers that his disappeared father is a transsexual woman who regularly travels miles to hire videos from him – the bond of parent and child is often unbreakable.

Veronica considers finding out for good and all whether Keith is her father or not, and eventually decides that she would rather not know if he is not. Later, he does the same DNA test and discovers, to his surprise and delight, that he is after all her father by blood as well as affinity. On the other hand, Veronica sacrifices her college fund to put her mother through alcoholism rehab, only to discover that her mother is still a drunk, and, moreover, a drunk who steals a small fortune from her, a cheque made out to Mars Investigations by the Kane family.

Duncan was made aware by his mother Celeste of the possibility that Veronica was his sister – this was part of the reason for their inexplicable break-up. However, both have moved on, and it seems unlikely that they will ever reunite; Duncan is in a more or less happy relationship with Meg. The fact that Veronica's virginity was taken by a drugged Duncan who overcame his fear of incest under the influence, and that she was conscious enough at the time to have seemed to have consented, a memory which she gradually recovers in part, is another factor here. The show has a nuanced and complex attitude to virginity and its loss – it is worth remembering that, technically, all of these characters are too young to have intercourse under Californian state law.

Veronica Mars is a show that often starts from the simple stock assumptions of the teen movie and renders them more complex. Logan, for example, originally appears to be entirely unpleasant – Veronica calls him the school's 'obligatory psychotic jackass' in the first episode – and this is borne out by, for example, his involvement in filming violent bouts between down-and-outs. We only gradually realize that Veronica's hatred of him is not entirely balanced – in 'The Return of the Kane' (1.6), Veronica assumes Logan, wrongly, to be guilty of both fraud and libel as campaign manager for Duncan in the Student Body President election. In fact, he is entirely innocent of both and justifiably says, 'I don't have time to be responsible for every little thing that goes wrong in your life.'

Then we, and later Veronica, discover that Logan is the victim of constant physical abuse by his movie star father, Aaron, who turns out in the show's last episode to have been both Lilly's lover and her murderer.

Moreover, his reasons for hating Veronica have their merits – she caught him in a momentary infidelity and told Lilly, who broke with him as a result. Had she not done so, he might have saved Lilly's life.

We have seen Aaron's violence and sexual promiscuity for ourselves, but have also seen the extent to which it is a consequence of his own physical abuse by his father. We have also found ourselves feeling more ambivalent towards Aaron when he beats up the director boyfriend who has been beating up his daughter, Trina. Logan is, at the same time, a young man whom Veronica might come to love and the person who supplied the date-rape drug that was used on both her and Duncan. Veronica forgave him this, but it is not clear that their relationship will survive the conviction of his father, even though he hates Aaron.

The debt of this show to many of the films discussed in the course of this book is clear. Rob Thomas has used the detective story structure to create a vast psychological investigation in which quite simple 'truths' are writ large. Where *Buffy*, in its classic first three seasons, used horror tropes to examine the simple truth that school life and adolescence are a nightmare, and in its sixth season turned this assumption on its head by arguing that reaching adulthood is being cast out of heaven, *Veronica Mars* uses detective tropes to point out that the truth of who you are and how you got to be that person is at once a necessary discovery and a painful one. The catharsis of its first season is similar to, merely vaster than, the catharsis of the end of *The Breakfast Club*.

Veronica is haunted throughout by memories of a happier time and by what appears to be Lilly's ghost. By the end of the series, we have received some confirmation of the ghost's status – Duncan also and independently is seen to experience her, and when Veronica has solved and avenged the murder, Lilly appears to her one last time to say goodbye. The memories are always confused and fragmentary, and shot in a blue light like that of a police car, or the water of the pool next to which Lilly died. The season's penultimate episode, 'A Trip to the Dentist', has a Rashomon-like structure in which Veronica gradually reconstructs the events leading up to her drugging and the loss of her virginity by interrogating the various other attendees at the party – each version of each event is shot in this same haunting blue light.

There are clear analogies between some of the show's principal characters and various figures from the teen genre's stock company, and most especially from the John Hughes films. Veronica Mars herself takes her first name from *Heathers* and her relationship with Lilly was in some respects that of Veronica in that film to Heather Chandler – to complicate matters further, Lilly is played by the actress (Amanda Seyfried) who plays Karen, one of Regina's acolytes in *Mean Girls*. Veronica Mars is forced to accept, as the first season proceeds, that in her days as an 09er she was as capable as anyone of mean behaviour to social outsiders.

Her relegation to pariah status after being part of the in-crowd links her to Amanda Jones in *Some Kind of Wonderful*, as does her poverty by comparison with the Kanes and the Echols of her world. Her close relationship with her father, and their sense of desertion by her mother, parallels that of Sam in *Pretty in Pink*, though Keith is never the traumatized hulk that Sam's father has become. In her endless invention of complex ploys, and her constant outwitting of the school authorities, and the growing sense around Neptune High that she is a competent individual to be feared and admired, she has much in common with Ferris Bueller, whose taste for anarchy is also a constant temptation to her.

The relationship between Logan Echols and Duncan Kane – mildly ambiguous in its element of the possessive – parallels that between Steff and Blane in *Pretty in Pink*, save that Logan has, as it turns out, very good reasons to detest Veronica Mars, rather than operating out of motiveless malignity. Though far more complex, Logan is quite closely parallel to Steff in his smug assumptions of social superiority, his desire to police the relationships of his friends and his sheer charisma.

The relationship between Logan and Veronica is precisely what would not normally happen in a teen movie where he would almost always remain an unregenerate villain, or go out with her on a dare or bet (like Freddie Prinz Jr. in *She's All That*). First the audience and then Veronica find, as the episodes unfold, that Logan is a more complex character than he at first seems. There is a particularly chilling moment when we see him selecting a belt from his father's wardrobe and only gradually realize that he has been sent to choose the belt with which he will be whipped. The suicide of his mother nearly breaks him, as does the revelation of the falsity of the hope that she has faked her death – and Veronica has to witness this. A casual remark by his thoughtless sister makes Veronica aware of what we have known by now for a while.

Similarly, he grows to value her, and she respects his confidences even though he has treated her badly in the past. He comes to enjoy her intelligence and capacity for control – there are areas where what they have disliked in each other is the recognition of abilities they share. In the episode 'Weapons of Class Destruction' (1.18), he protects her violently – though the person he attacks is actually a federal agent posing as a student at Neptune High. He stands by her in the most socially embarrassing of circumstances – their status as a couple is revealed, in 'MAD' (1.20), when they walk into what proves to be a surprise party thrown by his father for his friends, most of whom detest her. The status-conscious Logan accepts social death to be with a woman whose pariah status is largely of his own creation – there is a glorious irony to this exploitation of teen movie tropes.

(It should be added that there is another analogy to their relationship – the Draco/Hermione relationship in some Harry Potter fanfiction. Logan is not the Draco Malfoy of the books or films – he has, however, a resemblance to the redeemable Draco that exists in fanfiction. This distinction is sometimes referred to as the clash of canon and fanon.)

At the point of writing, between the first and second seasons of *Veronica Mars*, it is hard to see where Veronica's future lies. Duncan and she had sex when both of them had been drugged and it was Logan's fault, if indirectly, and it is hard to see whether it is Logan or Duncan whose future chances with her have been most damaged. She has suspected both of them of murdering Lilly, and the fact that she has exonerated both does not obscure the fact that both of them – Duncan to his parents as well – were objectively plausible candidates. One of the differences between Thomas and Hughes is that he is not working in a form which necessarily gives rise to happy endings.

Another obvious analogy is that between Weevil, the Hispanic bad-boy biker gang leader from the wrong side of town, and Duncan, the friendly thug who becomes Keith's guardian angel in *Some Kind of Wonderful*. Again, though, Thomas has the space that Hughes did not to take an essentially two-dimensional concept and open it out into a rich and complex person. Weevil originally dislikes Veronica as a former 09er, and bullies her sidekick Wallace; in early episodes she simply plays off his dislike and suspicion of her against his far greater reasons for hating Logan. His dislike of Logan parallels Duncan's dislike of Hardy, but has more grounds than mere class warfare – both young men were Lilly's lovers. This changes when she exonerates Weevil of criminal charges and reveals his betrayal by the cousin and lieutenant he trusted; he becomes her occasionally enthusiastic backup muscle, as when she has him and his gang loom menacingly in the fashion shop of an unwilling informant.

Like Hughes' Duncan, Weevil is capable of stepping outside the stereotype in a variety of unexpected ways; at one point, threatening Veronica with consequences if she breaks a deal between them, he adds, 'And your little dog too'. When the leader of a biker gang quotes the Wicked Witch of the West, we know that we are not in Kansas anymore. He also vocalizes some important truths about class and its ramifications: 'You still think like one of them,' he says to Veronica about the Duncan/Logan clique and he is not wrong.

At certain points, though, Weevil and Logan demonstrate a capacity for friendship with each other that exemplifies the greater canvas that Thomas is working on, as when they combine forces to destroy a teacher's car, and Logan confesses – professedly to get his share of credit for the prank – in order to save Weevil from expulsion. There is a bat squeak of homoeroticism between them that is not merely an echo of the fact that they were both Lilly's lovers and are both attracted to Veronica. When in the first season's final episode, we last see them about to engage in serious mutual violence, Logan steps forward with the come-hither gesture patented in the equally quasi-sexual sparring of Morpheus and Neo in the Wachowskis' *Matrix* movies. Thomas knows his audience and has created in these two the show's major 'slash' pairing in fanfiction.

Similarly, though this is as yet no more than a hint and may never be developed, it seems clear that the hacker Mac has more than a passing sexual interest in Veronica. Lilly on at least one occasion smooched Veronica as a piece of sexual display intended to arouse their respective boyfriends, Lilly's brother Duncan and Logan. One of the standard flashbacks – in fact a clue to Lilly's affair with Aaron – is of Lilly saying, 'I've got a secret, a good one.' In its original context, the remark happened during a charity car wash, which echoes the similar event in *Bring It On*, and thus brings to Lilly and Veronica's relationship the complex romantic associations of Torrance and Missy in that movie.

'Keep your friends close and your enemies closer,' says Kathryn in *Cruel Intentions* before quasi-seducing her rival Cecile; Duncan's new girlfriend Meg is not malevolent, and has been helped by Veronica, and is very inclined to spend time with her. Perhaps she is just a nice friendly girl, and then again, perhaps not. One of the many actions Veronica was talked into when drugged, and which have ruined her reputation, was a prolonged snog with another girl for the benefit of male voyeurs. Veronica Mars's cluelessness about all of this is analogous to Sam's failure to notice

Duckie's devotion to her or to Torrance's failure to understand nuances in her relationship with Missy that are blindingly obvious to the people who hate both of them. If queer subtext has become a part of the mature form of the teen genre, *Veronica Mars* has it in the proper quantity.

There are, of course, weaknesses here too. Thomas sometimes slips into teen genre default mode – the handling of the school's not especially bright principal and of Lamb, Keith Mars's replacement as sheriff, relies far too heavily on the clichéd humiliation of authority figures. The final revelation of Lilly's murderer is comparatively feeble and not entirely plausible depending as it does on a series of sudden shifts. We find out that Aaron is a child molester, that Lilly slept with the abusive father of her estranged boyfriend, that Lilly stole, and planned to use, the tapes of their intercourse – this is all a little much to swallow in a single episode.

This is particularly disastrous after the elegance of the solution of the rape mystery in the previous episode, where quite minor character points from the whole of the season come to fruition. The episode's culmination also places Veronica in serious physical danger from which she does not escape by her usual intelligence – she has to be rescued by her father. Elsewhere in the season, this might be tolerable because plausible and on a couple of occasions was; in the season finale, it is a worrying drift away from message.

It has been suggested in fandom that this over-rapid solution of the murder mystery was imposed by the network as a condition of the show's renewal, and that ideally these surprises would have been sprung one at a time over a period of weeks in the second season, had the studio not wanted this plot strand over and done with. The only objection to this theory is that it fails to take into account the extent to which even gifted creators of television can make major mistakes without network intervention – the magic=drugs=sex aspects of the sixth season of *Buffy the Vampire Slayer* are a good example here. Nonetheless, with *Veronica Mars*'s endless quotations and revisions from elsewhere in the teen genre, Rob Thomas has demonstrated, in the season as a whole, rather than its weak finale, both the genre's strengths and his own virtuosity in exploiting those strengths.

* * * *

Teenage Americans watch movies about themselves to make sense of their lives, to be reassured that the pangs of adolescence are a universal truth, not a personal wound. For them, to be told that bullies sometimes lose, that school principals are sometimes fallible or humiliated, that sometimes true love wins, is a necessary balm and encouragement to struggle. Above all they need to be told that nothing is forever and that there are second chances to get things right, that one day we will look back on these things and laugh.

For the rest of us, the teen genre means something else, and yet the same. In a sense, it has no more to do with the actual lives of existing teenagers than the Pastorals of Virgil had to do with actual shepherds. The teen genre is a stylized way of looking at the world which connects to that world but dresses it in artificial light. When youth is gone, we still need to connect to its hope through art. We still need Teen Dreams.

Index
of Films

Index